Multicultural Education for the 21st Century

Multicultural Education for the 21st Century

Carlos F. Diaz
Florida Atlantic University, Boca Raton

Longman

New York San Francisco Boston
London Toronto Sydney Tokyo Singapore Madrid
Mexico City Munich Paris Cape Town Hong Kong Montreal

Publisher: Priscilla McGeehon
Production Manager: Ellen MacElree
Project Coordination, Text Design, and Electronic Page Makeup: Electronic
    Publishing Services Inc., N.Y.C.
Cover Design Manager: John Callahan
Cover Designer: Mary McDonnell
Manufacturing Buyer: Al Dorsey
Printer and Binder: R.R. Donnelley & Sons Company
Cover Printer: Coral Graphic Services, Inc.

Library of Congress Cataloging-in-Publication Data
Multicultural education for the twenty-first century / Carlos F. Díaz, editor.--1st ed.
    p.   cm.
   Includes bibliographical references and index.
   ISBN 0-321-05417-2 (pbk.)
    1. Multicultural education--United States. 2. Effective teaching--United States. I. Díaz,
Carlos (Carlos F.)

LC1099.3 .M8163 2001
370.117'0973--dc21

                      00-039084

Please visit our website at http://www.awl.com

ISBN 0-321-05417-2

2 3 4 5 6 7 8 9 10—DOH—03 02 01

CONTENTS

Introduction

Carlos F. Diaz

T he third millennium has dawned. With it comes an opportunity to reflect on educational practices of the 20th century and which should be retained or altered in future.

Much has been written about the demographic revolution occurring in the United States. Some writers have termed this "the browning of America." This demographic shift is causing many Americans within and outside education to realize that this nation simply can no longer afford rates of educational failure similar to those we have had in the past. Students of color, as well as female students, should compose a significantly higher proportion of this nation's professional, scientific, and managerial workforce in the 21st century.

Being concerned about these issues is not a matter of liberal, moderate, or conservative philosophy. Pragmatism dictates that the United States of the future will not rely on white males to do many of the significant jobs of society to the extent that they have in the past; there simply will not be enough of them to meet the demands of a growing nation. Consequently, the education of people who historically have not fared too well in the schools of the United States becomes critically important. If the nation fails in this endeavor, a likely scenario for the future may be a declining standard of living. Despite the immense natural wealth of this nation, the bulk of its future lies in developing its intellectual capital. Multicultural education offers some promising avenues to improve achievement and to enrich curriculum for all students of this nation.

Imagine American classrooms where field-sensitive teaching practices are as common as field-independent ones. In these classrooms, cooperative learning would teach students the value of interacting well with others as well as the rewards of individual achievement. Multiple elements of intelligence would be recognized and rewarded, and students with significant elements of social and spatial intelligence would have avenues to display these skills, along with more traditional classroom talents such as inductive and deductive reasoning.

Teachers in these multicultural classrooms of the future would employ a wide array of teaching methods reflective of the variety of learning styles found among their students. Teachers would occasionally review their lesson plans to monitor the learning modalities being addressed as well as the content. Respect and sensitivity for gender, exceptionalities, and culture would permeate general school and classroom practices. These attitudes would serve as a magnet to increase levels of parental interest and participation in school matters.

If the day arrives when a multicultural curriculum represents the status quo in the schools of the United States, students will be far better prepared than they are currently to be caring and active participants in this democracy. A great deal of interethnic tension in the United States is rooted in ignorance about cultural or ethnic groups that are different from one's own. While no curriculum can promise a societal panacea, multicultural education can certainly diminish the gaps of ignorance that currently exist among various segments of the U.S. population. Knowledge is a powerful weapon against stereotypes, and a curriculum that delivers "transformative knowledge" also encourages critical thinking, the antithesis of prejudice.

Many Americans have realized that the isolationist tendencies in our educational practices have not and will not produce the globally literate citizens this nation needs for the 21st century. Therefore, the concept of global literacy has achieved a modicum of legitimacy and political currency. What is lacking, however, is the notion that we cannot create globally literate citizens who are simultaneously illiterate about the cultural variations in their own society. In other words, multicultural literacy is a precursor to global literacy. This message must reach more of our fellow citizens who have the ability to influence the educational process. American students must understand significant national and global variations of culture and achieve a level of academic mastery comparable or superior to their counterparts in other developed nations. To achieve this, educators and policy makers must be willing to "rearrange the furniture of the mind." Many school practices, ranging from tracking to presenting a monocultural curriculum, derive their legitimacy from tradition, but they need to be reevaluated with regard to their influence on student achievement.

Invariably, some will oppose any change in predictable practices and routines. Nevertheless, bureaucratic procedures, faculty preferences, and community priorities must be reexamined in light of their ultimate *raison d'être*: their impact on student achievement. If found lacking, these practices should be changed so that American schools can educate the students who will carry this nation in the 21st century.

It is hoped by the editor and authors that this volume will make a small contribution to encouraging educators to alter their teaching practices and teach content using multicultural perspectives. If this occurs, schools will move a little closer to educating students to reach their fullest potential.

I am indebted to the professionals who devoted a portion of their limited time to help with this publication. Particular gratitude is extended to the authors of this volume for their patience and courtesy in working with the editor through the various changes any book undergoes from the conception to the publication of the work.

Acknowledgments

I would like to acknowledge Amy Cronin, editor at Addison-Wesley Longman, and Matthew Ludvino, editorial assistant, for their patience and support during the preparation of this manuscript. Also, I would like to thank Marcella Centola and Evelyn Tracey for their assistance with various drafts of the chapters, and Janna Taft and McNeel Gordon for their research assistance. Finally, I would like to thank my wife, Diane, for her encouragement throughout this project.

Carlos F. Diaz, Editor
Florida Atlantic University, Boca Raton

chapter 1

The Third Millennium

A Multicultural Imperative for Education

Carlos F. Diaz

The United States has undergone a series of societal transformations during its history as a nation. The industrial revolution of the 19th century brought profound changes, as did the information and technological revolutions of the late 20th century. The 21st century, however, has brought this nation its most significant transition to date—a demographic revolution. What once was a country considered to be a microcosm of Europe is fast becoming a microcosm of the world.

Already one in four Americans is either an Asian, Hispanic, or African American, and students of color make up approximately one-third of the nation's public school students (Henry 1990). Projections for the year 2000 census indicate that the percentage increase of persons of color will be greater than the approximately 3.1% increase in this group from 1980 to 1990.

This demographic shift is occurring primarily for two reasons: (1) The birth rate among persons of color in our society is higher than that among whites, and (2) current and future immigrants are more likely to come from Latin American and Asian nations than from European ones. The implications of this demographic shift are very significant for educators. Historically, students of color have represented a disproportionate number of those who were unsuccessful in the schools of the United States. With the numbers of students of color rapidly increasing, what does this bode for the future? To improve the academic performance of these students, do schools need to change their approaches, or do these students merely need to try harder?

1

Policy makers in a number of states have responded by "raising the bar" on the assumption that if students know more is expected, they will deliver more. While high expectations are important, students in the United States take more tests than those of nearly any other nation. We need to also examine curriculum and instruction to see if they are preparing all segments of the student population. The wisdom of an old Vermont farmer is appropriate here. He cautioned, "You don't fatten your lambs by weighing them."

Curriculum

Despite demographic changes in the past two decades, Anglo- and Euro-centric curricula prevail in many of this nation's schools. When multicultural content is taught, it is frequently presented in an ethnic-additive manner (Banks 1994). Material that focuses on ethnic groups is concentrated in special courses and offered as electives in the curriculum. Carlos Cortes and others have suggested that this practice tends to "ghettoize" ethnic content within the curriculum.

Changing the curriculum to reflect more pluralistic content is not an easy task. In the mid 1990s, the National History Standards were presented to the U.S. Congress. They were supported by the American Historical Association and the Organization of American Historians. These standards were repudiated by Congress. Critiques centered around notions that the standards emphasized negative elements of history and celebrated "politically correct" causes (Cohen 1995).

A true multicultural curriculum integrates cultural content throughout subjects and grade levels, placing new content where it is pedagogically and contextually appropriate. This infusion approach involves a review of the entire curriculum and affects all of a school's faculty. Perhaps these far-reaching demands are what make the infusion method less prevalent than the ethnic-additive approach. Also, because the infusion approach reaches a much higher percentage of the student population, there is a greater likelihood that parents or students will raise the question, "Why do we study this nontraditional material?"

To date, we have not yet forged a national consensus that Americans, to be well educated, must have a significant measure of multicultural (and global) literacy. McGee Banks (1997) argues that what is missing from efforts to develop national standards is the inclusion of multicultural literacy as one of the standards. If such a consensus is reached in the future, it will have significant ramifications in teacher preparation, school district policies, and textbook content.

Textbooks play a critical role in the development of a basic curriculum and the ability of educators to make curricular changes. Some educators claim they don't currently teach their subjects in a multicultural manner because their textbooks impede such efforts. These educators may have a point. While textbooks have certainly improved in the past two decades, the wait for the optimal textbook would be a long one.

There is also a political dimension to the topic of textbook publication and adoption. For example, textbook publishers know they will not enhance the marketability of a new American history text by including an extensive and fair discussion of the United States' role in the Philippine Insurrection. Yet that background would be critical to understanding the notion of Philippine sovereignty as well as in analyzing the contemporary relationship between the two countries. Understanding the Philippine Insurrection would also help students understand U.S. tactics during the Vietnam war. Prior to Vietnam, the insurrection was the only major guerilla war in Asia involving the United States.

However, textbook publishers invest heavily in a new history textbook for the public school market. Editors are well aware that their futures will be judged by the percentage of market share their products garner. Therefore, it is critical for publishers to have their texts adopted, particularly in large states like California, Texas, and Florida, which have state-adopted lists of texts.

The more heavily educators rely on a textbook as a source of information in a course, the more critical its content becomes. Most educators would agree they should not limit their teaching to information in textbooks. However, multiple demands on their time often leave them with few hours left for selecting and incorporating supplemental materials.

Nevertheless, educators across the United States need to understand that multicultural education is not a fleeting topic whose need and purpose will disappear in a year or two. Schools serve as arbiters of knowledge for every society and provide legitimacy for the information and perspectives they purvey. When they fail to inform students about specific cultural groups, they convey a picture of marginality about those groups in society.

If we were to ask this year's class of high school seniors to name the Hispanic Americans they have studied in the past 12 years, what would the results be? Most would give no response, some might mention Spanish explorers (who were Spaniards and not Hispanic Americans), and there would be the occasional correct response. It should be noted that the ancestors of Hispanic Americans arrived in North America before the English. Hispanic Americans will soon become more numerous than African Americans, making them the largest minority group in the United States. Yet, in a curricular sense, they remain largely invisible.

What are the intellectual, normative, and public policy implications for a nation which knows relatively little about one of its fastest-growing groups of citizens? What are the consequences to Hispanic Americans when the curriculum does not include them among those who helped to forge the nation? Inaccurate perceptions of Hispanic Americans are conveyed to Hispanic and non-Hispanic students alike, but the ramifications are doubly serious for the former group.

Restructuring the curriculum to reflect multicultural perspectives requires reconceptualizing our canon of knowledge, not simply injecting selected ethnic heroes or events into an otherwise unreconstructed curriculum. Restructuring requires the willingness to share "transformative knowledge" that allows students to develop new perspectives on the traditional academic canon (Banks 1996). Acquiring new realizations is one of the most profound effects of multicultural education. A curriculum that raises significant questions about history, literature, public policy, or ethical issues in science tends to move students from being spectators of knowledge to being active participants (in the Freirian sense) in their own education (Freire 1993).

Not everyone is eager to raise, or have their students raise, these difficult questions in the classroom. Yet a curriculum with significant amounts of transformative knowledge will boost students' interest as they realize that subjects may be studied from diverse, contrasting, and often fascinating perspectives.

Teaching Practices

A study of secondary school students conducted at Michigan State University in East Lansing found that one-third of all students actively resisted the curriculum, and an additional one-third resisted it passively (Sedlack et al. 1986). Clearly, a great deal more needs to be done in our classrooms to heighten the level of enthusiasm and participation among all students. For students of color, this situation is particularly significant because their rates of academic success are generally below the national average.

Banks (1999) cites a study by Darling-Hammond, which found that the academic achievement of students of color and low-income students increased when they had high-quality teachers who were experts in pedagogy, content, and child development. Banks also relates a study by Dreehan that found when African American students received high-quality reading instruction, their reading achievement was as high as that of white students.

These studies raise the question of access to high-quality teachers. Are these teachers typically found randomly assigned to all schools in a district? How prevalent are high-quality teachers in schools with high proportions of students of color, low-income, or immigrant students? The consensus of the research on teaching practices indicates that the most effective teaching practices are found in classes for academically advanced (high-track) students. Conversely, the least effective teaching practices tend to be more prevalent in classes for academically deficient (low-track) students.

As teachers improve their professional skills with added experience and advanced degrees, a curious pattern develops. They are less likely to be found teaching the most academically needy learners. There are some exceptions to this pattern in teachers who choose to remain with academically needy students. Yet, in most school districts with tracking or socioeconomic segregation of students, new vacancies are far more prevalent for teaching low-track than high-track students.

If there is often an inverse correlation between the quality of teaching and the achievement of learners, how does this situation occur? In the public educational system of the United States, an arena of finite material and intellectual resources, the distribution of these resources is not dictated primarily by academic need. Despite protests to the contrary, political factors influence nearly every district in the nation to concentrate financial resources and the most effective teachers on students who are most academically advantaged. At the same time, political leaders often stress that the system of public education in the United State provides a level playing field for all students.

The types of instructional methods used in the classroom are of paramount importance. A massive observational study by John Goodlad (1984) showed that instruction based on rote questions and answers is still very prevalent in our nation's schools. Most teachers were field-independent students who performed reasonably well in an individualistic and fairly competitive classroom environment. Therefore, it is not surprising that a look at instructional methods in our nation's schools reveals a large preponderance of field-independent teaching techniques.

However, field-sensitive teaching approaches, which capitalize on human associations, correspond much more closely with the learning preferences of many students. This is especially true for minority students. All students prefer to learn in environments that are most consistent with their learning styles. Approaches like cooperative learning show great promise for involving high- and low-achieving students in common learning tasks. In fact, students of color have shown (Slavin 1983; Cohen 1986) far greater academic gains in cooperative-learning situations than in traditional classrooms. Other approaches that involve significant interaction, such as peer tutoring or older students mentoring younger ones, also provide promising alternatives for instructing students who are deterred by formal and impersonal teaching approaches.

Among the other findings by Goodlad (1984) and supported by other authors (Gillette and Chinn 1997) is that "teacher talk" tends to dominate classrooms, but few students learn best by merely listening. Oral instruction should be amply supported by visual cues and hands-on experiences. Additionally, Goodlad found that textbook content accounts for approximately 90% of what is taught, and only 1% of time in the classrooms he examined was spent on critical thinking. These last two points are especially significant when viewed against the general tendency to have somewhat more time spent on critical thinking in schools where students have higher socioeconomic profiles.

We also need to consider instructional time as well as instructional methods. Time-on-task studies have shown that low-achieving students receive considerably less instructional time than their high-achieving counterparts (Frederick 1977). Because larger numbers of African American and Hispanic students are found in lower-track school curricula, these students are denied the same instructional time as pupils in higher-track courses. This is rather ironic, since those students who are least academically independent should receive the greatest instructional time.

Classroom atmosphere is important, too. After all, this is the setting in which teaching and learning occur. Positive classroom morale has a direct effect upon student achievement. One study found that when students felt relaxed and positive in a classroom, they performed better. When they were anxious, their academic performance and self-concepts declined (Walberg 1984).

It is clear that the affective domain plays a significant role in effective teaching. Not enough emphasis is placed on the pivotal role of classroom climate in the education of teachers. Research in this area needs to be an integral part of teacher education if we are to be effective in teaching the increasingly heterogeneous student population of the United States.

Teachers

Teacher attitudes and expectations play a significant role in classrooms. The bulk of research in this area indicates that racial, ethnic, and social stereotypes affect teachers' perceptions of their pupils. The classic Pygmalion Study (Rosenthal and Jacobson 1968) found that Mexican American students who made high achievement gains were still rated low in curiosity by their teachers.

Other research indicates that teacher ratings of like and dislike for students also paralleled social stereotypes. In other words, teachers possessed more negative opinions of pupils of color and students of lower socioeconomic status (Graybill 1997; Sheets 1996). The body of research strongly suggests that pupils who violate teacher expectations are likely to suffer teacher rejection. This is true even if students who are expected to do poorly perform well (Brophy and Good 1974).

A study was done in Texas to test the applicability of the Banks Ethnic Identity Typology to a cross section of teachers. In that typology, the *ethnic identity clarification stage* is the minimum stage of attitudinal development teachers must meet to work effectively in schools. Fewer than one-fifth of the more than 400 teachers sampled were found to have reached the ethnic identity clarification stage. These results were true for minority-group as well as majority-group teachers. Four-fifths of the sample were quite probably unprepared or unable to function in heterogeneous classrooms. Yet the entire sample was composed of in-service teachers (Ford 1979).

A departure point for teachers becoming cross-culturally competent is developing an understanding of their own ethnicity and cultural background. Approximately 90% of teachers in the United States describe themselves as White and emanating from the middle class (Snyder, Hoffman, and Geddes 1997). When questioned about their own ethnicity, White middle-class teachers have often described themselves as American, without any ethnic culture (Ladson-Billings 1994). Teachers who fail to recognize that most citizens of the United States, in spite of assimilation, have heritages from outside this nation are unlikely to value the ethnicities of their students. This issue should be addressed in in-service training of teachers or university courses that aim to develop cross-cultural competency.

The consensus of the literature on teacher attitudes toward minority and lower socioeconomic status (SES) students seems to indicate that these students, although granted access to our nation's public schools, encounter a rather different climate from their peers. This climate is often less attentive and sometimes even hostile to their educational needs. The typical school has a series of microclimates rather than a single school climate. Finally, it is interesting that the data on teacher attitudes show that these factors are true on the aggregate, although few teachers or administrators would admit to reflecting these patterns individually.

Students

Given the manner in which public schools in the United States function, a number of student characteristics correlate with academic success. Let's start with the fact that two-thirds of secondary students resist the curriculum, either actively or passively (Sedlack et al. 1986) Clearly, that resistance doesn't begin in high school but often considerably earlier. Students who show limited progress in their early years of schooling fall farther and farther behind in succeeding years (Stanovick 1986). There are two main factors behind this phenomenon: (1) such students continue to find the curriculum pedantic and unstimulating; and (2) teaching practices tend to be unvaried and teacher-centered. The combination of these factors causes many students to become increasingly passive and unmotivated with each succeeding year of school.

Educators need to understand that students' cognitive styles are different. While field-independent and field-sensitive students are found in all cultural and racial groups, research seems to indicate that Hispanic and African American students are more likely to be field-sensitive learners. Curriculum presented in a more humanistic and relational manner would be better suited for them (Ramirez and Price-Williams 1974).

The relationship between race, ethnic background, and mental ability has been the subject of much controversy and speculation. One revealing study attempted to evaluate the role of social class in determining mental ability. In this study, an examination was conducted of African American children who were adopted by two types of middle-class families: one White and the other African American. The study found those African American children adopted by White families scored significantly better on the Weschler Intelligence Scale for Children (W.I.S.C.) test. The 13.5 point difference between the two groups of African American children mirrored the gap on W.I.S.C. scores between Whites and African Americans in the larger society (Moore 1985).

A study of socialization practices found that fewer analytic and self-dependent skills were being fostered in Hispanic homes in comparison with socialization practices in Anglo-American homes (Bermudez 1986). This finding supports other studies that conclude that Hispanic students are less numerous among field-independent learners.

Another student characteristic that affects academic achievement is locus of control. Students with an internal locus of control feel better able to affect their environment. Conversely, those with an external locus of control are more likely to feel that factors that influence their lives are controlled by outside forces. When this topic has been related to the socioeconomic status of students, it was found that higher SES students are more likely to have an internal locus of control than lower SES students. In turn, an internal locus of control has also been found to correlate positively with higher academic achievement in our nation's schools (Leftcourt 1982).

Galguera (1998) examined the influence of gender, ethnicity, and bilingualism on the cognitive aspects of students' attitudes toward teachers. He found that all three factors had a significant influence, and the influence of bilingualism was strongest. These findings underscore the need to recruit, educate, and retain a diverse population of teachers to instruct an increasingly diverse student population.

When you summarize the student characteristics that currently correlate with high academic achievement (i.e., field-independent learner, White, middle/upper class, internal locus of control), it becomes evident that these are not the characteristics that abound in the most rapidly growing segments of this nation's public school students. Without significant changes in the *modus operandi* of schools, the consequences for the 21st century will be significant.

Conclusion

American education must make significant adjustments to meet the challenge of the demographic changes of the 21st century. The cultural and ethnic differences between our teacher and student populations are growing. We cannot continue to assume that all current practices are appropriate, especially in light of the school failure rates for students of color that are frequently more than twice those found for mainstream students.

One place to begin this change is in teacher-education programs. Traditionally, prospective teachers learned about the role of culture in education either vicariously or on the job. A number of universities have strong multicultural education components in their teacher-education programs, but these institutions are currently the exception rather than the rule. In most institutions of higher education, multicultural education is interspersed in other education courses or often taught in separate courses by faculty with minimal background in the field.

Ideally, teachers should enter the profession with a sufficient knowledge of the research base in education so they can relate their activities in the classroom to it. Teachers with these abilities would truly practice their profession in a manner more analogous to that of other professionals. This research base should include thorough familiarity with how race, ethnic background, socioeconomic status, gender, and exceptionality interact with the learning process.

A strong component of teacher education should be aimed at assessing a candidate's level of multicultural functioning, with specific strategies for developing respectful and caring attitudes toward all students. Currently, even though teacher attitude is a major factor in the learning process, only in extreme cases would biased perspectives cause teacher candidates to fail to complete their certification programs.

Colleges of education also need to help future teachers develop teaching skills that are relational and cooperative as well as factual and analytical. (Equal time and attention should be paid to the former and the latter.) Prospective teachers need to internalize the notion that the educational product is much more significant than the educational process. If traditional teaching approaches are not yielding satisfactory results, teachers should not be reluctant to restructure their methods.

School systems across this nation that have not already done so should examine their curricula to see whether or not they present content that incorporates multicultural perspectives. When those perspectives are integrated and permeate entire curricula, they also create an interesting side effect: prejudice reduction. This is certainly another worthy objective for our schools.

It has now become common for educators and community leaders to advocate that global literacy should be a product of American education. The economic impact of not having an internationally literate populace in a global economy is self-evident. However, many have not realized that before persons can be literate in the cultural contexts of other nations, they must first be cognizant of the cultural diversity within their own society. In other words, multicultural literacy is a precursor to global literacy. The economic value of multicultural literacy will, in time, become as obvious as that of global sophistication.

Public school systems in this nation need to provide incentives for veteran teachers to become familiar with the research base in multicultural education, either through workshops or the recertification process. Nearly all teachers in our schools are interested in improving the level of their practice if new information is presented concisely and is related to classroom activity. Teachers and administrators must be able to analyze their schools' atmosphere, curriculum, and evaluation practices through multicultural perspectives. If these elements are found lacking, changes should be made.

Finally, educators need to redouble efforts aimed toward students who are malcontent with school or who feel hopeless in their efforts to gain an education. Those pupils need to feel that we, their teachers, believe there are no disposable students.

References

Banks, J. (1994). *Teaching strategies for ethnic studies* (3rd ed.). Boston: Allyn and Bacon.

Banks, J. (1996). Multicultural education and curriculum transformation. *Journal of Negro Education, 64*(4), 390–400.

Banks, J. (1999). Multicultural education in the new century. *The School Administrator, 56*(5), 8–10.

Bermudez, A. (1986). Examining the effects of home training on problem-solving styles. E.R.I.C., ED 187107.

Brophy, J., and Good, T. (1974). *Teacher-student relationships: Causes and consequences.* New York: Holt, Rinehart, and Winston.

Cohen, E. (1986). *Designing group work-strategies for the heterogeneous classroom.* New York: Teachers College Press.

Cohen, R. (1995). Moving beyond name games: The conservative attack on U.S. history. *Social Education, 60* (January), 49–54.

Ford, M. (1979). The development of an instrument for assessing levels of ethnicity in public school teachers. Ed.D. dissertation, University of Houston.

Frederick, W. (1977). The use of classroom time in high schools above or below the mean reading score. *Urban Education, 11*(4), 459–465.

Freire, P. (1993). *Pedagogy of the oppressed.* New York: Continuum.

Galguerra, T. (1998). Students' attitudes towad teachers' ethnicity, blinguality, and gender. *Hispanic Journal of Behavioral Sciences, 20*(4), 411–428.

Gillette, M., and Chinn, P. (1997). Multicultural education: Responding to a mandate for equitable educational outcomes. *Teacher Education and Practice, 13*(1), 1–13.

Goodlad, J. (1984). *A place called school.* New York: McGraw-Hill.

Graybill, S. W. (1997). Questions of race and culture: How they relate to the classroom for African American students. *Clearing House, 70,* 311–318.

Henry, W. A. (1990). Beyond the melting pot. *Time, 135*(15), 28.

Ladson-Billings, G. (1994). *The dreamkeepers: Successful teachers of African American children.* San Francisco: Jossey-Bass.

Leftcourt, H. M. (1982). *Locus of control: Current trends in theory and research.* Mahwah, NJ: Lawrence Erlbaum.

McGee Banks, C. (1997). The challenges of national standards in a multicultural society. *Educational Horizons* (Spring), 126–132.

Moore, E. G. (1985). Ethnicity as a variable in child development. In M. G. Spencer, G. K. Brooklins, and W. R. Allen (Eds.), *The social and affective development of black children* (pp. 101–115). Mahwah, NJ: Lawrence Erlbaum.

Ramirez, M., and Price-Williams, D. R. (1974). Cognitive styles of children of three ethnic groups in the United States. *Journal of Cross-Cultural Psychology, 5*(2), 212–219.

Rosenthal, R., and Jacobson, L. (1968). *Pygmalion in the classroom: Teacher expectation and pupils' intellectual development.* New York: Holt, Rinehart, and Winston.

Sedlack, M., Wheeler, C. W., Pullin, D. W., and Cusick, P. M. (1986). *Selling students short.* New York: Teachers College Press.

Sheets, R. H. (1996). Urban classroom conflict: Student teacher perception: Ethnic identity, solidarity, and resistance. *Urban Review, 28,* 165–183.

Slavin, R. E. (1983). *Cooperative learning.* New York: Longman.

Snyder, T. D., Hoffman, C. M., and Geddes, C. M (1997). *Digest of education statistics.* Washington, DC: National Center for Education Statistics, Office of Research and Improvement.

Stanovick, K. (1986). Matthew effects in reading: Some consequences of individual differences in the acquisition of literacy. *Reading Research Quarterly, 21*(4), 360–407.

Walberg, H. (1984). Improving the productivity of America's schools. *Educational Leadership, 41*(8), 19–27.

chapter 2

Multicultural Education: Goals, Possibilities, and Challenges

James A. Banks

Well, we just see it that kids are kids. Besides, the early grades are all about skill building. We don't have time to add extra stuff and we don't have diversity anyway.

This statement was made by a veteran elementary school teacher in a predominantly white school when a novice teacher asked her how she incorporated multicultural issues into her teaching. Her confused and essentialized conception of multicultural education is not uncommon among educational practitioners and the general public. However, multicultural scholars and researchers have reached agreement on some of the major components and dimensions of multicultural education within the last decade. A significant gap exists between the conception of multicultural education among specialists and among practitioners and the public. The definition presented by Banks and Banks (1995) in the *Handbook of Research of Multicultural Education* reflects the emerging consensus among multicultural education scholars and researchers:

> Multicultural education is a field of study designed to increase educational equity for all students that incorporates, for this purpose, content, concepts, principles, theories, and paradigms from history, the social and

behavioral sciences, and particularly from ethnic studies and women's studies. (p. xii).

Banks and Banks describe multicultural education as a "metadiscipline." The consensus among specialists centers around a primary goal for multicultural education, which is to increase educational equality for both gender groups, for students from diverse ethnic, cultural, and language groups, and for exceptional students (Banks and Banks 2001; Gay 2000; Grant 1999).

The Meaning and Goals of Multicultural Education

A major assumption of multicultural education is that some groups of students, because of their cultural and language characteristics, are more consistent with the school's culture, norms, and expectations than other groups of students. Students whose cultures are more consistent with the school culture have greater opportunities for academic success than students whose cultures conflict with the school culture. Low-income African American males, for example, tend to have more problems in school than middle-class Anglo-American males (Nettles and Perna 1997).

Increasing educational equality for students from diverse groups requires significant school restructuring and more income parity between low-income schools and schools in affluent communities (Darling-Hammond 1997; Anyon 2001). Some of the basic assumptions, beliefs, and structures within schools, such as tracking and the ways in which educators interpret and use mental-ability tests, need to be reformed. New paradigms about the ways students learn, about human ability, and about the nature of knowledge should be institutionalized within schools (Banks 1996; Gardner 1999; Gould 1996). School restructuring also requires teachers who believe that all students can learn, regardless of their social class or ethnic group, and that knowledge be conceptualized as a social construction that reflects social, political, and normative assumptions (Banks 2000). Implementing multicultural school reform is a continuous process that cannot be completed within a few weeks or over several years. It requires a long-term commitment to school improvement, restructuring, and transformation.

Another important goal of multicultural education, acknowledged by authorities in the field but neither fully understood nor appreciated by many teachers, journalists, and the public, is to help all students, including white mainstream students, develop the knowledge, skills, and attitudes they need to survive and function effectively in a culturally diverse society. The U.S. Census projects that Latinos, African Americans, and other groups of color will make up 38% of the U.S. population in 2025, and 48%

in 2050 (cited in Martin and Midgley 1999). Our survival as a strong and democratic nation depends on the ability of students to function effectively in a pluralistic civic community. As Martin Luther King Jr. said so eloquently: "We will live together as brothers and sisters or die separate and apart as strangers" (King 1987).

Multicultural education and global education share important goals. Global education seeks to help students develop cross-cultural competency in cultures beyond their national borders and to acquire the insights needed to recognize that all peoples living on earth have highly interconnected fates (Diaz, Massialas, and Xanthopoulos 1999). Citizens who have an understanding and empathy for the cultures within their own society are probably more likely to function effectively in cultures outside of their nation than citizens who do not have this knowledge (Banks 2001).

Although multicultural and global education share important aims, the two fields should be distinguished in theory and practice. Components of both global and multicultural education should be incorporated into the curriculum. However, one should not substitute for the other. Some teachers are more comfortable teaching about Mexico than about Mexican Americans who live within their own cities and states. Other teachers and some publishers do not differentiate between multicultural and global education.

Multicultural Education Is for All Students

We need to think seriously about why multicultural educators have not been more successful in conveying to teachers, journalists, and the general public the idea that multicultural education is concerned not only with students of color but with all students. It is also not widely recognized that many of the reforms designed to increase the academic achievement of students of color—such as a pedagogy that is sensitive to learning styles and cooperative learning techniques—will also help white mainstream students to increase their academic achievement and to develop more positive intergroup attitudes and values (Ladson-Billings 1994; Delpit 1995).

Multicultural education must be conceptualized as a strategy for all students for several important reasons. U.S. schools are not working as well for any groups of students as they should (Oakes et al. 2000). Most students of color (with the important exception of some groups of Asian American students) and low-income students are more dependent on the school for academic achievement than are most mainstream, white middle-class students for a variety of complex reasons. However, school restructuring is needed for all students because most groups of students are not achieving at levels that are essential for the cyberage world in which we live (Darling-Hammond 1997).

Multicultural education should also be conceptualized as a strategy for all students because it will become institutionalized and supported in the nation's schools, colleges, and universities only to the extent that it is perceived as universal and in the broad public interest. An ethnic-specific notion of multicultural education stands little chance of success and implementation in the nation's educational institutions.

Challenges to the Anglocentric Curriculum

The Anglocentric, male-dominated curriculum that is institutionalized within the nation's schools, colleges, and universities has been seriously challenged within the last two decades by transformative academic scholars (Banks 1996) and the ethnic studies, women's studies, and multicultural education movements. Attempts to transform the mainstream curriculum in the nation's educational institutions experienced significant success during the 1980s and 1990s. Curriculum reform has been uneven and has been more substantial at the college and university levels than in the nation's schools. However, ethnic groups of color are much more visible in the textbooks of the 1990s than they were in the textbooks of yesteryear. Many teachers throughout the United States completed required multicultural education courses and experiences during the 1980s and 1990s. These teachers are more able and likely to incorporate components of multicultural education and diversity into their teaching than teachers of the past who took no multicultural course work. Some highly respected scholars of the classics, such as Martha C. Nussbaum (1997), have crafted thoughtful rationales for including multicultural content into the college and university curriculum.

An Anglocentric education dominated the 20th but will not dominate the 21st century. The Anglocentric curriculum that is institutionalized within our nation's schools, colleges, and universities is being seriously challenged today and will continue to be contested until it is transformed to accurately reflect the experiences, voices, and struggles of people of color, women, and other cultural and social groups in U.S. society.

The historical, social, and economic factors are different today than they were when Anglo-Americans established dominance over the nation's major social, economic, and political institutions in the 17th and 18th centuries. The economic, demographic, and ideological factors that led to the establishment of Anglo-hegemony early in U.S. history are changing even though Anglo-Americans are still politically, economically, and culturally dominant.

Groups such as African Americans and Latinos are demanding full structural inclusion and a reformulation of the canon used to select the content for the school, college, and university curriculum. Many compassionate and informed whites are joining groups of color to support reforms in the nation's social, economic, political, and educational institutions (Dilg 1999; Howard 1999). Therefore, it would be a mistake to perceive the educational reform movements related to diversity as confrontations between people of color and whites.

One of the pervasive myths within our society is that whites are a monolithic group. In fact, the word *white* conceals more than it reveals. Whites are a very diverse group in terms of ethnic and cultural characteristics (Waters 1990), experiences with discrimination and exclusion (Ignatiev 1995; Brodkin 1998), political affiliations, and attitudes towards ethnic and cultural diversity (Jacobson 1998). While most whites have benefited from and sanctioned institutionalized racism throughout U.S. history (Zinn 1999), many groups of whites as well as individual whites have supported social movements to increase the rights of African Americans and other people of color (Smith 1949/1994; Dees 1991). Reform-oriented white citizens who are pushing for a more equitable and just society are an important factor that will make it increasingly difficult for mainstream white American perspectives, paradigms, and values to continue to dominate U.S. educational institutions.

Whites play an important role in social-reform movements and in the election of politicians of color. In 2000, the executive of King County (Seattle metropolitan area) was African American and the governor of Washington state was Chinese American. Norm Rice, an African American, served as mayor of Seattle for eight years. Mayors of a number of U.S. cities and an African American governor of Virginia would not have been elected without substantial support from white voters during the last three decades. Many white students on university campuses formed coalitions with students of color to demand that the university curriculum be reformed to include content about people of color and women. These student movements experienced major victories in the 1970s and 1980s. Ethnic studies and multicultural requirements exist on a number of college and university campuses, the result of student action.

In 1995, 35% of the students enrolled in public schools in the United States were students of color (Pratt and Rittenhouse 1998). Demographers project that they will make up about 46 percent of the nation's school-age youths by 2020 (Pallas, Natriello, and McDill 1989). The Anglocentric curriculum needs to be reformed to include the voices and experiences of a range of ethnic, cultural, and language groups. The significant percentage of people of color, including African Americans and Latinos, who are in positions of leadership in educational institutions will continue to work to get the experiences of their peoples integrated into the school and university curriculum. These individuals include researchers, professors, administrators, and authors of textbooks. Students of color will continue to form coalitions with reform-oriented white students and demand that the school and university curriculum be reformed to reflect the ethnic, cultural, and language realities of American life. Parents and community groups will continue to seek a school, college, and university curriculum that gives voice to their experiences, hopes, dreams, and struggles. African American parents and community groups are the major agents pushing for a curriculum that reflects African civilizations and experimental schools for African American males (Chmelynski 1990).

Feminists also will continue to challenge the Anglocentric curriculum because they view it as male oriented, patriarchal, and sexist. Significantly, much of the new research in women's studies deals with the cultures of women of color (Guy-Sheftall 1995; Garcia 1997).

The Challenges to Multicultural Education

Multicultural education is frequently challenged by conservative writers and scholars (Schlesinger 1991; D'Souza 1995). Some of the misunderstandings surrounding multicultural education result from attempts by conservative scholars to portray it as a movement against Western civilization, as anti-white and, by implication, anti-American (Schlesinger 1991; D'Souza 1995). The popular press frequently calls the movement to infuse African American and African perspectives into the curriculum *Afrocentric*, and it has defined the term to mean an education that excludes whites and Western civilization.

Afrocentric has different meanings to different people. Because of these diverse interpretations, conservative scholars have focused many of their criticisms of multicultural education on Afrocentrism. They have not described the ways in which multicultural education and Afrocentrism differ. Molefi Kete Asante (1987) defines Afrocentricity as "placing African ideals at the center of any analysis that involves African culture and behavior" (p 6). In other words, he defines Afrocentricity as looking at African and African American behavior from an African or African American perspective. His definition suggests that Black English, or *Ebonics*, cannot be understood unless it is viewed from the perspective of those who speak it.

Afrocentricity, when Asante's definition is used, can describe the addition of an African American perspective to the school and university curriculum. A sound multicultural curriculum makes it possible for a variety of ethnic and cultural perspectives, including Afrocentric perspectives, to be incorporated into the curriculum. *Africana: The Encyclopedia of the African and African American Experience*, edited by Appiah and Gates (1999), is an excellent source of information for incorporating content into the curriculum about people of African descent in the United States and throughout the world.

The Canon Battle: Special Interests Versus the Public Interest

The push by people of color and by women to get their voices and experiences institutionalized within the curriculum and to transform its canon has evoked strong reactions from conservative scholars (Schlesinger 1991; D'Souza 1995). Many of the arguments presented by conservative critics, however, are smoke screens for a political agenda designed to promote dominant-group hegemony and the interests of a small elite. A clever tactic of the conservative scholars is to portray their own interests as universal and in the public good, and the interests of women and people of color as *special interests* that are particularistic. When a dominant elite describes its interests as the same as those of the public, it marginalizes the experiences of structurally excluded groups, such as women and people of color.

Special interest implies a particular interest inconsistent with the overreaching goals and needs of the nation-state or commonwealth. To be in the public good, interests must extend beyond the needs of a unique or specific group. It is important to identify who formulates the criteria for determining what is a special interest. Because the dominant group has already shaped the curriculum, institutions, and structures in its images and interests, it views its interests not as special, but as identical with the common good. Special interests, as seen by those who control the curriculum and other institutions within society, are therefore those that challenge their power, ideologies, and paradigms, particularly if the interest group demands that the canons, assumptions, and values of the institutions be transformed.

Only a curriculum that reflects the experiences and interests of a wide range of groups in the United States and the world is in the national interest and therefore consistent with the public good. Any other kind of curriculum reflects a special interest and is detrimental to the needs of a nation that must survive in a pluralistic and highly interdependent world. Special-interest history and literature, such as history and literature that emphasize the primacy of the West and the history of European American males, undermine the public good because they will not help students acquire the knowledge, skills, and attitudes essential for survival in this century.

An important aim of the ethnic studies and women's studies movements is to reform the curriculum so that it will be more truthful, more inclusive, and more reflective of the histories and experiences of the diverse groups and cultures that make up American society. Rather than being special-interest reform movements, these groups contribute to the democratization of the school and the university curriculum. They support the public good rather than the strengthening of special interests.

We need to rethink concepts such as *special interests*, the *national interest*, and the *public good*, and to identify which groups are using these terms and for what purposes. We must also evaluate the use of these terms in the context of a nation and world that are rapidly changing. Powerless and marginalized groups accurately perceive efforts to label their visions and experiences as *special interests* as an attempt to make their voices silent and their faces invisible.

Our concept of cultural literacy should be broader than the one presented by E. D. Hirsch (1987) in *Cultural Literacy: What Every American Needs to Know*. He depicts knowledge as neutral and static, and his book contains a list of important facts that he believes students should master in order to become culturally literate. *Knowledge, however, is dynamic, changing, and constructed within a social context, not neutral and static as Hirsch implies.* He recommends transmitting knowledge in a largely uncritical way. When we help students learn, we should teach them to recognize that knowledge reflects the social context in which it is created and that it has normative and value assumptions (Banks 1998).

I agree with Hirsch that there is a need for all U.S. citizens to have a common core of knowledge. However, the important question is: *Who will participate in the formulation of that knowledge, and whose interests will it serve?* Scholars and educators from diverse racial, cultural, ethnic, and language groups must participate in the identification, construction, and formulation of the information that we expect all of our citizens to master. This knowledge should reflect cultural democracy and serve the needs of all the people. It should contribute to public virtue and the public good, and it cannot serve only the needs of dominant and powerful groups, as much of it currently does. Rather, it should reflect the experiences of all of the nation's citizens and should empower all people to participate effectively in a democratic society.

A Transformed Curriculum and Multiple Perspectives

Educators use several approaches to integrate cultural content into the school and university curriculum (Banks 1997). Among these is the *contributions approach*, in which content about ethnic and cultural groups is limited primarily to holidays and celebrations, such as Martin Luther King Jr.'s Birthday and Women's History Week. This approach is used often in the primary and elementary grades.

Another frequently used approach to integrate cultural content into the curriculum is the *additive approach*. In this method, cultural content, concepts, and themes are added to the curriculum without changing its basic structure, purposes, and characteristics. The additive approach is often accomplished by inserting a multicultural unit or course into an otherwise unchanged curriculum.

Neither the contributions nor the additive approach challenges the basic structure or canon of the curriculum. Cultural celebrations, activities, and content are inserted into the curriculum within its existing framework and assumptions. When these approaches are used, the selection of people, events, and interpretations related to ethnic groups and women often reflects the norms and values of the dominant culture rather than those of the cultural communities. Consequently, most of the additions reflect the values and roles of the dominant culture. Men and women who challenged the *status quo* and established institutions are less likely to be selected for inclusion into the curriculum. Thus Sacajawea, who helped whites to conquer Indian lands, is more likely to be chosen for inclusion than Geronimo, who resisted the takeover of Indian lands by whites.

The *transformative approach* differs fundamentally from the contributions and additive approaches. It changes the canon, paradigms, and basic assumptions of the curriculum and enables students to view concepts, issues, themes, and problems from different perspectives. Important goals of this approach include helping students to understand concepts, events, and people from diverse ethnic and cultural perspectives and to understand knowledge as a social construction. In this approach, students are able to read and listen to the voices of the victors and the vanquished. They also analyze the teacher's perspective on events and situations and are given the opportunity to formulate and justify their own versions of them. A key aim of the transformation approach is to teach students to think critically and to develop the skills to formulate, document, and justify their conclusions and generalizations.

When using the transformation approach to teach a unit such as "The Westward Movement," the teacher would assign appropriate readings and then ask the students such questions as: What do you think "The Westward Movement" means? Who was moving west, the whites or the Native Americans? What region in the United States was referred to as "the West"? Why? The point of these questions is to help students understand that "The Westward Movement" is a Eurocentric term because the Lakota Sioux were already living in the West and consequently were not moving. This phrase is used to refer to the movement of European Americans who were headed in the direction of the Pacific Ocean. Furthermore, the Sioux did not consider their homeland the West, but the center of the universe.

The teacher could ask the students to describe the Westward Movement from the point of view of the Sioux. The students might use such titles as "The End," "The Age of Doom," or "The Coming of the People who Took our Land." The teacher could also ask students to give the unit a name that is more neutral than "The Westward Movement." They might name the unit "The Meeting of Two Cultures."

The *decision-making* and *social-action* approach extends the transformative curriculum by enabling students to pursue projects and activities that allow them to take personal, social, and civic actions related to the concepts, problems, and issues they have studied. For example, after studying different perspectives on "The Westward Movement," the students might decide that they want to learn more about contemporary Native Americans and to take actions that will enable the school to depict and perpetuate more accurate and positive views of America's first inhabitants (Stedman 1982; Hoxie 1996; Churchill, 1998). The students might decide to view a videotape about the Westward Movement and discuss the extent to which it gives an accurate description of relationships between Native Americans and whites. They might also compile a list of books written by Native Americans for the school librarian to order and present a pageant for the school's morning exercise entitled: "The Western Movement: A View From Both Sides."

Conclusion

Multicultural education is necessary to help all of the nation's future citizens acquire the knowledge, attitudes, and skills needed to survive in the 21st century. Nothing less than the nation's survival is at stake. The rapid growth in the nation's population of people of color, the escalating importance of nonwhite nations such as China and Japan, and the widening gap between the rich and the poor make it essential for our future citizens to have multicultural literacy and cross-cultural skills. A nation whose citizens cannot negotiate on the world's multicultural global stage will be tremendously disadvantaged, and its very survival will be imperiled.

References

Anyon, J. (2001). Inner cities, affluent suburbs, and unequal educational opportunities. In J. A. Banks and C. A. M. Banks (Eds.), *Multicultural education: Issues and perspectives* (4th ed.) (pp. 85–102). New York: John Wiley and Sons.

Appiah, A., and Gates, H. L., Jr. (Eds.). (1999). *Africana: The encyclopedia of the African and African American experience.* New York: Basic Books.

Asante, M. K. (1987). *The Afrocentric idea.* Philadelphia: Temple University Press.

Banks, J. A. (Ed.). (1996). *Multicultural education, transformative knowledge, and action: Historical and contemporary perspectives.* New York: Teachers College Press.

Banks, J. A. 1997. *Teaching strategies for ethnic studies* (6th ed). Boston: Allyn and Bacon.

Banks, J. A. (1998). The lives and values of researchers: Implications for educating citizens in a multicultural society. *Educational Researcher, 27*(7), 4–17.

Banks, J. A. (2000). The social construction of difference and the quest for educational equality. In R. Brandt (Ed.), *Education in a new era* (ASCD Yearbook) (pp. 21–45). Alexandria, VA: Association for Supervision and Curriculum Development.

Banks, J. A. (2001). *Cultural diversity and education: Foundations, curriculum, and teaching* (4th ed.). Boston: Allyn and Bacon.

Banks, J. A., and Banks, C. A. M. (Eds.). (1995). *Handbook of research on multicultural education.* New York: Macmillan.

Banks, J. A., and Banks, C. A. M. (Eds.). (2001). *Multicultural education: Issues and perspectives* (4th ed). New York: John Wiley and Sons.

Brodkin, K. (1998). *How the Jews became white folks and what that says about race in America.* New Brunswick: Rutgers University Press.

Chmelynski, C. (1990). Controversy attends schools with all-black, all-male classes. *The Executive Educator, 12*(10), 16–18.

Churchill, W. (1998). *Fantasies of the master race.* San Francisco: City Lights Books.

Darling-Hammond, L. (1997). *The right to learn: A blueprint for creating schools that work.* San Francisco: Jossey-Bass.

Dees, M., with Fiffer, S. (1991). *A season for justice: The life and times of civil rights lawyer Morris Dees.* New York: Scribner's.

D'Souza, D. (1995). *The end of racism: Principles for a multicultural society.* New York: Free Press.

Delpit, L. (1995). *Other People's children: Cultural conflict in the classroom.* New York: New Press.

Diaz, C. F., Massialas, B. G., and Xanthopoulos, J. A. (1999). *Global perspectives for educators.* Boston: Allyn and Bacon.

Dilg, M. (1999). *Race and culture in the classroom: Teaching and learning through multicultural education.* New York: Teachers College Press.

Garcia, A. M. (Ed.). (1997). *Chicana feminist thought: The basic historical writings.* New York: Routledge.

Gardner, H. (1999). *The disciplined mind: What all students should understand.* New York: Simon and Schuster.

Gould, S. J. (1996). *The mismeasure of man* (Rev. and Expanded ed). New York: W. W. Norton.

Gay, G. (2000). *Culturally responsive teaching: Theory, research, and practice.* New York: Teachers College Press.

Grant, C. A. (Ed.). (1999). *Multicultural research: A reflective engagement with race, class, gender, and sexual orientation.* Philadelphia: Falmer.

Guy-Sheftall, B. (Ed.). (1995). *Words of fire: An anthology of African-American feminist thought.* New York: New Press.

Hirsch, E. D. (1987). *Cultural literacy: What every American needs to know.* Boston: Houghton-Mifflin.

Howard, G. (1999). *We can't teach what we don't know: White teachers, multiracial schools.* New York: Teachers College Press.

Hoxie, F. E. (Ed.). (1996). *Encyclopedia of North American Indians.* Boston: Houghton Mifflin.

Ignatiev, N. (1995). *How the Irish became white.* New York: Routledge.

Jacobson, M. F. (1998). *Whiteness of a different color: European immigrants and the alchemy of race.* Cambridge: Harvard University Press.

King, M. L., Jr. (1987). *The words of Martin Luther King Jr.* (selected by C. S. King). New York: Newmarket Press.

Ladson-Billings, G. (1994). *The dreamkeepers: Successful teachers of African American children.* San Francisco: Jossey-Bass.

Martin, P., and Midgley, E. (1999). Immigration to the United States. *Population Bulletin, 54*(2), pp. 1–44. Washington, DC: Population Reference Bureau.

Nettles, M. T., and Perna, L. W. (1997). *The African American databook: Preschool through high school education* (Vol. 2). Fairfax, VA: Frederick D. Patterson Research Institute.

Nussbaum, M. C. (1997). *Cultivating humanity: A classical defense of reform in liberal education.* Cambridge: Harvard University Press.

Oakes, J., Quartz, K. H., Ryan, S., and Lipton, M. (2000). *Becoming good American schools: The struggle for civic virtue in education reform.* San Francisco: Jossey-Bass.

Pallas, A. M., Natriello, G., and McDill, E. L. (1989). The changing nature of the disadvantaged population: Current dimensions and future trends. *Educational Researcher, 18*(5), 16–22, ff. 46–48.

Pratt, R., and Rittenhouse, G. (Eds.). (1998). *The Condition of education 1998.* Washington, DC: U.S. Government Printing Office.

Schlesinger, A. M., Jr. (1991). *The disuniting of America: Reflections on a multicultural society.* Knoxville, TN: Whittle Direct Books.

Smith, L. (1949/1994). *Killers of the dream.* New York: Norton.

Stedman, R. W. (1982). *Shadows of the Indian: Stereotypes in American culture.* Norman: University of Oklahoma Press.

Waters, M. C. (1990). *Ethnic options: Choosing identities in America.* Berkeley: University of California Press.

Zinn, H. (1999). *A people's history of the United States, 1492–present* (20th anniversary ed.). New York: HarperCollins

chapter 3

Effective Multicultural Teaching Practices

Geneva Gay

When teachers are challenged to be more sensitive to the cultural heritages and life experiences of ethnically diverse students, they frequently respond in one of three ways. One is, "When I look at my students, I don't see race, class, ethnicity, or gender. I see *children*, and I treat them all the same." This response seems to be motivated by a desire to demonstrate that teachers are free of biases and discrimination in their interactions with students. It also is a declaration that ethnic identity and cultural diversity are not (or should not be) issues of concern in classroom instruction.

Another frequent response comes from teachers who recognize the need to do something about ethnic and cultural diversity in their classroom, but they are not sure what this is. They say, "Tell us what to do, and we will do it." While more constructive than the first one, this reaction is still problematic. Teachers who make this declaration seem to be looking to someone else to provide definitive answers to all of the possible challenges multicultural education provides for classroom instruction. They do not seem to realize that this is an impossible request. No one can ever provide failure-proof strategies for classroom use, especially if they are not active, regular participants in the classroom dynamics. They can offer some very useful guidance in the form of principles for practice, and examples to illustrate the principles, but teachers will still have to extrapolate the messages of these for use in their own classrooms. This is an unavoidable reality—classroom teachers cannot abdicate the responsibility for translating general instructional ideas into specific techniques that will be effective for their own classroom settings and instructional interactions with students. In commenting on this necessity, Good and Brophy (1978, p. 341) explain that consulting educators from outside of the classroom "can say that certain things should take place, but the frequency of their occurrence and the ways they are performed depend, in part, upon teacher style and situational variables." Therefore, teachers must act as *decision makers*, determining how general principles apply to their particular classrooms.

The third common response to the challenge to implement multicultural education in classrooms comes from teachers who are more overtly opposed to the idea. They express this opposition in statements like, "Multicultural education is not appropriate for my subject or discipline (especially math and science)," "Why lower academic standards (or have a different set) for African, Native, Latino, and Asian American students," and "They are all in the USA now, and they have to learn to be Americans." The motivation behind these reactions seem to be the misconception that multicultural education, civic citizenship, high-quality academic performance, and the disciplinary integrity of certain subjects are inherently contradictory. Nothing could be further from the truth. All of these are both independent and interconnected goals and missions of achieving educational excellence for all students. Neither one can be fully accomplished without attending simultaneously to the other.

Confronting Conventions and Challenges of Change

The need to apply multicultural knowledge, values, and skills to classroom instruction will intensify as traditional instructional efforts become less effective for ethnically, racially, and linguistically diverse students, and as teachers experience increasing frustrations and doubts about working with these different populations. These changes will require more of teachers than simply being aware, respectful, and tolerant of cultural diversity among students from a wide variety of ethnic groups. They must do something fundamentally different in their instructional interactions than what many are currently doing if more diverse students are to achieve higher levels of school success.

The demands for changes are so great and the need so pressing that it is tempting to respond by creating lists of multicultural classroom practices and strategies for teachers to use. But yielding to this temptation may reinforce fallacious assumptions that effective multicultural education can be implemented easily and expeditiously with little professional preparation. In fact, preparation is imperative. It should include three major types of tasks. One has to do with acquiring a knowledge base for and engaging in the process of making multicultural instructional decisions; another involves assessing the adequacy of the decisions made; the third deals with how to place multicultural interventions into the proper scope, sequence, and context of other classroom operations.

Compiling catalogs of learning activities, resources, and materials about the heritages, experiences, perspectives, and contributions of a variety of ethnic groups is not sufficient to accomplish these tasks. However good such instructional aids are, they are never good enough for most teachers and classroom situations. They tend to be overly general, and reflective of the personal preferences, purposes, and perspectives of the individuals who create them. They also can quickly become outdated. For example, activities that are part of the personal experiences of students in one decade (such as the ethnic self-determination and protest movements of the 1970s) are merely historical artifacts for those in another decade. Furthermore, catalog listings *per se* of multicultural strategies and activities do not adequately inform potential users about *how the ideas and techniques evolved, how to determine the goodness of fit* of these strategies for their own classrooms, or *how to improve the quality of their own pedagogical decision-making skills*. Catalog listings of multicultural instructional strategies can inadvertently perpetuate a sense of powerlessness and intimidation among teachers.

To break this cycle of dependency and to achieve greater instructional success in teaching ethnically diverse students, teachers need to be *empowered* to make decisions about what is best for their own places, purposes, times, and circumstances. This chapter attempts to respond to this need. It endorses the principle of multicultural *infusion*, which means information about and responsiveness to the cultures and experiences of different ethnic groups should be incorporated into *routine* educational operations. This inclusion is especially needed for those groups of color who historically have been oppressed, marginalized, or excluded from mainstream society and institutions.

Three additional guidelines underlie the ideas discussed and proposals made in this chapter. First, instructional decision making should honor the key definitions, concepts, goals, and parameters of multicultural education (Gay 1994a, 1994b). This requires some fundamental knowledge and understanding of the basic content, conventions, and convictions of multicultural education. For example, advocates generally agree that while multicultural, global, and international education are similar and complementary in mission, spirit, and principle, they are not identical. Teaching about Japan, the Philippines, or Mexico is not the same as teaching the history, culture, and experiences of Japanese Americans, Filipino Americans, and Mexican Americans. Multicultural education is concerned primarily with ethnically and culturally different issues within a national context. Furthermore, multicultural education is fundamentally an affective and transformative endeavor, with improved academic performance for underachieving students of color, and greater sociocivic equality, justice, power, and privilege for all ethnic groups as its ultimate outcomes. Simply teaching factual information about the histories, contributions, and experiences of different ethnic groups of color or merely adding multicultural materials to existing curricula is not enough. Effective multicultural education requires that the clarification of values and beliefs related to ethnic, cultural, and racial diversity, institutional and attitudinal reform, and social action accompany the acquisition of factual information.

Second, multicultural education is a means to achieving *greater relevance in the curriculum content and instructional strategies* for ethnically diverse students. This principle applies the logic of a general theory of learning that teaching tools and techniques that are personally meaningful to students increases their learning interests, efforts, and outcomes. Thus, including information about their ethnic groups' contributions and teaching in ways that are compatible with their learning styles improve the school achievement of African, Asian, Latino, and Native American students. This is true whether the achievement is better test scores, participation in instructional discourse, school attendance and persistence records, positive self-concepts, and social relations, or fewer disciplinary referrals (Gay 2000). Additionally, multicultural education can reduce racial and ethnic prejudices and stereotyping and help students learn to be agents of change for greater social justice and equality. Several researchers have provided empirical evidence in support of these effects (see, for example, Allen and Boykin 1992; Deyhle 1995; Fullilove and Treisman 1990; Lee 1993; Mathews 1988; Tharp and Gallimore 1988).

Third, multicultural education should not enter into classroom instruction in capricious, haphazard, or incidental ways. Some *carefully conceived and well-planned schemata* should govern its *deliberate and systemic* implementation. Several possible schemes are available from scholarly literature (Banks 1997a; Sleeter and Grant 1994; Bennett 1995). However, these frameworks apply more to program planning and curriculum development than to classroom instruction. They are more theoretical and conceptual than operational and practical. That is, they suggest what should be done and why, but they do not necessarily explain, with sufficient procedural clarity, how to translate the prescriptions into actual behaviors within the context of real classroom instruction. Teachers must learn how to make these principle-to-practice translations. Otherwise, very good theoretical advice for how to do multicultural teaching will be wasted. *Contextual decision-making* skills are essential to these translations because particular classrooms have many discrete characteristics and instructional dynamics.

Systematic Analysis of the Teaching Process

Any problem-solving or decision-making process begins with acknowledging and identifying specific issues or situations that require resolution. Then the problem situation needs to be carefully analyzed to determine its

nature and elements, alternative solutions or decisions, and ways to evaluate appropriate options for the given circumstances. Therefore, before
quality decisions can be made about what multicultural instructional practices are best suited for particular classroom climates and learning tasks,
the most problematic aspects need to be determined. This can be accomplished by (1) doing systemic analyses of the *habitual tasks, functions, and
features* of the teaching process; (2) identifying the conflict points between
these and their operations in working with students from different ethnic
and cultural backgrounds; (3) making decisions and choices about the
kinds of changes needed to resolve these conflicts; and (4) determining the
best ways to implement the desired changes.

In general, systems analysis involves identifying observable unifor-
mities, patterns, and interactions between structures and functions that
exist in a phenomenon being studied (Levy 1968). When applied to teaching, these analyses are somewhat analogous to constructing an anatomy of
the process. The act of teaching is dissected to discern and describe its
most *characteristic features or normative* tasks and activities. These analyses
are similar to, but more inclusive than, techniques that have been used in
classroom interaction analysis research (Flanders 1970; Gage 1963). Goodlad (1984) used some of these techniques in his seminal study of schooling.
He conducted site observations of more than 1,000 classrooms throughout
the United States to describe the *habitual* instructional processes that were
being employed, and to deduce from them "who … was doing what … to
whom … how … and in what [teaching] context" (p. 226).

Structural analysis of teaching is based on several key assumptions.
Among these are: (1) the process or act of teaching includes some common
tasks and functions that prevail across time, place, setting, circumstance,
and individual teacher characteristics; (2) these functions are systematic,
habitual, and occur with a high degree of regularity; (3) they have substantive, organizational, and procedural traits; and (4) all regular teaching functions have direct implications for implementing multicultural education.
These assumptions are supported by the thinking and research of other
educators as well. Bossert (1979), for instance, suggests that every classroom activity can be described according to its structural and functional
characteristics. Goodlad (1984) found some strikingly similar patterns of
teaching functions and behaviors across teachers, grade levels, and subjects.
Adams (1970) contends that the classroom is a social and behavioral setting
with its own rituals, rules, regularities, and persistent patterns of behavior.

These claims about teaching can be extended to yet another level of
operations. Not only is teaching a system, but there are other systems (or
subsystems) within it, each of which has its own system. Classroom management, feedback provisions, performance appraisal, curriculum design,
and classroom discourse are persistent components (or subsystems) of
teaching. None of these is monolithic or uni-dimensional; each has its own
elements, structures, and regularities. Once identified, those in need of

change can be more effectively remediated. Hudgins (1971, p. 71) states that "teachers must understand how classrooms function if they are to operate effectively and comfortably in them," and that "such understanding is a prerequisite to the design and implementation of reasoned and viable educational change." Some significant changes in the conventional ways of teaching are needed if more students from ethnically diverse backgrounds are to achieve greater success in schools.

Several different classification schemes are available for viewing teaching systematically. Individually and collectively, they describe teaching as including methodological and managerial tasks; having preactive (preparatory) and interactive (face-to-face encounters) components; involving logical (thinking and reasoning), strategic (planning, organizing, and directing), and institutional (keeping records, chaperoning, etc.) acts; and unfolding through a progressional sequence of review, presentation, guided learning practice, corrective feedback, supervision of independent practice, performance assessment, and reteaching (Haysom 1985; Hudgins 1971; Jackson 1968; Rosenshine and Stevens 1986).

A composite profile of teaching functions emerges from further explanations of these general characteristics. All teachers, in some form or another:

- Develop and administer instructional plans
- Set goals and objectives
- Select content and skills to be taught
- Create climates and environments for learning
- Establish relationships with students
- Teach social, academic, personal, and moral skills and values
- Choose instructional materials, teaching techniques, and learning activities
- Provide praise, evaluation, encouragement, and criticism of student performances
- Group students for instruction
- Model and transmit values, beliefs, and standards of social decorum, knowledge acquisition, codes of acceptable behavior, and performance expectations
- Discipline student behavior

Within and across each of these general functions, some specific structures and behaviors dominate. Among these are the passive role of students, whole-group instruction, teacher control, and teacher talk. An emotional tone prevails in most classrooms that Goodlad (1984) describes as "flat," meaning it is neither harsh nor punitive, warm or joyful, passionate or compassionate, very friendly or antagonistic. Nor is it highly exhilarating and engaging. According to Goodlad, regardless of what approaches are used to understand what routinely goes on in the classroom, the teacher emerges as the dominant and directive force—sometimes in the form of coach, quarterback, referee, rule-maker, and too often as autocrat. There is little about how most conventional classrooms function to indicate that students routinely engage in cooperative and collaborative efforts to achieve shared learning objectives. Goodlad adds further that "the most successful classrooms may be those in which teachers succeed in creating commonly shared goals and individuals cooperate in ensuring each person's success in achieving them. The ultimate criterion becomes group accomplishment of individual progress. But this would be countervailing to prevailing practice" (p. 108).

Effective Multicultural Teaching Practices

Four major features and functions of teaching and how to use structural analysis in adapting them to be more multicultural are discussed in this section. They are classroom discourse, substantive anchors of instruction, transforming curriculum, and creating classroom climates for learning. All of these play a significant role in the overall instructional process. They also are consistent with the underlying message of *infusion* as the best way to determine the placement and alignment of multicultural content, experiences, perspectives, and responses in the total educational enterprise. In other words, they support the belief that multicultural education teaching should impact the *significant, mainstream, and regular* operations of the classroom, instead of being relegated to the insignificant, peripheral, and special occasions aspects.

Talking in the Classroom

When it comes to classroom discourse, teachers are the dominant force. This dominance is exhibited through the magnitude of their own verbal initiations and the control they have over who else will talk, when, and under what circumstances (Cazden 1986). According to Hudgins (1971, p.71) "someone is talking in classrooms about two-thirds of the time, and about two-thirds of that time it is the teacher." Teachers spend great amounts of time informing, demonstrating, questioning, illustrating, directing, monitoring, evaluating, and managing. Obviously, then, teacher talk should be high among the priorities targeted for change in developing effective multicultural teaching strategies.

Hurt, Scott, and McCroskey (1978) and Smith (1971) declare that effective communication is fundamental to successful teaching and learning. Montagu and Matson (1979) extend the importance of communication to an even greater plane by explaining that it is the "foundation of community" and "the essential human connection" (p. vii). Most certainly "community" and "human connection" are critical components of teaching and learning. Classroom discourse includes, among other things, teacher and student vocabularies, questioning and thinking strategies, use of time and space, relationships between speakers and listeners, wait-time for responses, turn-taking rules, and a host of nonverbal nuances. A wide variety of "symbolic talking," such as decorations, images, and icons, is also an important part of classroom instruction. Classroom instructional discourse involves how students interact with each other as well. Analyses of these various dimensions of instructional talk can identify patterns of activities, tasks, relationships, and interactions that compose the *mainstay* of teaching. This is the first step in making the instructional process more effective for ethnically diverse students. The next action needed is to examine how these students experience the various aspects of classroom discourse.

Other researchers explain that communication styles are shaped by culture and ethnicity and, in turn, influence how people think, learn, and teach. This is Vygotsky's (1962, p. 51) point when he explains that "thought development is determined by language ... and by the sociocultural experience of the child." Bruner (1996) adds that learning and thinking are always situated in cultural settings and use cultural resources. Sociolinguistic and ethnography communication research provides several different structural, substantive, and procedural components of communication that affect the kinds of opportunities culturally different students receive to participate in the instructional process. They are turn-taking rules, attending and attention-getting behaviors, wait-time for responses, length of speech exchanges, and feedback mechanisms (Philips 1983; Cazden, John, and Hymes 1985; Samovar and Porter 1991).

Many teachers assume that there is a "right way" for all students to participate in classroom discourse that applies to virtually every situation. It includes (1) serialized turn-taking with only one person speaking at a time; (2) students raising hands and waiting to be recognized by the teacher before talking; (3) maintaining eye contact with the teacher as a sign of paying attention; (4) posing questions to specifically targeted individuals instead of to the group as a whole; and (5) creating a dichotomous relationship between speaking and listening in which the listener assumes a passive, receptive posture. Philips (1983) calls these patterns of interacting *switchboard participation structures*, and Kochman (1981) refers to them as *passive-receptive modes of communication.*. Teachers also tend to use rather lengthy speech segments in giving information and instructions, but they provide small amounts of wait-time for students to formulate and present responses. Questions that require higher-order thinking skills, physical action, and genuine affective reactions are used infrequently in classroom discourse. Similar elements and emphases are apparent in written communication as well. They take the form of preferences for focusing on one idea, issue, or topic at a time, descriptive details, linear development of thoughts, dispassionate reporting of factual information, and making narrative relationships very explicit. These styles of communication are referred to as *topic-centered* (Au 1993).

The conventional ways of communicating in the classroom are not shared by all ethnic groups, and they can have profound negative effects on the classroom participation and academic performance of some students. Philips (1985) explains why. Although she speaks specifically about the effects of cultural inconsistencies in communication styles on Native Americans, her observations apply to many students from other groups of color as well. She says, "Indian children fail to participate verbally in classroom interactions because the social conditions to which they have become accustomed in the Indian community are lacking. The absence of these appropriate social conditions for communication performances affects the most common and everyday speech acts that occur in the classroom" (p. 392). Who gets what kinds of opportunities to participate in what kinds of instructional talking correlates highly with the race, ethnicity, culture, language, ability, and gender of students. Those who are middle class, European American, male, and native English-speaking are most advantaged in talking with teachers and engaging in instructional opportunities. They participate more frequently and more qualitatively, are assisted more in working through instructional challenges, are questioned more thoroughly and thus have better opportunities to practice higher-order thinking and problem solving, and are given more complex academic tasks to accomplish (Oakes 1985; Oakes and Guiton 1995) .

Students who are poor and members of ethnic groups of color are frequently treated conversely; they receive fewer and lower-quality opportunities to engage in instructional interactions, and they are assisted less often and in less enabling ways in their academic problem solving. These "second-class instructional engagement opportunities" are a direct result of the failure of teachers to know, respect, and incorporate the culture and communicative styles of ethnically different students into classroom instruction. In addition to obstructing academic learning, these exclusions can create feelings of personal and cultural inferiority for students of color (Philips 1983; Cazden, John, and Hymes 1985; Perry and Delpit 1998). For example, many students from certain ethnic groups will not look directly at a teacher when the teacher is talking. Yet they can be listening intently. Interpreting these behaviors as disrespectful and not paying attention is incorrect. Students resent these unfair indictments, which indeed may cause them to not pay attention or not participate in the instructional discourse. Some students of color and non-native English speakers may require more wait-time to provide responses than teachers routinely give because of their cultural socialization and the processes involved in foreign language production.

African American and Latino students are often very dramatic, emotional, active, inquiring, and interactive in their responding behaviors. These preferences may result from the prominence of storytelling affective expressions and communal values in their traditional cultures. They use *topic-chaining* approaches to organizing their thoughts in both written and oral forms of communication. This means writing and speaking are episodic, anecdotal, and circular with a seamless weaving together of contextual information, descriptive facts, narratives, personal feelings and opinions, multiple topics, and advocacy and evaluation. Asian American students tend to be more passive, quiet, conforming, and accommodating in classroom discourse. These behaviors may reflect cultural values that emphasize harmonious relations and moderation. They also may be misinterpreted by teachers as assurance of high interest in and mastery of learning tasks (Fox 1994; Au 1993; Cazden, John, and Hymes 1985; Philips 1983; Kochman 1981).

All aspects of classroom communication are amenable to including multicultural content and perspectives. These modifications might include:

- Extending and varying wait-time, and changing turn-taking rules to fit more closely with the time and pacing patterns of different ethnic and cultural groups. This is more feasible for effective muticultural teaching than trying to find the ideal amount of time that should elapse between a prompt or invitation to participate in instructional discourse and when students' responding should begin. Some students take longer than others and some can naturally disengage more quickly. Variability in wait-time by ethnic groups may get more students actively involved in *significant instructional communication* and thus improve their overall performance.

- Using alternative cues to indicate attending behaviors, such as asking students to summarize points previously made, to restate another's point of view, or to declare their personal preferences on issues under discussion.

- Shortening the length of teacher speech exchanges. Not only do teachers talk too much, they talk too long at a time for students from some ethnic groups. Less teacher talk in shorter durations can provide windows of opportunity for more students to "get into" classroom conversations, as will more horizontally directed (student-to-student) classroom talking. Thus, teachers should use *more multi-directional routing in facilitating classroom discourse,* including teacher-to-student, student-to-student, student-to teacher, individually guided, and group constructed talking.

- Minimizing teacher talk through the use of more student-focused and active learning strategies, such as small-group tasks, simulations, role playing, dramatic readings, student-led discussions, and cooperative learning.

- Providing opportunities for students to establish, manage, and correct their own rules of classroom discourse. This may cultivate a multiplicity of accepted ways of communicating instead of the "one way only" typically expected in schools.

- Using the naturalistic discourse patterns of different ethnic and cultural groups for some instructional experiences. For example, teachers might encourage students to use cultural styles of storytelling and dramatic performance to develop and appraise translation and comprehension skills in reading, to present critical incidents in social studies, or to report the results of inquiry exercises and research topics.

- Asking more divergent, high-order cognitive, and affective questions that allow all students the chance to respond, and accepting their affective reactions as legitimate contributions to the learning process.

- Converting knowledge acquired in one communicative form to another, such as from reading written text to having a verbal conversation, depicting it in some visual or symbolic image, and using nonverbal gestures, facial expressions, and body movements to convey understanding. Students also could be asked to translate the meaning of an essay into a poem, a script for a play, a newspaper feature (e.g., headline story, editorial, classified, etc.), or a television commercial. Another possibility is to ask students to convert something written or spoken topic-chaining formats into topic-centered expressive styles and vice versa. These are examples *of communicative style-shifting skills*—something all students should learn.

- Providing practice opportunities and guided assistance for students to learn how to become consciously aware of, monitor, and edit cultural nuances in their communication styles.

Substantive Anchor of the Instructional Process

A careful look at how time is allotted across the content of instructional talk is as revealing as its structural characteristics. Much of the actual process of teaching is devoted to providing examples, illustrations, vignettes, scenarios, and anecdotes to demonstrate the appearances, meanings, and functions of the concepts, ideas, facts, principles, and skills being taught. The process begins with naming, defining, and explaining the phenomenon being taught. All other subsequent instructional efforts are devoted to illustrating how, when, and where the object of instruction operates. Examples and illustrations in teaching act as pedagogical bridges between what is being taught in its abstract form and its connection to the life experiences of learners. They are the conduits or transmitters of meaningfulness in learning. Thus, the theory of probability, a literary analogy, a moral dilemma, or the concept of interdependence are most meaningful and easily mastered for more students when the examples used to illustrate the topics reflect the experiences, perspectives, and frames of references of a variety of cultural, ethnic, and social groups. Conversely, when teachers fail to use instructional examples that reflect and connect to the cultures and experiences of ethnically diverse students, they minimize their own instructional effectiveness and make learning more problematic for students.

Incorporating *multicultural* examples into classroom instruction requires that teachers understand the function of examples in their teaching behaviors, the types of examples they currently use, and the cultural limitations they contain. They then need to determine what kinds of examples are best suited for different ethnic and cultural groups; how to create, locate, and solicit them; and how to incorporate them into regular teaching repertoires and routines. For instance, what is heroism according to the standards of different ethnic groups, and which individuals best meet these criteria and should be presented to students as ethnic role models or cultural heroes and heroines. None of these decisions can be made without a working knowledge of different groups' cultural traditions, value systems, learning styles, communications patterns, contributions, and styles of interpersonal interactions.

Multicultural teaching examples serve many teaching and learning functions simultaneously. In addition to being "bridges of meaningfulness" between academic abstractions and practical living, they help all students learn about ethnic and cultural pluralism as they develop academic skills; they demonstrate that multiculturalism is a real, normative, and valued fact of daily life in the classroom; and they model how ethnic and cultural diversity penetrates the inner core of the teaching and learning processes. For instance, showing how basic mathematical forms or shapes like lines, circles, squares, and triangles are applied in different types of ethnic art and architecture (such as Native American long houses, Moslem mosques, Jewish synagogues, indigenous African American and Native American clothes, paintings, and carvings). These cultural applications of mathematical concepts make understanding the concepts (and thus improving math achievement) easier for more diverse students. Using multiethnic examples of protest poetry in the process of teaching literary criticism will improve students' understanding of concept, expressive technique, genre, and analytical skills in relationship to each other. This type of *integrated teaching* is much better for learning than acquiring knowledge in isolation. Multiethnic examples in teaching also facilitate the development of several different kinds of general intellectual abilities, such as critical thinking, synthesizing information from multiple sources, comparative analysis, transfer of learning, and personal empowerment, along with specific multicultural skills like ethnic and cultural literacy, appreciation of cultural diversity, and prejudice reduction (Lee 1993; Gay 1994; Krater, Zeni, and Cason 1994; Banks 1997b).

Multicultural Curriculum Development

A third area of regular teaching behavior that can be a powerful conduit of multicultural teaching is curriculum development. Teachers are always designing and modifying plans for instruction. They should understand this function systematically and know how to incorporate multicultural content and perspectives within it. That is, they should be able to modify the curriculum to make it more culturally and ethnically pluralistic.

Typically, curriculum as a plan for instruction includes six components: rationale, goals, objectives, content, activities, and evaluation. Materials, resources, and timelines are often included as well. These components can be further grouped by function and value into two categories. One is substantive and intrinsic; the other is methodological and instrumental. Substantive curriculum components are the achievement outcomes expected of all students. They are *standards of performance* and are, therefore, non-negotiable. In current educational thinking and improvement initiatives, they are variously called core learnings, essential academic learnings, and standards for educational excellence. They appear in the curriculum as goals and objectives. All other components are means, methods, and tools—instruments—to assist in the achievement of goals and objectives. These should be diversified to accommodate different ethnic, cultural, and social contexts, settings, and clients in the schools and society. That is, multiple, culturally relevant pathways to learning should be used to achieve common outcomes for ethnically diverse student populations. Thus, rationales, content, activities, evaluation procedures, resources, materials, and timelines serve functions in planning for instruction similar to those performed by examples and illustrations in the process of teaching. They, too, are conduits through which intended learning becomes personally meaningful to students, and they are the components of curriculum designs most amenable to change.

Without question, all students should learn to read, write, think critically, and solve problems as well as master the disciplinary knowledge, principles, and skills of the subjects commonly taught in schools, such as mathematics, science, social studies, humanities, fine arts, vocational education, and computer literacy. But how these skills and knowledges should be acquired is less consensual. Answers to this question depend upon for whom, as well as when and where, the teaching takes place. African American students may learn to read better by using curriculum materials and instructional techniques that are quite different from those used with European Americans, but similar to Navajos and Mexican Americans. Similar approaches to learning English might work well for Filipino and Mexican Americans, but Hmong, Cambodian, and Russian immigrants may be different enough for each to require discrete instructional materials, methods, and activities. This means that curriculum content, activities, resources, and evaluation procedures should *always* be varied across and within domains of learning, subjects, and skills to reflect the experiences, contributions, lifestyles, and learning styles of a wide variety of ethnic groups.

Additionally, in planning curricula, multicultural literature, arts, aesthetics, and personal experiences should complement factual information; more active learning, participatory partnerships, cooperative arrangements, and creative expressions should be included in learning activities; and more diverse combinations of written, oral, and kinesthetic opportunities should be provided for students to demonstrate task and skill mastery. For instance, the study of critical issues in social studies might include the struggle for social justice in the United States. The study would involve examining the struggle from the perspectives of different ethnic groups; in different time periods; through different mediums (such as nonviolent social activism, laws, court decisions, literature, art, music, political elections, and theater); separate, collaborative, and comparative efforts and effects across ethnic groups; and gender-based efforts within ethnic groups. As part of these learning experiences, students could design and execute their own action-based contributions to the struggle to achieve social justice by designing a media campaign against ethnic profiling by the police, participating in community service projects earmarked for particular ethnic groups, and boycotting industries and agencies that engage in discriminatory practices against people of color. Multicultural music lyrics, children's and adolescent literature, folktales, personal stories, newspapers, and magazines are as routinely used as basal texts (if not more so) to teach reading, writing, and spelling. These kinds of learning materials and experiences are effective for ethnically diverse students because the content enrichment, multiple perspectives, varied formats, and multisensory stimulations they offer are more compatible with their cultural values and learning styles.

Creating Multicultural Climates for Learning

Teaching involves more than creating curriculum designs and engaging in classroom discourse. Another essential component of the process is the physical, social, and interpersonal climates or environments created for learning. According to Moos (1979), all classrooms are social environments, and they have several common dimensions, such as relationships among students and teachers, climate conditions, task orientation, and managerial rules and regulations. Together, these elements form the sociocultural contexts and settings for learning.

Research shows that students achieve greater satisfaction, personal growth, and levels of performance in classrooms that include high student involvement, strong personal student-teacher relationships, innovative teaching methods, clarity of roles, affective concern and caring for students as people, and hard work for academic rewards—all within a coherent, well-organized context (Moos 1979). These characteristics are especially significant to learning for ethnically different students whose learning styles and cultural values are people-centered, affective, humanistic, and group-based (Nodding 1992; Mehan et al. 1996; Gay 2000). In most U.S. classrooms, students operate largely on an individual basis, have a limited range of movement and involvement, and are expected to function in a rather rigidly organized and sterile physical space. Relationships between students and teachers are formal and somewhat distant, and classroom decorations are too often limited to the mechanical tools (maps, books, machinery, laboratory equipment, and so on) of various subject areas. The notable exceptions are elementary classrooms, which tend to use more comprehensive and creative decorations, and where students and teachers work in closer harmony with each other.

Students of some cultural and ethnic groups, especially African American, Latino, Native American, and Native Hawaiian, find "cold," formal, and passive learning environments distractive to concentrating on academic tasks. Most mainstream classroom procedures use linear, compartmentalized, individualistic, and competitive structures for learning (from lining up to enter and exit the classroom, to sitting in straight rows, to serialized participation in discussions, to how information is arranged and presented, to giving awards to "the best ones"). The cultural structures of most ethnic groups of color are circular, holistic, group-centered, and collaborative. In learning situations, students from these groups are more likely to prefer cooperative learning arrangements; integration of affective, cognitive, and psychomotor abilities in learning challenges; and active and affective interaction among all environmental factors (humans, objects, space, and emotional tone) in the learning setting. A warm, emotionally supportive, caring, and vibrant environment is fundamental to their learning.

Given the environmental conditions that many students of color prefer for learning, what are some specific ways in which classroom climates can be modified to embrace more multicultural principles, perspectives, and experiences? Obviously, they will vary somewhat according to the specific setting, circumstances, and people involved. The suggestions offered here are only *guidelines*, not dictum, for helping teachers create more effective multicultural learning environments. Possible practices include:

- Employing cooperative group, team, and pair arrangements for learning as the normative structure instead of as the occasional exception.

- Using learning stations, multimedia, and interactive video to present information instead of being overly dependent on didactic teaching.
- Varying the format of learning activities frequently to incorporate more affective responses, motion, and movement along with passive listening, reading, and writing.
- Establishing friendships between students and teachers.
- Creating genuine partnerships with students so that they are active participants in making decisions about how their learning experiences will occur and will be evaluated.
- Changing the roles and procedures that govern life in the classroom so they reflect some of the codes of behavior, social etiquette, and participation styles of culturally different students.
- Devising ways for students to monitor and manage their own and each other's classroom behaviors.
- Developing an esprit de corps of "family" to give cohesion and focused meaning to interpersonal relationships in the classroom.
- Routinely incoporrating a wide variety of multicultural images, artifacts, icons, events, and individuals in classroom decorations and instructional materials. Ethnically specific books, music, magazines, posters, and student-created art are valuable tools to use.

Conclusion

The ultimate answer to creating effective multicultural teaching practices is *empowering* teachers to make better decisions for themselves within their own classrooms. Empowerment here means having the knowledge, will, and skill to incorporate ethnicity and diversity into all routine teaching functions. Having "the knowledge" *means understanding how culture affects teaching and learning*, being familiar with the cultural contributions of different ethnic groups to the various disciplinary domains of knowledge and humankind, and knowing how various teaching tasks converge to form systems of teaching functions. Having "the will" is *possessing beliefs and values* that accept the legitimacy of cultural diversity for people, schools, and society, as well as being enthusiastic in affirming, celebrating, and using these differences to enrich the educational process for all students. Having "the skill" is *being competent* to translate multicultural education knowledge and systematic understanding of the nature of teaching into instructional practices that are more culturally responsive to ethnically diverse students.

While the specific multicultural instructional practices that are most effective for particular settings, purposes, and students vary, the analytical, diagnostic, and decision-making processes out of which they emerge are similar. These include a systematic analysis of routine teaching tasks and functions, and modifying them so that they incorporate information about and sensitivity to the life experiences, heritages, contributions, and learning styles of students from different ethnic, cultural, racial, and social backgrounds.

The mission of multicultural teaching is somewhat analogous to the creation and function of a democratic government. Both are supposed to be of, by, and for the people. This means that teaching in the United States should provide a thorough understanding of who composes society; those who constitute society should be involved, either directly or through representation, in determining what teaching will be; and teaching should be conceived and delivered in ways to best serve the needs of those for whom it is intended. Since U.S. society and students are ethnically and culturally pluralistic, there is no way that teaching can be most effective in meeting its academic and sociocivic obligations unless it, too, is culturally pluralistic. Thus, multicultural teaching for all students is a civic responsibility and a moral imperative, as well as a viable pedagogy for improving the quality of educational opportunities and outcomes for all students. The issue now is not whether multicultural teaching should be done, but how soon and how best to do it.

References

Adams, R. S. (1970). The classroom context. In W. J. Campbell (Ed.), *Scholars in context: The effects of environments on learning* (pp. 261–283). New York: John Wiley and Sons.

Au, K. H. (1993). *Literacy instruction in multicultural settings.* New York: Harcourt Brace.

Banks, J. A. (1997a). Approaches to multicultural curriculum reform. In J. A. Banks and C. A. Banks (Eds.), *Multicultural education: Issues and perspectives* (3rd ed.) (pp. 189–207). Boston: Allyn and Bacon.

Banks, J. A. (1997b). *Teaching strategies for ethnic studies* (6th ed.). Boston: Allyn and Bacon.

Bennett, C. I. (1995). *Comprehensive multicultural education: Theory and practice* (3rd ed.). Boston: Allyn and Bacon.

Bossert, S. T. (1979). *Tasks and social relationship in classrooms: A study of instructional organization and its consequences.* Cambridge: Harvard University Press.

Bruner, J. (1996). *The culture of education.* Cambridge, MA: Harvard University Press.

Cazden, C. B. (1986). Classroom discourse. In M. C. Wittrock (Ed.), *Handbook of research on teaching* (3rd ed.) (pp. 432–463). New York: MacMillan.

Cazden, C. B., John, V. P., and Hymes, D. (Eds.). (1985). *Functions of language in the classroom.* Prospect Heights, IL: Waveland Press.

Deyhle, D. (1995). Navajo youth and Anglo racism: Cultural integrity and resistance. *Harvard Educational Review, 65*(3), 403–444.

Flanders, N. A. (1970). *Analyzing teacher behavior.* Reading, MA: Addison-Wesley.

Fox, H. (1994). *Listening to the world: Cultural issues in academic writing.* Urbana, IL: National Council of Teachers of English.

Fullilove, R. E., and Treisman, P. U. (1990). Mathematics achievement among African American undergraduates at the University of California, Berkeley: An evaluation of the Mathematics Workshop Program. *Journal of Negro Education, 59*(3), 463–478.

Gage, N. L. (Ed.). (1963). *Handbook of research on teaching.* Chicago: Rand McNally.

Gay, G. (1994a). *A synthesis of scholarship in multicultural education.* Oak Brook, IL: North Central Regional Educational Laboratory.

Gay, G. (1994b). *At the essence of learning: Multicultural education.* West Lafayette, IN: Kappa Delta Pi.

Gay, G. (2000). *Culturally responsive teaching: Theory, practice, and research.* New York: Teachers College Press.

Good, T. L., and Brophy, J. E. (1978). *Looking in classrooms.* New York: Harper and Row.

Goodlad, J. I. (1984). *A place called school: Prospects for the future.* New York: McGraw-Hill.

Haysom, J. (1985). *Inquiring into the teaching process: Toward self-evaluation and professional development.* Toronto: Ontario Institute of Studies in Education.

Hudgins, B. B. (1971). *The instructional process.* Chicago: Rand McNally.

Hurt, H. T., Scott, M. D., and McCroskey, J. C. (1978). *Communication in the classroom.* Massachusetts: Addison-Wesley.

Jackson, P. W. (1968). *Life in classrooms.* New York: Holt, Rinehart and Winston.

Kochman, T. (1981). *Black and white styles in conflict.* Chicago: University of Chicago Press.

Krater, J., Zeni, J., and Cason, N. D. (1994). *Mirror images: Teaching writing in black and white.* Portsmouth, NH: Heinemann.

Lee, C. (1993). *Signifying as a scaffold to literary interpretation: The pedagogical implications of a form of African-American discourse.* Urbana, IL: National Council of Teachers of English.

Levy, M. L. (1968). Structural-functional analysis. In D. L. Sills (Ed.), *International encyclopedia of the social sciences* (Vol. 6) (pp. 21–29). New York: Free Press.

Mathews, J. (1988). *Escalante: The best teacher in America.* New York: Henry Holt.

Mehan, H., Hubbard, L., Villanueva, I., and Lintz, A. (1996). *Constructing school success: The consequences of untracking low-achieving students.* New York: Cambridge University Press.

Montagu, A., and Matson, F. (1979). *The human connection.* New York: McGraw-Hill.

Moos, R. H. (1979). Educational climates. In H. J. Walberg (Ed.), *Educational Environments and effects: Evaluation, policy, and productivity* (pp. 79–100). Berkeley, CA: McCutchan.

Noddings, N. (1992). *The challenge to care in schools: An alternative approach to education.* New York: Teachers College Press.

Oakes, J. (1985). *Keeping tracks: How schools structure inequality.* New Haven, CT: Yale University Press.

Oakes, J., and Guiton, G. (1995). Matchmaking: The dynamics of high school tracking decisions. *American Educational Research Journal, 32*(1), 3–33.

Perry, T., and Delpit, L. (Eds.). (1998). *The real Ebonics debate: Power, language, and the education of African-American children.* Boston: Beacon Press.

Philips, S. U. (1983). *The invisible culture: Communication in classroom and community on the Warm Springs Indian Reservation.* Prospect Heights, IL: Waveland Press.

Philips, S. U. (1985). Participant structures and communicative competence: Warm Springs children in community and classroom. In C. B. Cazden, V. P. John, and D. Hymes (Eds.), *Functions of language in the classroom* (pp. 370–394). Prospect Heights, IL: Waveland Press.

Rosenshine, B., and Stevens, R. (1986). Teaching functions. In M. C. Wittrock (Ed.), *Handbook of research on teaching* (3rd ed.) (pp. 376–391). New York: MacMillan.

Samovar, L. A., and Porter, R. E. (Eds.). (1991). *Intercultural communication: A reader* (6th ed.). Belmont, CA: Wadsworth.

Smith, B. O. (1971). On the anatomy of teaching. In R. T. Hyman (Ed.), *Contemporary thought on teaching* (pp. 20–27). Englewood Cliffs, NJ: Prentice-Hall.

Sleeter, C. E., and Grant, C. A. (1994). *Making choices for multicultural education: Five approaches to race, class, and gender* (2nd ed.). Columbus, OH: Merrill.

Tharp, R. G., and Gallimore, R. (1988). *Rousing minds to life: Teaching, learning, and schooling in social context.* Cambridge: Cambridge University Press.

Vygotsky, L. S. (1962). *Thought and Language.* Cambridge, MA: The M.I.T. Press.

chapter 4

Creating Effective Urban Schools

The Impact of School Climate

Valerie Ooka Pang and Andre J. Branch

> *Despair is paralyzing. I urge you to remember that chaotic, distressed, impoverished, and underachieving schools have been turned around by individual efforts, just as our distressed and underachieving students were able to become productive through individual efforts. I am suggesting that most schools and school systems can become more productive and happier places to be than they are right now. Nothing is wrong with public schools that programs to revitalize communities and families cannot improve through participation, cooperation, and an atmosphere of trust* (Comer 1980, p. 247).

In 1968, Martin Luther King Jr. Elementary School was one of the lowest-achieving schools in New Haven, Connecticut (Comer 1988). The school was 99% Black, and more than 70% of the students received Aid to Families with Dependent Children. The school had serious discipline and attendance problems. Its students and their parents felt frustrated with and alienated from the school. Its teachers were depressed and exhausted from trying to cope within a hostile environment. But miraculously, by 1984 the school was one of the highest achieving in math and reading in the district, and the attendance rate was one of the best in the district (Comer 1997).

How did these successes occur? During 1968, the school became the focal point of university consultants, administrators, teachers, parents, and students. As these groups joined forces and discussions evolved, everyone became hopeful, and this hope transferred into commitment. Administrators, teachers, parents, and students began working together with the common vision that all children have enormous potential. Those students and parents who once felt frustrated and alienated became actively involved in the learning process; students, in particular, challenged their teachers and themselves to know more. Teachers, in turn, rose to the challenges.

The purpose of this chapter is to focus upon the question: What are the factors that create a successful urban school, one where students from diverse populations exhibit competence in basic skills and where the total school environment reflects cultural diversity?

The School Climate

Numerous factors contribute to an overall climate of either hope or despair in schools. Schools are institutions where many social phenomena, such as ethnicity, economic level, race, gender, religion, and sexual orientation meet and interact. Children may come from families that have behaviors and values that differ from those of middle-class schools. District policies, school practices, faculty makeup, curriculum content, instructional strategies, and school routines may force these students to choose between cultural identity and school success. This distressing dilemma can cause them to suffer from depression, frustration, and confusion (Fordham 1988). In addition, school faculties may suffer from low morale, lack of respect, and a heavily burdened curriculum that requires them to deal with issues such as nuclear war, AIDS, drug abuse, teenage pregnancies, and day care of young children.

To create successful urban schools, learning must be seen from a systemwide approach that (1) promotes respect for and forges cooperation of all community-school personnel, and (2) reflects cultural diversity in its curriculum and instructional programs.

The characteristics of successful urban schools should not be perceived as a shopping list of research-proven factors that can be selected from the shelf, purchased, and then used. Educators and parents must engage in discussions about their vision for their local school and how these characteristics work simultaneously to support a "can do" school climate.

Before examining the characteristics of successful urban schools, one must recognize seven important factors about the research on effective schools. First, the research literature on effective schools includes studies of both high-middle-class White schools and poor, culturally diverse schools. Initially, James Coleman was commissioned to conduct a national study of equality of educational opportunity in 1965. His research found that family background was a large determinant of school success. Many educators interpreted this to mean that schools did not have much impact on the learning process (Coleman 1966).

More recently, however, the literature on effective schools has shifted, and professionals have adopted the belief that schools have the responsibility and ability to teach all children (Coleman 1987; Gordon 1999). One of the pioneers in this research was Ronald Edmonds. His studies focused attention on successful schools that served poor, culturally diverse schools. He believed that once he identified common characteristics of these successful schools, it would be possible to transfer those elements to schools that were failing their students (Edmonds 1979).

Research on thriving, culturally diverse schools centers on building supportive school communities. There is a strong sense of "we" in these schools. The collaborative effort of teachers, parents, and students working together as responsible, interdependent allies builds an educational climate that offers a predictable, encouraging, and supportive environment (Comer 1980).

Second, schools are like people; every school has individual strengths and needs. Something that may be exceptionally successful at one school may only be moderately effective in another. In reviewing the components that correlate with school success, one should remember that there is no single recipe for healthy learning ecology. The culture of each school may differ not only in ethnicity, but also in aspects like social class, rural or urban setting, and language groups. Schools will journey toward school success on different roads and in different vehicles.

Third, one must be aware that although much of the professional literature points to correlations between various components, it does not explain cause and effect relationships based within well-defined theoretical models. This can limit the applicability of some effective schools literature (Comer, Haynes, and Hamilton Lee 1987–1988).

Fourth, although research has provided important information about school reform, the quantitative examinations of successful schools often ignores intangible and other hidden factors that contribute to achievement (Pang 1988). They do not explore the following questions: How are working interpersonal relationships formed between teacher and parents? Between student and parent? Between teacher and administrator? How can the cultural background of students be integrated into the curriculum and instruction of schools? How do teachers acknowledge and value the lifestyles that students bring to school? How are cultural diversities seen in schools, as deficits or differences? The differing ways in which teachers, administrators, and parents view these questions will also have a definite impact upon the climate of schools. The Funds of Knowledge project was a collaborative project among teachers, parents, and students that incorporated the knowledge of local households into the curriculum (Moll, Amanti, Neff, and Gonzalez 1992). These interactions changed the dynamics in the classroom and placed great value upon the life experiences of students and their families.

Fifth, one must recognize that schools are important social organizations. Schools tend to reflect mainstream values in their structures, curricula, and interactions. The historically reinforced stratifications of American society, which are based on levels of wealth, social status, and student ethnicity, are often seen as principal determinants of school success (Wilson and Fergus 1988). School staff members should examine their own values and beliefs about student potential in light of these factors. Do school members operate from a belief that students from low-income, culturally diverse communities are not as capable as those from affluent, White neighborhoods? Some school staff members reinforce the social status by mirroring an overall atmosphere of schools as places where teachers "know best" about schooling. They may regard parents as persons who send their children to school with comments like, "You don't have to listen to the teacher." This mind-set may have developed from negative experiences parents had when they were in school. These attitudes will not contribute to the development of a cohesive school community.

Sixth, the movement toward effective school research, in part, represents a strong corporate agenda found in today's schools. Many of the tools that have been brought forth in school reform reflect an organizational and management orientation. Though these tools can strengthen the school structure, schools should not be equated with factories or offices. Schools are unique institutions whose purpose is to develop fulfilled, responsible citizens who are active participants in a democratic society (Goodlad 1984).

Seventh, one of the most important components for school change is changing power relationships. Sarason wrote, "if you want an institution, any institution, to change, then you must seek to change the power relationships between what are the equivalents of faculty and administration. You may make other changes that are far from trivial, but if the faculty-administration type of relationship is not altered, the basic character of the institution—that characteristic which if altered has the most pervasive consequences—is likely to survive" (p. 245). Most schools are hierarchical in nature; to create more equal status among faculty and administrators, schools must allocate much time to the process. It cannot be forced.

One of the strategies that is demonstrating significant success is to include the comments and input of students in the school reform process (Betchel and Reed 1998; SooHoo 1993). Several approaches have been used to gather input from students, such as focus group discussions, written questionnaires, and student responses to written prompts. The input has been used by schools to understand what students viewed as the major problems in their schools.

As school personnel look for successful examples of individual schools, it is critical to review not only the school practices that set the institution aside from others, but also the values and philosophy that motivate and drive them toward reform. Changing school policies and practices alone will not assure success. Educators must understand the belief system that led to the change in school practices and policies (Sarason 1996).

As educators move toward more partnerships with the business sector of society, it is important to focus on the inherent goal of schooling. Many educators see their goal as preparing and developing responsible, educated, and fulfilled citizens (Goodlad 1984). While schools want students to be economically self-sufficient, their principal function is not to exclusively produce workers for business. The complexity of the relationship between business and school is due, in part, to the assumption that the underlying economic infrastructure of society is dependent on schools to produce workers for business. Yet, if schools see their mission as preparing responsible citizens, there may be a vast difference in purpose between schools and businesses. Schools are not profit-driven and so do not view students as commodities being produced or managed. Transferring what works in a factory or office may not always be suitable for schools.

Characteristics That Foster Successful Schools

The research on effective schools has been uneven, and definitions of success vary. Yet specific characteristics emerge that seem to impact healthy school climate and academic achievement (Murphy 1989). The following such characteristics will be discussed as key to the implementation of successful schools in diverse communities:

1. The school community engages in lengthy discussions about curriculum, organizational structure, assessment instruments, and educational purpose.
2. The school community believes in the ability of all areas of school.
3. Parents are participating partners in schools.
4. Teachers are involved in the decision-making process.
5. The principal is a key leader in guiding and directing the collective effort of the learning community.
6. Instruction is founded on developmental and social skill needs of students.
7. Teachers consistently monitor and reinforce student academic performance.

School-Community Dialogue

Establishing dialogue between parents and school faculty as well as among faculty members is an important first stage in constructing a cohesive school community. These ongoing, continuous discussions create trusting, interpersonal relationships among parents, teachers, and administrators, which, in turn, lead to shared vision and effective decision making. Through this process, consistent role models at home and school develop and reinforce similar academic, behavioral, and social expectations.

Teachers who have the opportunity to discuss concerns and problems with each other are more likely to develop supportive professional networks. By sharing ideas and effective instructional approaches to curriculum and discipline problems, teachers minimize individual isolation. Moreover, dialogue with parents can help develop understanding and support for school programs. Parents become better informed about the kinds of pressures teachers face, and how they can aid teachers as volunteers and as role models at home.

In a recent study at Bethune Elementary School (a pseudonym for an urban school whose student body is 70% African American), Sarah (also a pseudonym) reported that she found it helpful to consult with the school counselor to resolve conflicts among some of the African American girls in her kindergarten class. She admitted that as a White teacher she was not as adept as the African American counselor at resolving ethnic conflicts in her classroom, so she readily seeks and accepts the assistance of her African American colleague. Sarah looks to this African American professional as a valuable part of her professional network (Branch 1999).

High Expectations

Successful schools possess high expectations for all students. Often students from culturally diverse communities have been told through overt and covert avenues that they are not as good as White students and will not do as well because of their background. They overhear teachers say things like, "Well, you can't expect anything from these children. Their parents don't care and they come from transient families." After a while, children internalize these attitudes and begin to believe them. For children who are members of a disenfranchised minority group that has historically been victimized by society, this message is almost insidious (Comer 1980; Comer 1997; Sarason 1996). Teachers must reinforce the belief that all students can achieve by conveying high expectations.

One way teachers convey high expectations to students is through teacher-student interactional patterns (Cohen 1987). Teachers wait longer for responses from high-achieving students than they do from low-achieving students, and they respond to their questions more often. They also give them more praise and extensive feedback because they expect high achievement.

One way that schools reinforce low expectations is through ability grouping. Though many teachers believe that these grouping methods are the most effective means of instruction, Robert Slavin has found that ability grouping is not more effective than heterogeneous placement of students. Ability grouping has the most negative effects on lower-track pupils because it reduces their expectations (Slavin et al. 1989). Alternatives to traditional ability-grouping practices are beginning to be developed that should change the way students see themselves and the manner in which teachers deal with academic and cultural diversity. They will enhance school climate by (a) conveying the belief that all students can reach their enormous potentials, and (b) developing instructional practices and curricula that reinforce that vision.

Parent/Community Involvement

Parents are children's first teachers and their most important role models (Herenton 1987-1988). Unfortunately, they often do not know how the educational process operates or how they can participate in it in a way that will help their children. Schools can solicit effective community and parent participation in two major ways: by recruiting parents to become involved in daily school activities and by eliciting a broad-based community effort in the educational enterprise.

James Comer and his colleagues designed the School Development Program in New Haven, Connecticut, specifically to promote active parent involvement in schools. The Comer schools instituted three levels of parent participation. The first level was a broad-based participation in which parents were invited to whole-school activities, such as potluck suppers, gospel music nights, and general meetings. These events served as bridges between home and school. The second level involved participation in day-to-day school affairs and brought parents into the classrooms to work as assistants and tutors. Some parents became volunteers and others received minimum wage for about 15 hours of employment. The third level supported parent participation in school governance. It aimed "to develop patterns of shared responsibility and decision making among parents and staff" (Comer 1980, p. 68). The schools encouraged parents to act as partners in schooling rather than as separate advisors. Teachers, principals, and members of the Comer team trained these parents in intervention, developmental, and instructional strategies.

This model has been extremely successful. Students at Martin Luther King Jr. and Katharine Brennan Elementary Schools in New Haven from 1969 through 1984 produced continual gains in math and reading scores (Comer 1980, p. 47). When the project first began, these schools ranked lowest in achievement among the district's 33 schools. By 1984, the fourth-grade students were found to be third and fourth in the district on the Iowa Test of Basic Skills. In addition, the attendance rates became some of the best in the city, and behavior problems declined drastically. Comer believed that the success of the program was due to their ethos, or structured approach of collaborative decision making, rather than defining school climate in terms of rules, discipline, or teacher expectations (Comer, Haynes, and Hamilton-Lee 1987–1988, p. 196). Parents were key to their effective school model.

Parents are an important part of the instructional program at Bethune Elementary School. Sarah, one of the most effective teachers, invites parents to assist her in the classroom as she teaches students content specific to the various ethnic groups represented in her classroom (Branch 1999). Sarah has the reputation of being one of the best teachers in the district because each year she teaches new classes of kindergartners to read by the end of their first year in school. Sarah, a White female, is proud to live in, and be an active member of, the African American community where the school is located.

Another successful avenue for encouraging parental involvement is the community-based approach. The Rochester Education Initiative, designed by the Urban League, fostered a grassroots program to inform the community of the low achievement of Black students and the need for a holistic and community-organized program to address the serious educational needs of young people (Johnson, Dwyer, and Spade 1987–1988). The League received assistance from businesses, churches, human services, and governmental agencies in developing a comprehensive educational plan.

The project began with public forums that featured speakers from educator, student, and parent groups. These speakers addressed the key question: "What can we do to improve the academic performance of Rochester's students?" Later, community leaders conducted town meetings where educators and community representatives formed school-action committees to develop a range of school improvement projects that included job incentives for student achievement, a marketing program that highlighted the importance of education, and management expertise from the business sector.

The early stages of the plan showed improvement in student achievement levels for African American ninth, tenth, and eleventh graders. In particular, the number of those students who had B or higher grade averages increased from 226 students in 1986 to 346 in 1987 (Johnson, Dwyer, and Spade 1987–1988, p. 226).

Teacher Involvement in Decision Making

Teachers comprise the largest segment of school faculty, yet often they may not be involved in important school decisions. Successful schools have the participation of the total faculty in planning and executing school reform. In the Comer project, teacher representatives were elected to the school's governance and management team (Comer 1988, 1997). This team examined school curriculum and structure and its relationship to student behavior and academic performance. The principal, although an authority figure, considered the input of this team before making decisions. Major decisions were made by consensus because Comer and his colleagues felt shared decision making resulted in a broader feeling of ownership.

Other schools have adopted site-based management for their schools. Meier shared how her staff, when she was teacher-director of Central Park East in East Harlem, created a community-based school that was run by teachers. Meier described it in this way: "Our experience suggested that a strong school culture requires that most decisions be struggled over and made by those directly responsible for implementing the decision, not by representative bodies handing down dictates for others to follow" (Meier, 1995, p. 24). Most of the students were African American and Latino from low-income families. Central Park East became an extremely successful school where approximately 90% of the students went on to college. The teachers created a collaborative vision of a school that believed in the ability of every child and changed the school structure so that every child became an affirmed and academically successful person.

Effective Leadership of the Principal

Principals are key leaders in developing bridges of communication among staff, students, and community. Effective principals understand and view instruction from a systemwide perspective. They can clearly articulate the goals of their schools and can integrate policy into practice by using shared decision making with teachers and parents.

Understanding learning from an ecological perspective, effective principals create mechanisms for dialogue and rapport in which parents and teachers develop a sense of ownership that supports the learning process (Comer 1980, pp. 233–235; Comer 1997). Additionally, these principals provide administrative support for community decisions about schooling. They often have financial and human resources that can assist in funding structural and innovative changes (Wilson and Firestone 1987).

Focus on Developmental and Social Skills

Successful schools create instructional programs that focus on both cognitive and social skill development. Educators in these schools do not perceive their students as empty vessels, but as active learners (Devaney and Sykes 1988). They know that rote facts and worksheets will not prepare students to tackle social problems; they know that they must find better ways to develop the critical-thinking skills needed to do so—and they find those ways. These teachers can move from their reliance on textbooks and prepackaged materials to active investigation of social problems connected to students' lives (Goodlad 1984). They know that meaningful relationships between curriculum and life need to be built; otherwise, schools will be removed from reality.

A curriculum that is relevant to the daily lives of students also helps build positive school climate (Firestone and Rosenblum 1988). High school students, in particular, often seek connections between the curriculum and the many personal judgments and decisions that they make. For example, students want to know how learning U.S. history is going to have any bearing on their ability to earn money or make important decisions. They are more motivated to learn when school content considers their life situations.

In one instance, a group of students requested that their high school examine the underlying issues of racism found at school. They successfully organized a series of schoolwide discussions on racism and instituted a pilot course on human behavior that included a large unit on racism. As a result of these activities, the students were able to present school administrators with a list of recommendations for structural changes in the curriculum and in district policies that would address racial problems in their school (Polakow-Suransky and Ulaby 1990). Their actions are an example of how students can force schools to make their education more relevant to the social conflicts that exist in their lives.

At Apex Middle School (a pseudonym), Kendra Katahira wanted the students in her sixth-grade social studies class to learn about prejudice and stereotyping in a way that was meaningful to them. While participating in a study of teachers' role conceptions on ethnic identity development, she reiterated a portion of the directions she gave to her students regarding a class assignment. "Saying, 'Oh, just be nice to everybody, treat everybody equal,' is a load of crap; that's so easy. I want to know specific things that I can do to put a stop to prejudice and stereotyping" (Branch 1999, p. 77). From this challenge the students created a "stereotypes brochure" and large posters that hung on the walls inside and outside the classroom. Each poster had the following stem: "Prejudice is contagious. We can stop it by ..." Following this item, each poster listed ten concrete actions people might take to end prejudice. This social studies lesson and the students' responses to it, complete with pictures of Katahira's students, were front-page news in the northwest city where she teaches.

In a positive climate for learning, children also have social skills that reinforce the educational process. For example, teachers may have helped them develop skills that support cooperative-learning activities, risk taking, and positive interpersonal interactions.

Regular Monitoring of Student Progress and Reinforcement of Success

Successful schools institute monitoring programs that measure student achievement and performance. These schools are constantly assessing their own areas of weakness. Some schools have instituted criterion-referenced tests for evaluating students' progress, which helps teachers to continually check students' knowledge levels in basic skill areas, reinforce successes, and adjust instruction accordingly (Firestone 1989). Some teachers include the use of student portfolios (Gordon 1999). Portfolios can be more comprehensive than test scores in presenting an integrated assessment of what students are learning, how they are applying their new knowledge, and what reflections they are making about their own learning. By making students accountable for their learning, teachers create an environment that reflects high expectations (Meier 1995).

Conclusion

We have too many at-risk schools, institutions that are struggling to serve our diverse student population. Instead, we need more risking schools, institutions that challenge themselves to create new structures where the climate is based on mutual respect, the ethic of care, and the importance of community—schools that encourage the infusion of content and strategies that are effective and meaningful to diverse students.

Building a school community is central to the academic and social success of all students. This community made up of parents, students, teachers, administrators, and other community people must be a compassionate one which focuses on the needs of students. Addressing the issue of power relationships in building schools in which people have equal status and feel a sense of ownership of the process is critical to true school reform.

Cultural and class background may be pivotal elements in the communities from which students come. Unfortunately, literature on effective schools offers scattered findings or little research that focuses on the impact of cultural context on the school environment. Cultural factors may not be easily quantified into existing models of school reform. While separate school programs may not be needed for inner-city and suburban schools, there is no one model for school success. Though massive databases have been gathered on urban schools, the intangible effect of culture on the psychosocial development of students often is overlooked. Securing parent involvement, using educational materials relevant to the community life of students, and understanding that students' motivational system may have cultural roots can help build strong academic and individual self-concepts.

When educators do not understand how schools' values and behaviors may conflict with community lifestyles, students face the dilemma of choosing between their cultural identity and fitting in at school; these students can suffer from depression, frustration, and confusion. Schools need to understand that the social-cultural context of learning has a major impact on the interactions and structure of schooling. When schools deny the role of culture and the existence of a hidden as well as a stated curriculum, the learning environment cannot provide students with an equal educational opportunity.

The process of urban schooling is complicated. Educational equity can only occur when we make courageous systemic school changes. We face tremendous problems in schools today; among these are resegregated patterns of student school assignments, escalating dropouts rates, and the continued growth of the underclass. To deal with these problems effectively, we must continue to strengthen the relationship between ethnic communities and schools through dialogue, collective goal setting, and cooperative planning. Ultimately, all children can be successful in schools.

References

Betchel, D., and Reed, C. (1998). Students as documenters: Benefits, reflections, and suggestions. *NASSP Bulletin, 82*(594), 89–95.

Branch, A. (1999). Teachers' conceptions of their role in the facilitation of students' ethnic identity development. Unpublished doctoral dissertation. University of Washington.

Cohen, M. (1987). Improving school effectiveness: Lessons from research. In V. Richardson-Kowhler (Ed.), *Educator's handbook* (pp. 474–490). New York: Longman.

Coleman, J. (1966). *Equality of education opportunity*. Washington, DC: U.S. Office of Education.

Comer, J. (1980). *School power*. New York: Free Press.

Comer, J. (1988). Educating poor minority children. *Scientific American 259*(5), 24–28.

Comer, J. (1997). *Waiting for a miracle: Why Schools can't solve our problems—and how we can*. New York: Dutton.

Comer, J., Haynes, N., and Hamilton-Lee, M. (1987–1988). School Power: A model for improving black student achievement. *Urban Review 11*(1–2), 187–200.

Devaney, K., and Sykes, G. (1988). Making the case for professionalism. In A. Lieberman (Ed.), *Building a professional culture in schools* (pp. 3–22). New York: Teachers College Press.

Edmonds, R. (1979). Some schools work and more can. *Social Policy 9*, 28–32.

Firestone, W. A. (1989). Beyond order and expectations in high schools serving at-risk youth. *Educational Leadership 46*(5), 45.

Firestone, W. A., and Rosenblum, S. (1988). Building commitment in urban high schools. *Educational Evaluation and Policy Analysis 10*(4), 285–299.

Fordham, S. (1988). Racelessness as a factor in black students' school success: Pragmatic strategy or Pyrrhic victory? *Harvard Educational Review 58*(1), 54–84.

Goodlad, J. I. (1984). *A place called school*. New York: McGraw-Hill.

Gordon, E. W. (1999). *Education and justice: A view from the back of the bus*. New York: Teachers College Press.

Herenton, W. (1987–1988). Memphis inner-city school improvement project: A holistic approach for developing academic excellence. *Urban Review 11*(1–2), 211–226.

Johnson, W. A.; Dwyer, B.; and Spade, J. Z. (1987–1988). A community initiative: Making a difference in the quality of black education. *Urban Review 11*(1–2), 217–226.

Meier, D. (1995). *The power of their ideas*. Boston, MA: Beacon.

Moll, L., Amanti, C., Neff, D., and Gonzalez, N. (1992). Funds of knowledge for teaching: Using a qualitative approach to connect homes and classrooms. *Theory Into Practice 31*(2), 132–141.

Murphy, J. (1989). Education reform in the 1980s: Explaining some surprising success. *Educational Evaluation and Policy Analysis 11*(3), 209–221.

Pang, V. O. (1988). Ethnic prejudice: Still alive and hurtful. *Harvard Educational Review, 58*(3), 375–379.

Polakow-Suransky, S., and Ulaby, N. (1990). Students take action to combat racism. *Phi Delta Kappan 71*(8), 601–606.

Sarason, S. B. (1996). *Barometers of Change*. San Francisco: Jossey-Bass.

Slavin, R. E., Braddock, J. H., Hall, C., and Petza, R. J. (1989). *Alternatives to ability grouping*. Johns Hopkins University. Research funded by a grant from the National Education Association.

SooHoo, S. (1993). Students as partners in research and restructuring schools. *Educational Forum, 4*, 386–393.

Wilson, B. L., and Firestone, W. A. (1987). The principal and instruction: Combining bureaucratic and cultural linkages. *Educational Leadership 45*(1), 18–23.

Wilson, B. L., and Fergus, E. O. (1988). Combining effective schools and school improvement research traditions for achieving equity-based education. *Equity and Excellence 24*(1), 54–65.

chapter 5

Learning Styles: Implications for Teachers

Karen Swisher and Dilys Schoorman

The search for more effective ways to serve an increasing number of students who have not been well served by our nation's schools has never been more important than it is now. The increasing diversity of the USA is giving our schools a different complexion. In addition to an increasing presence of ethnically and culturally diverse children, the number of children who live below the poverty line and/or are homeless is increasing, and the high number of "at-risk" or "school-weary" students has caused alarm. All of these factors are reported among the many concerns in the call for reforming or restructuring U.S. schools.

The purpose of this chapter is to focus on the construct of learning styles as a promising, yet not "panaceaistic," view of successful schooling for our multicultural population of students. As Irvine and York (1995) point out, research on learning styles has significant possibilities for enhancing the achievement of culturally diverse students. As this knowledge has become more accessible to practitioners, "some teachers have begun to experiment with *learning styles*, persuaded that the concept helps them to both understand differences better and to provide for those differences, thereby improving learning" (Brandt 1990, p. 3). It goes without saying that some expert teachers have intuitively been doing this for years. They have always accommodated students' individual differences by varying their style of instruction or by giving students options for demonstrating competence.

This chapter is intended to validate the convictions and spirit of those expert teachers and to provide information for those who want to know more. It is also intended that a discussion of learning styles will remind teachers "to be attentive not only to individual students' learning styles but to their own actions, instructional goals, methods and materials in reference to their students' cultural experiences and preferred learning environments" (Irvine and York 1995, p. 484).

Learning Styles Defined

The definition of *learning style* has been discussed and debated for several years. In 1983, the National Task Force on Learning Style and Brain Behavior offered the following definition:

> *Learning style* is that consistent pattern of behavior and performance by which an individual approaches educational experiences. It is the composite of characteristic cognitive, affective, and physiological behaviors that serve as relatively stable indicators of how a learner perceives, interacts with, and responds to the learning environment. It is formed in the deep structure of neural organization and personality [that] molds and is molded by human development and the cultural experiences of home, school, and society. (Keefe and Languis 1983, p.1)

This definition, with emphasis on "cultural experiences of home, school, and society," is the basis for the following discussion of learning styles and its implications for teaching and learning in a multicultural society. Cooper Shaw (1996) emphasizes four aspects of a learning style: everyone has a learning style; it is relatively consistent over time; no particular learning style is innately superior to another (even though they may be more or less effective in certain situations); and it is pervasive and observable in diverse contexts of the individual's life.

Dimensions of Learning Styles

Cooper Shaw (1996) identified three dimensions of learning styles that teachers need to consider in order to exemplify instructional pluralism in their classes: the conceptual, perceptual, and social dimensions. These dimensions are interrelated and often seem to overlap, but they are a useful framework for synthesizing the diverse array of approaches to education observed among students.

The conceptual dimension draws attention to students' cognitive approach to information or learning tasks. The earliest and most widely researched aspect of learning styles has pertained to field-dependent (also known as field-sensitive, relational, or global) and field-independent learners. Herman Witkin and his associates in 1954 began to study the field-dependent and field-independent dimensions of cognitive style. Their work was concerned with how people use the visual environment around them; in other words, the extent to which the surrounding organized field influences the person's perception of an item within it. For example, in an embedded-figures test, participants were asked to locate a simple figure; they saw the items as separate from the surrounding field and were designated field independent. Those who could not locate the figure in the time allotted were designated field dependent because their perception was dominated by the surrounding field (Witkin, Goodenough and Cox 1977).

Field-independent learners have a perception of discrete parts and are good at abstract analytical thought. They tend to be individualistic, less sensitive to the emotions of others, and may have poorly developed social skills. They favor inquiry and independent study and can provide their own structure to facilitate learning. Field-independent learners are intrinsically motivated and less responsive to social reinforcement.

Conversely, field-dependent learners have a global perspective and are less adept at analytical problem solving. They tend to be highly sensitive and attuned to the social environment; their social skills are highly developed. They favor a spectator approach to learning and to organizing the information to be learned in the form it is given. They are extrinsically motivated and responsive to social reinforcement (Witkin et al. 1977).

Several researchers have applied other names to describe the ends of the cognitive style continuum. For example, Rosalie Cohen (1969) described the dimensions as analytical and relational. Ramirez and Castañeda (1974) believed that the term "dependent" implied negative connotations and substituted the term "sensitive" in its place; thus, "field-sensitive" and "field-independent" are terms identified with their work. Castañeda and Gray (1974) provide a more detailed discussion of these learners and appropriate teaching practices to address their needs.

Another aspect of the conceptual dimension is students' need for structure in learning tasks. As Bennett (1999) points out, students differ in their ability to rely on themselves, to take on new assignments, to make choices, to organize themselves and their materials, and in their need for reassurance from their teachers. They also differ in their need for explanation of instructions on learning tasks and assignments. Research by Hunt (1979) reveals that students who require much structure have short attention spans, find it difficult to sit still for long periods, ask for directions often, tend to be literal, and find it difficult to make inferences or interpretations. They want to know the basic information, find it difficult to handle general questions, and tend to guess when they have to think through problems. In contrast, students with low need for structure want to solve problems themselves and seek the teacher's help only as a last resort, display greater ability in making interpretations and drawing inferences, stay on task for longer periods of time, and work with limited supervision. Hunt recommends that teachers provide specific guidelines and step by step instructions, make goals and deadlines short and definite (give them a topic, required pages/lines, how it is to be done), and provide immediate feedback on each step for students who require a high level of structure. For students who require little structure, Hunt advises teachers to provide choices, set weekly or monthly assignments, allow students to make decisions about timetables, and provide students freedom to pursue projects on their own.

The perceptual dimension pertains to students' preferred perceptual mode. Researchers have identified three general classifications of learners based on their preferred perceptual modality: visual, auditory, and kinesthetic (or tactile) learners. Visual learners learn best when they can take in new information through their eyes. Reinhart (1976) made further distinctions in this category, noting that some learn best when they can actually see objects and activities or when concepts are presented in terms of a visual depiction. Films, pictures, demonstrations, and models are appropriate learning tools to use with these students. On the other hand, there are visual learners who learn best by reading.

Auditory learners learn best when they hear new information. Teachers can accommodate these learners through the use of listening labs or audiotapes. These learners tend to be good listeners and do not like external sounds that interfere with the listening process.

Kinesthetic learners are those who learn best through demonstration or hands-on experiences. Activities such as field trips and nature walks work well with these students. Kinesthetic learning has been associated with the learning aproach of many American Indian children, who prefer to observe and then practice the necessary skill to be mastered in an apprenticeship-style relationship before they feel confident to demonstrate it themselves. Drawing on the work of Reinhart (1976), Bennett (1999) notes that kinesthetic learners are compulsive underliners and note takers but seldom refer to these notes because the act of note taking itself has helped them to internalize that knowledge.

The social dimension addresses the particular social context that is preferred by the learner. Some students prefer to work alone, whereas others prefer to work in cooperative groups. This particular dimension overlaps considerably with the field independent and field dependent classification. The system of education in the United States has traditionally favored individual learners through the assignment of individual and often competitive tasks, seating arrangements where students are separated from one another in rows, and a classroom climate that has exemplified individualistic values (favoring field-independent or analytical learners). More contemporary classrooms have introduced several opportunities for cooperative work through the rearrangement of furniture, the design of cooperative projects and activities, and an encouragement of interdependence. These practices have emerged following research that has demonstrated that many underrepresented cultural groups are oriented toward more cooperative work. Research in this area has been extensive; detailed descriptions of types of cooperative activities can be found in the work of Slavin, DeVries, and Edwards (1983) and summarized by Bennett (1999) and Cooper Shaw (1996). Teachers must be cautioned to ensure that the cooperative work enables all students to share equal status and equal responsibility toward achieving the group goal instead of merely facilitating dependence among students. Variations in social environment can be achieved by allowing work in pairs or in a large group, as well as having individual and small-group activities.

Dunn and Dunn (1993) also drew attention to other factors that characterize a student's learning style. These factors can be linked to either global (or relational) learners or analytic learners. With regard to environmental factors, they noted that global learners prefer what many think of as "distractions," such as music, low lighting, and informal lounging positions, whereas analytics prefer silence, bright lights, and conventional or formal studying positions. Emotional factors pertain to students' motivation, persistence, and need for structure. Global learners tend not to be persistent, working in short bursts with frequent breaks during the task. They are also able to work on multiple tasks simultaneously and can begin an assignment in the middle or at the end. Analytic learners tend to be more persistent and have a strong emotional urge to continue with a task once it is begun. Physiological factors also characterize learning style. Global learners tend to eat while studying and sometimes need to be mobile (to pace or walk around). Analytics rarely eat while studying. Two other factors identified by Dunn and Dunn, sociological factors (preferred social context) and psychological factors (global vs. analytical) have already been discussed. The extent to which a student is left or right brain dominant and whether the learner is impulsive or reflective were also included as facets of psychological factors.

Multiple Intelligences

Although not always included in discussions of learning style, the work of Gardner (1993) on multiple intelligences is pertinent to our understanding of diverse students' orientation to learning. Gardner posited that every human being was capable of several relatively independent forms of information processing which could be seen as a unique "intelligence." He identified the following intelligences: logical-mathematical, linguistic, musical, spatial, kinesthetic, interpersonal, intrapersonal and, more recently, naturalist. The first two are the types typically regarded by schools as the primary forms of intelligence.

Gardner's theory of multiple intelligences is important to multicultural education for several reasons. First, it addresses the fact that all students have the ability to learn. Second, it highlights the "hegemony of a single intelligence" that has characterized traditional education. Finally, it draws attention to the need for teachers to create opportunities for multi-dimensional learning whereby students can discover and combine their particular strengths with areas where they lack experience (Nieto 2000; Oakes and Lipton 1999).

Communication Styles

Students also differ in their expectations of, and their orientations toward, the learning process. This is often manifested in the diverse communica-tion patterns evident among cultures. For some, the classroom is a place where only the teacher should talk, and students' obligations are to listen attentively and follow directions. When student participation occurs, it is by invitation of the teacher. This is particularly evident among many Asian students, especially recent immigrants, and among many American Indi-ans. On the other hand, there are many students who learn best through constant interchange with their teachers or peers. The call-and-response pattern among African Americans and the participatory nature of African American audiences remind us that many students are used to contexts in which they learn through active, affective, and ongoing participation or debate. Teachers will need to be prepared for classrooms that may have students who dread being called on to answer questions and others who learn primarily through such interactions. There may be students who view academic discussions as "objective" or "neutral," while others demonstrate their interest through impassioned participation.

The social relationship expected between students and teachers also varies. Many students expect the teacher to be an authority figure who maintains a formal and distant relationship with students. They see teach-ers as experts not to be questioned. Many such students are puzzled by what they perceive to be "too much praise," especially when they know they could make significant improvement in their work. Others, while viewing the teacher as an authority figure, expect more of a parental role, with greater emotional involvement between teachers and students. These students look for constant praise, emotional support, and ongoing inter-action with the teacher. Others do not see teachers in such hierarchically distant roles and expect a more casual and informal relationship. These students are more comfortable initiating discussions, pointing out teacher errors, and engaging in conversations about nonacademic interests with the teacher. These divergent perspectives have a significant impact on stu-dents' approaches to the learning process.

Students' nonverbal communication patterns (typically rooted in their cultural background) also have an impact on the learning process and classroom interactions. Differences in eye contact, though seemingly insignificant, have led to misunderstandings among teachers and students. Tales abound about teachers who have severely reprimanded students for being disrespectful because they didn't look their teachers in the eye. In fact, these students' home cultures dictate that they look away when showing respect and they presumed that eye contact with an authority figure was disrespectful. Nieto (2000) describes how a teacher failed to realize that Puerto Rican students wrinkle their noses as an indication of puzzlement and, as a result, missed several opportunities for instruction. Scarcella (1992) warns that many Asian students will smile and nod their heads as a sign of respect to the teacher. This should not be taken as an indication that they are enjoying, agreeing with, or even understanding what is being said.

There are infinite ways in which students' nonverbal behavior can affect how they learn, and it is impossible for teachers to know all such nuances for all cultures. However, it is important for all teachers to be in touch with the cultures represented in their classrooms and the dominant cultural patterns of expression and expectations of learning that their students have. Furthermore, teachers should recognize that their own classroom interactions and expectations are also culturally rooted and be open to the fact that what one takes for granted as "universal practice" might seem strange and even detrimental to some children. As Delpit (1988) notes, it is important for teachers to explain explicitly the rules and expectations for classroom interactions and learning so that students who are strangers to the classroom culture will not be at a disadvantage.

The Relationship Between Culture and Learning Styles

The relationship between culture and cognitive style, as conceptualized by Witkin and others, has been of interest to researchers for many years. For example, Ramirez and Castañeda (1974) built upon the research of Witkin (1967), indicating that socialization practices play a large role in determining learning behavior preferences in children. A framework set forth by Ramirez and Castañeda in 1974 suggests that cultural values influence socialization practices, which affect the ways children prefer to learn. Cox and Ramirez (1981) explained it this way:

> Clearly, the task, the situation, and the materials influence the ways that children are encouraged to learn or behave, and few families encourage only field-independent or field-sensitive learning, even though, on the average, they may use one type of strategy more than the other. The predominant or general teaching style of a family may thus be of basic importance in deciding the direction a child's learning preferences may take. Insofar as these teaching styles reflect a certain set of values held by parents and family, values that in many cases are clearly culturally determined, one may posit that cultural differences in learning-style preferences develop through children's early experiences (p. 63).

While there is evidence of the relationship between culture and learning styles, educators generally have expected learning styles to be more analytical or field independent. As a result, some learners whose styles may be more relational or field dependent/sensitive have not done well in our schools. Therefore, it is vital that educators become more familiar with the cultural background of their students and understand its potential impact on their learning.

Learning Style Differences

An awareness of the characteristics of groups of people is important. We must also realize that this knowledge helps us to understand groups, not just individual learners. Diversity within each cultural or ethnic group exists and is demonstrated in aspects such as language use, child-rearing practices, and socialization methods. Diversity is also determined by the degree to which members of a particular group have assimilated aspects of the larger society, or macroculture, and the social class to which the family "belongs." Because of this intragroup diversity, it is unrealistic to think that all members of a certain group will have the same learning style. However, there are general characteristics that provide a basis for further investigation into the individual characteristics that constitute style. Presenting information about the learning styles of African Americans, American Indians, Alaskan Natives, Asian Americans, and Hispanics may contribute to greater understanding, but it may also reinforce stereotypical notions about the relationship between learning styles and cultural-group membership. Furthermore, Cox and Ramirez (1981) cautioned us to not ignore the great diversity within any culture. They remind us that the learning-styles construct should be a tool for individualization, rather than a label for categorizing and evaluating. It is with these cautions that the following information is presented.

African Americans

Hale-Benson (1986) and Hilliard (1976) have described African American youth as more relational (field dependent/field sensitive) than analytical (field independent). This relational orientation to learning is produced by family socialization patterns in which members share functions, thereby socializing their members to be more relational in their learning styles. Boykin (1986) identified nine interrelated dimensions of African American culture that had implications for students' learning styles. As summarized by Irvine and York (1995), these were: (1) spirituality—an approach in which life is viewed as vitalistic rather than mechanistic; (2) harmony—the idea that humans and nature live interdependently; (3) movement—an emphasis on rhythm, music, and dance; (4) verve—a propensity for high levels of stimulation; (5) affect—an emphasis on emotions and feelings; (6) communalism—a commitment to social connectedness; (7) expressive individualism—a value on genuine personal expression; (8) oral tradition—a value on genuine oral/aural communication; and (9) social time perspective—an orientation to time as social rather than material space. These observations suggest that African American students learn best through physical movements, personal teacher-student relationships, cooperative groups, and oral/aural communication.

In their review of the research on African American learning styles, Irvine and York (1995) noted that these students tend to respond to things in terms of the whole instead of isolated parts, prefer inferential reasoning as opposed to deduction or induction, approximate space and numbers rather than adhere to exactness or accuracy, focus on people rather than on things, prefer learning characterized by variation and freedom of movement, prefer kinesthetic/active instruction, choose social over nonsocial cues, and prefer "vervistic" learning experiences. As Shade (1982; Shade, Kelly, and Oberg 1997) and Gay (1975) point out, African Americans' learning styles are often antithetical to the assumptions and expectations of mainstream teachers. Success in school requires sequential, analytical, or object-oriented cognitive styles; African Americans tend to be universalistic, intuitive, and very person oriented. African Americans also tend to be mutually supportive in work tasks but intensely individualistic and competitive in play. This is totally opposite to the mainstream expectation that students work independently on academic tasks and cooperate on the playground.

American Indians and Alaskan Natives

What do we know about the learning styles of American Indian and Alaskan Native children who come from more than 500 tribal groups? We have very little empirical data available when one considers that, as an indigenous group, American Indians are among the most researched of all cultures in this country.

A review of the literature regarding American Indian learning styles by Swisher and Deyhle (1989) presented some anecdotal and empirical information from various researchers about several tribal groups. Similarities exist, perhaps because of the indigenous nature shared by all groups, but there are differences as well. For example, Navajo, Oglala Sioux, and Yaqui cultures teach that competence should precede performance. Observation and self-testing in private are important steps that must be taken before one demonstrates competence of a task. The review also cited visual strengths of Kwakuitl and Eskimo children of the Northwest and of Navajo and Pueblo children of the Southwest, as well as the cooperative nature of Cherokee and Kwakuitl children.

A summary of research findings by Irvine and York (1995) indicates that American Indian learners tend to prefer visual, spatial, and perceptual information rather than verbal; learn better privately rather than in public; use mental images to understand and remember words and concepts rather than word associations. They also watch and then do, rather than employ trial and error; have well-formed spatial ability; learn best from nonverbal mechanisms rather than verbal; learn experientially and in natural settings and have a generalist orientation with an interest in people and things. Additionally, American Indian students value conciseness of speech, have slightly varied intonation and limited vocal range, and prefer small-group work, holistic presentations, and visual representations.

Gaining communicative competence and participation in classroom interactional structures were areas studied by Susan Philips (1983) in her work with Indian children in Warm Springs, Oregon. She found that community norms as well as socialization practices greatly influenced the way children gained communicative competence and their preference for participation in small cooperative-learning groups. It has been speculated that American Indians tend to be field dependent; however, exploratory work in learning styles of Jicarilla Apache children by Swisher and Page (1990) indicates that intragroup differences exist to the point that no general tendencies could be determined.

Asian Americans

Although Asian Americans constitute a highly diverse group of people in terms of culture and socioeconomic background, such intragroup diversity has often been overlooked in favor of a recent characterization of Asians as the "model minority." Asian students have been typified as hard working, high achieving, polite, and docile. This style of learning appears to be compatible with what is expected in American classrooms; therefore, research into this dimension of their educational experience has been limited. Pang (1990; Pang and Cheng 1998) has done extensive work on Asian American students and identifies the following as general themes in their approach to learning: students view schooling as a serious endeavor and demonstrate a strong work ethic; they value technical or "academic" skills and see music or sports as activities to be pursued only if time permits; teachers are seen as authority figures to be respected, obeyed, and not to be questioned; humility and modesty are important values, which means that students might be reluctant to volunteer in class; cooperation and harmony are valued; and students tend to help one another, sometimes violating educators' rules about "cheating." Fuller (1996) notes that Asian American students prefer highly structured activities. Difficulties with the English language and the propensity to memorize have facilitated students' success in mathematics and science. Students' orientation to schoolwork is linked with their high value of the family; students view their performance in school as bringing honor or shame to their families.

Scholars have challenged the "model minority" stereotype for several reasons. First, it fails to capture the experiences of the wide range of Asians in U.S. schools. Second, it puts enormous pressure on students to perform well, especially in mathematics. When this school-based pressure is exerted in addition to already existing family-based pressure, the results could be severe or even tragic. Third, the "model minority" stereotype has caused teachers to ignore the problems that many students experience in the classroom because of the assumption that, as Asians, they will "somehow get by." Teachers have viewed students' passivity as an indication of understanding, and Asian students who do not demonstrate the "model" characteristics have often been more severely reprimanded than their colleagues from other cultures. Additional information on the myths and stereotypes of Asian Americans and recent Southeast Asian newcomers is provided in the works of Valerie Ooka Pang (1990; 1995), and Don Nakashini and Marsha Hirano-Nakashini (1983).

Hispanics

"Hispanic" is a term that encompasses people from Spanish-speaking ancestry, nations, or territories, regardless of race. They are all people with different histories. Heterogeneity characterizes this large group of Spanish-speaking people, although they do share some religious, social, and cultural values.

The landmark work of Ramirez and Castañeda on learning styles of Mexican American children has provided a definitive lens through which the relationship between culture and learning can be viewed. Their research indicated that Mexican American children tend to be field sensitive in their learning styles. For example, they prefer to work with others to achieve a common goal, and they tend to be more sensitive to the feelings and opinions of others (Ramirez and Castañeda 1974).

This conclusion has been supported by most researchers, who note that Hispanic students tend to prefer group learning situations, are sensitive to the opinion of others, and remember faces and social words. They also tend to be extrinsically motivated, learn by doing, prefer concrete representations to abstract ones, and prefer people to ideas (Irvine and York 1995). Fuller (1996) also noted that research described Hispanic students as warm and concerned about others, more physically affectionate (demonstrating more touching behaviors in communication), and viewing teachers as authority figures (often as equivalent to a parent figure). As Nieto (2000) and Fuller indicate, teachers who work with this population of students would do well to establish a sense of community within the classroom, where the teacher plays an active nurturing role in a warm and friendly classroom.

Multicultural Education and Learning Styles: Implications for Practice

Multicultural education recognizes that there are multiple ways of perceiving, evaluating, believing, and behaving. We recognize that people perceive and learn about the world in different ways, and that they demonstrate this understanding in unique ways. How they have learned to learn about their world is characteristic of the socialization practices within the cultures from which they come. While we can articulate the importance of this concept, we are still not very good at determining what this means in terms of providing education that is multicultural. Thus, we believe it has to do with providing each child an equal opportunity to develop to full potential; we understand that attending to individual differences may mean treating children unequally; and we prefer to talk about treating children equitably and fairly rather than identically.

Facilitating Instructional Pluralism

As Banks (1997) suggests, equity will exist for all students "when teachers modify their teaching in ways that will facilitate the academic achievement of students from diverse racial, cultural, gender and social class groups" (p. 22). Such equity pedagogy can be achieved through instructional pluralism, a sensitivity to diverse learning styles demonstrated through the incorporation of diverse and meaningful learning activities in a lesson (Cooper Shaw 1996). Bennett (1999) cautions teachers to build classroom flexibility slowly, adding one new strategy at a time. She encourages teachers to consider all models of teaching new concepts and skills. Multisensory approaches should be an important consideration in all instructional delivery.

The emphasis on multidimensional teaching is important, especially when teachers may limit their instructional strategies to "style matching," where activities are chosen only to match students' perceived learning styles. While it is appropriate to provide students the opportunities to work in areas of strength, it is also important to provide them a chance to increase their own repertoire of learning or coping strategies.

Analyzing One's Teaching Style

Swisher and Deyhle (1989) propose that teachers who are empathetic and want to change do so only when they have had the time to reflect, research, and restructure their teaching styles. There may never be enough time to do this, but it is an essential element in understanding the learning styles of all children in our classrooms. Bennett (1999) encourages teachers to know their own learning and teaching styles and then determine how far they can comfortably stray from these strengths and preferences.

Learning About Students' Cultures

Getting to know our students and their home backgrounds should be a requisite beginning-of-the-year activity. Fuller (1996) suggests that beginning teachers ask the following questions about their students' cultures: What is the group's history? What are the important cultural values of the group? Who are outstanding individuals who claim membership in this group? What are the group's major religions and beliefs? What are the current political concerns? What are the group's political, religious, and social celebration days? What are the educational implications of the answers to the preceding questions? Fuller advises teachers to gather this information through academic sources in libraries; reading community-based newspapers and magazines; visiting cultural centers, museums, and students' homes; and, when possible, actually living and working within the community.

Identifying Students' Learning Styles

Central to a teacher's ability to draw on the information on learning styles is his or her ability to identify students' learning preferences. Several informal and formal guides have been developed to assist in this task. According to Irvine and York (1995), more than 30 learning-style instruments have been constructed. These researchers offer a summary of the most frequently used tests, providing information on the type of assessment, the category of learners, the format and duration. Bennett (1999) also provides a detailed summary of four instruments. These are the Embedded Figures Test (EFT, also known as the Hidden Figures Test) pioneered by Witkin and associates to identify field independent and dependent learners; the Edmonds Learning Style Identification Exercise (ELSIE) created by Reinhart to identify visual, auditory, and kinesthetic learners; the Learning Style Inventory by Dunn, Dunn, and Price (1978) that identified 21 elements of learning styles; and the paragraph completion task designed by Hunt (1979) to identify a student's need for structure. Cornett (1983) also offers a summary of instruments designed to assess cognitive style, perceptual modality, and multidimensional aspects. Informal student and teacher observable behavior checklists have been developed by Ramirez and Castañeda (1974). They provide valuable tools in the identification of both learning and teaching style tendencies.

Applying Research Appropriately

The message to be gleaned from the research on learning styles isn't always clear. As Bennett (1999) notes, decades of research have presented more questions than answers. Irvine and York (1995) point out that research linking learning style and culture has methodological, conceptual, and pedagogical problems. Hence, one has to be extremely cautious when applying the knowledge generated through such research. Perhaps the most effective way to use this wide information base is to view it as the range of ways in which an individual might approach learning. It is best used as a guide, not a stereotype, for understanding individuals in our schools.

Unfortunately, many students have suffered the consequences of their teachers' simplistic applications of the knowledge about learning styles. Nieto (2000) describes the case of Latino students in a multicultural class having to share textbooks when there was no shortage of textbooks in the class. It was assumed that, since Latinos were more cooperative learners, they would prefer to share books instead of each having one as other students had. American Indian students have not been offered parts in school plays or leadership roles because of the assumption that they did not like public attention. Not only do these cases reveal inappropriate applications of the knowledge about learning styles, but they also demonstrate how well-meaning teachers can engage in instructional practices that are inherently inequitable and deprive students of equal opportunities to learn and succeed in school. It is important that we make the knowledge about learning styles an asset, rather than a hindrance, to teaching and learning.

Conclusion

Understanding learning styles is a powerful element in a teacher's repertoire of effective instructional tools. Use of knowledge about learning styles demonstrates, in an observable manner, the valuing of diversity. The fundamental values of fairness and equitable treatment of all children are manifested in teachers' personal behaviors as they adapt their instruction and interact with learners. However, as Bennett (1999) advises, "We must be careful, however, not to view learning styles as the panacea that will eliminate failure in the schools. To address learning styles is often a necessary, but never sufficient, condition for effective teaching" (p. 179).

References

Banks, J. A. (1997). Multicultural education: Characteristics and goals. In J. A. Banks and C. M. Banks (Eds.), *Multicultural education: Issues and perspectives* (3rd ed.) (pp. 3–31). Boston: Allyn and Bacon.

Bennett, C. (1999). *Comprehensive multicultural education: Theory and practice* (4th ed.). Boston: Allyn and Bacon.

Boykin, A. W. (1986). The triple quandary and the schooling of Afro-American children. In U. Neisser (Ed.) *The school achievement of minority children.* (pp. 57–92). Hillsdale, NJ: Lawrence Erlbaum Associates.

Brandt, R. (1990). If we only knew enough. *Educational Leadership, 48*(2), 3.

Castañeda, A., and Gray, T. (1974). Bicognitive processes in multicultural education. *Educational Leadership, 32,* 203–207.

Cohen, R. A. (1969). Conceptual styles, cultural conflict, and nonverbal tests of intelligence. *American Anthropologist, 71,* 828–856.

Cooper Shaw, C. (1996). Instructional pluralism: A means to realizing the dream of multicultural, social reconstructionist education. In C. Grant and M. L. Gomez (Eds.), *Making schooling multicultural: Classroom and campus* (pp. 55–76). Englewood Cliffs, NJ: Prentice Hall.

Cornett, C. E. (1983). *What you should know about teaching and learning styles.* Bloomington, IN: Phi Delta Kappan Foundation.

Cox, B. G., and Ramirez, M. (1981). Cognitive styles: Implications for multiethnic education. In J. A. Banks (Ed.), *Education in the '80s: Implications for multiethnic education* (p. 61). Washington, DC: National Education Association.

Delpit, L. (1988). The silenced dialogue: Power and pedagogy in educating other people's children. *Harvard Education Review, 58,* 280–298.

Dunn, R., and Dunn, K. (1993). *Teaching secondary students through their individual learning styles.* Boston: Allyn and Bacon.

Dunn, R., Dunn, K., and Price, G. E. (1978). *Learning style inventory.* Lawrence, KS: Price Systems.

Fuller, M. L. (1996). Multicultural concerns and classroom management. In C. Grant and M. L. Gomez (Eds.). *Making schooling multicultural: Classroom and campus* (pp. 133–158). Englewood Cliffs, NJ: Prentice Hall.

Gardner, H. (1993). *Multiple intelligences: The theory in practice.* New York: Basic Books.

Gay, G. (1975). Cultural differences important in the education of Black children. *Momentum* (October), 30–33.

Hale-Benson, J. E. (1986). *Black children: Their roots, culture, and learning styles* (Revised ed.). Baltimore: Johns Hopkins University Press.

Hilliard, A. (1976). Alternatives to IQ testing: An approach to the identification of gifted minority children. Final report to the California State Department of Education.

Hunt, D. E. (1979). Learning style and student needs: An introduction to conceptual level. In *Student learning styles: Diagnosing and describing programs.* Reston, VA: National Association of Secondary School Principals.

Irvine, J. J., and York, D. E. (1995). Learning styles and culturally diverse students: A literature review. In J. A. Banks and C. M. Banks (Eds.), *Handbook of research on multicultural education* (pp. 484–497). New York: MacMillan.

Keefe, J. W., and Languis, M. (1983). *Learning Stages Network Newsletter, 4*(2), 1.

Nakanishi, D. T., and Hirano-Nakanishi, M. (Eds.). (1983). *The education of Asian and Pacific American: Historical perspectives and prescriptions for the future.* Phoenix, AZ: Oryx.

Nieto, S. (2000*). Affirming Diversity: The sociopolitical context of multicultural education* (3rd ed.). New York: Longman.

Oakes, J., and Lipton, M. (1999). *Teaching to change the world.* Boston: McGraw-Hill College.

Pang, V., and Cheng, L. (1998). *Struggling to be heard: The unmet needs of Asian Pacific American children.* New York: State University of New York.

Pang, V. O. (1995). Asian Pacific American students: A diverse and complex population. In J. A. Banks and C. M. Banks (Eds.), *Handbook of research on multicultural education* (pp. 412–424). New York: MacMillan.

Pang, V. O. (1990). Asian American children: A diverse population. *The Education Forum, 55,* 49–66.

Philips, S. U. (1983). *The invisible culture.* New York: Longman.

Ramirez, M., and Castañeda, A. (1974). *Cultural democracy, bicognitive development, and education*. New York: Academic Press.

Reinhart, H. (1976). One picture is worth a thousand words? Not necessarily! *Modern Language Journal, 60,* 160–168.

Scarcella, R. (1992). Providing culturally sensitive feedback. In P. A. Richard-Amato and M. A. Snow (Eds.), *The Multicultural classroom: Readings for content-area teachers* (pp. 126–141). White Plains, NY: Longman.

Shade, B. J. (1982). Afro-American cognitive style: A variable in school success? *Review of Educational Research, 52*(2), 219–44.

Shade, B. J., Kelly, C., and Oberg, M. (1997). *Creating culturally responsive classrooms.* Washington, DC: American Psychological Association.

Slavin, R., DeVries, D., and Edwards, K. (1983). *Cooperative Learning.* New York: Longman.

Swisher, K., and Deyhle, D. (1989). The styles of learning are different, but teaching is just the same: Suggestions for teachers of American Indian youth. *Journal of American Indian Education,* (August), 1–14.

Swisher, K., and Page, B. (1990). Determining Jicarilla Apache learning styles: A collaborative approach. Paper delivered at the Annual Meeting of the American Educational Research Association, Boston, MA, 18 April 1990.

Witkin, H. A. (1967). A cognitive style approach to cross-cultural research. *International Journal of Psychology, 2,* 233–250.

Witkin, H. A., Moore, C. A., Goodenough, D. R., and Cox, P. W. (1977). *Cognitive style and the teaching/learning process.* Cassette series 3F. Washington, DC: American Educational Research Association.

chapter 6

Gender Effects in Schooling

Jane Bernard-Powers

When my daughter, Michelle, was 12, she reminded me of a powerful stereotype that emerged in early adolescence and shadowed young women through their high school years. She said that "brainy" girls are not popular. Almost a decade later, Mary Pipher, author of *Reviving Ophelia*, observed that girls and young women are suffering because they choose to "be quiet in class rather than risk being called a brain" (Pipher 1994, p. 40). The notion that women could not and should not aspire to intellectual goals reverberates through the history of education in the United States, coupled with the reality of women's pursuit of learning (Kerber 1988).

In contrast, boys and young men have been expected to perform intellectual and physical feats while commanding the sound space in classrooms. The history of education for males in the United States, which was mainly for White propertied men up to the 20th century, was predicated on the notion that schools and schooling were for men and boys—girls and women were the interlopers (Kerber 1988, p. 19). As Annie G. Porritt, a conservative from Hartford, Connecticut, wrote in 1911, "the training for politics and for the larger life of the nation is necessary for boys; it is manifestly absurd to give such training for girls—training which would unfit them for their own sphere" (Porritt 1911). Myths and realities associated with gender may not be as manifest at the turn of the 21st century, yet they persist in the fabric of school life, shaping the experience of schooling and influencing the benefits realized for boys and girls and young women and men.

Gender is a dynamic phenomenon of social experience in the United States and elsewhere. Distinguished from sex, which refers to biology and anatomy, gender is the socially constructed meaning assigned to being a girl or woman, or a boy or man. Comparisons between girls and boys, men and women are implicit in the term, and gender is viewed through a relational frame by researchers and educators. The goal of gender-fair education is to foster research, understanding, and practices that lead to equal or comparable opportunities for males and females at all levels and in all dimensions of educational life.

Research on gender dynamics and gender effects in schooling has flowered in the United States and elsewhere in the last 30 years. It has resulted in a deep appreciation for the tenacity and complexity of gender phenomena in school life. Gender-fair education encompasses both knowledge of systemic issues—such as shifting school populations and community change precipitated by political and social forces in the United States and across the globe—as well as attention to specific school contexts and change strategies.

This chapter explores the influence of gender, that is, the significance of being male or female on educational experiences and achievement in the United States. Given the breadth of the field, it is an edited montage that begins with an introduction to current perspectives on gender in education and then discusses gender biases in specific contexts and content areas.

Theoretical Considerations

Statistics from a 1995 publication, *The World's Women 1995: Trends and Statistics,* indicate that 60% of illiterate humans are women, less than 1% are heads of states, and less than 10% are cabinet ministers. Men earn 70% of income on a global basis, while 70% of the world's women live in poverty and are refugees with their children (United Nations 1995). In the United States, the labor market is still conspicuously segregated, with women concentrated in pink-collar and service occupations and with segregation across and within occupations (Peterson and Runyan 1999, p. 90).

The correlative relationship between opportunities in school and opportunities in life has been a consistent focus of gender equity advocates since the early 1970s. *Equity* has been a central goal that encompasses fairness in the distribution of funding and human resources, access to courses and curriculum materials that reflect the range of human experiences, and the elimination of gender stereotypes that demean females and limit males.

Equity remains a central goal of programs and research that focus on gender. Yet the gendered landscape of schools and education is considerably more complex than it was conceived in the 1970s, and our understanding has changed. The landmark work *How Schools Shortchange Girls* published in 1992 by the American Association of University Women (AAUW) has been followed by a new study entitled *Gender Gaps: Where Schools Still Fail Our Children* (AAUW 1999). The contrast in titles signals that the lens of gender-fair education is shifting to include all children—boys and girls.

Three key concepts are useful for understanding gender issues. These are *difference, salience,* and *negotiation. Difference* refers to the idea that gender is a fluid category. There are differences and connections that come into focus and are useful for understanding schooling, education, and opportunities. Masculine and feminine are comparative: there are similarities and differences between categories and within each category. Multiple perspectives and multiple identities influence how we understand and enact gender in education. For example, students who take physics constitute a small population of the high school population. We might wonder why only a small group of students enroll in physics classes. Within that group of physics students, however, we find a gender gap: fewer females than males enroll in physics.

Using lenses that focus on both similarities and differences strengthens our abilities as educators to understand the significance of race, class, ethnicity, immigration status, cultural histories, and other dimensions of identity as they interact with gender. Scholars have developed language to characterize this notion, referring to diversities, masculinities, and femininities (Arnot, M. et. al. 1999; Biklen and Pollard 1993).

The second key concept, *salience,* is closely related to the first. Barrie Thorne (1990), an ethnographer who studies gender as a participant-observer in classrooms, lunchrooms, and playgrounds, noted that gender separation in a physical sense did not happen all the time, but seemed to be situational. She found, "The occasions when girls and boys are together are as theoretically and socially significant as when they are apart." Thus, to understand gender relations, one must understand context as an important dynamic (Thorne 1990, pp. 103, 111).

The third concept is *negotiation.* Students and teachers are participants in a system whereby gender constraints and gender relations are negotiated, sometimes consciously and often unconsciously. The confusing and conflicting array of norms and rules that young females and males encounter in the classroom, lunchroom, playground, and halls necessitates negotiation through *accommodation* and *resistance.* As Jean Anyon (1983) found in her study of fifth graders, girls can resist the middle-class feminine-gender prescriptions by dressing and behaving in ways that teachers find provocative (Anyon 1983, p. 33). Similarly, boys resist the perceived feminine culture of classrooms by setting up disruptions. Students are active participants in school culture, and they respond collectively and individually to cultural messages. Given the choice of accommodating or resisting a middle-class attitude and behavior toward school and work, many will choose the latter. It seems to help them maintain their independence.

The idea that social structures and values are mainly responsible for the underachievement of groups of students is limiting because it masks the subtleties and complexities of processes that work in schooling. Students are not passive victims in these processes; nor are teachers hapless victims of cultural reproduction systems. Students, teachers, and administrators may contribute to the factors that limit opportunities as well as to those that expand them. Our challenge is to identify crucial structures and processes that will increase life opportunities for all students and maximize the potential of our diversity.

Gender Gaps and Issues in School

The following sections examine gender effects in important areas of schooling: in testing, content areas, classroom organization and school climate, and athletics, with a brief commentary about newcomers to U.S. schools.

Testing and Assessment: How Normative Data Are Used

Standardized testing is a fact of life in U.S. schools. While the phenomenon is not new, the 1980s and 1990s gave rise to increased interest in general and content-based standards, along with more testing to measure what students and teachers know. For students, parents, teachers, and other interested educators, there are important questions embedded in the design, administration, outcome, and use of standardized testing, with special implications for gender. Research which has focused on gender and assessment provides insight into some persistent issues. A fundamental question is: "Are there gender differences in responses to standardized tests as indicated by outcomes?" The answer is yes, according to the Educational Testing Service (ETS), publishers of *The ETS Gender Study*. The analysis of data from 74 tests for twelfth graders indicated that, in general, young men do better on standardized tests in math concepts, spatial skills, natural science, and geopolitical knowledge (ETS 1997, p. 12). The degree of difference is, according to the authors of the study, small but persistent. Young women performed better on measures of verbal-vocabulary reasoning, abstract reasoning, verbal-reading, study skills, verbal language use, and verbal-writing. The differences in the latter two areas are identified as small to medium, and thus significant (ETS 1997, pp. 12–14)

Another question is: "Are gender differences in standardized tests stable over time?" Gender differences in particular areas changed over time, favoring males in gains in math and science from grades 8 to 12, and favoring females in language subjects from grades 4 to 8. The spread in scores was "found to change over the grades as well." The spread was greater at grade 12 than at grade 4, with males registering a greater spread in grade 12, with higher upper-end scores in math and science as a result (ETS p. 15).

The implications of testing format for gender is a third area of interest. Willingham and Cole (1997) report that in some instances the format—multiple-choice questions or writing—influences response. Data from 27 advanced placement exams in the AP Program of the College Board favored males in the multiple-choice questions section, with minimal advantage for either males or females reported in the free-response sections, which rely heavily on writing (Willingham and Cole 1997, p. 174).

A final area of interest is the "high-stakes test." The Preliminary Scholastic Assessment Test (PSAT), the Scholastic Assessment Test (SAT), and the American College Testing Program (ACT) determine who will receive scholarships. The most consistent finding on high-stakes tests is that males perform better in natural sciences and math, and they dominate the upper percentiles (AAUW 1999). The impact of this phenomenon is financial—males have garnered more National Merit Scholarships than females.

Phyllis Rosser, author of the *The SAT Gender Gap: Identifying the Causes* (1989), asserts that women were eligible for only 36% of the 6,000 college scholarships based on their lower qualifying scores in 1987–1988 (p. 4). Moreover, opportunities for academic enrichment programs in high schools are also lost as a result of lower scores on high-stakes tests (Rosser 1989).

If grades were used as primary predictors of performance and the basis for scholarship awards, young women would probably fare much better. As the ETS study indicates, "Females, on average, have higher grades than males in all major subjects" (ETS 1997, p. 18). Female grades exceed male grades most substantially in English, with smaller differences reported in social studies, science, and math. Grades are a measure of a broader complex of practical skills, including study habits, and they are considered a highly reliable predictor of performance in the first year of college. Thus, many would argue, grades should more heavily influence college entrance and scholarship awards.

The most serious problem with a heavy reliance on test scores is how some young women interpret them. According to Rosser (1989), young men and women believed that a standarized test was a fair measure of their abilities. That means that young women see themselves as less able than their male contemporaries. For some young women, especially minority women for whom scholarship monies and belief in self are critical, the consequences of this assumption could include opting out of college.

Content Areas

Social Studies

Social studies presents a mixed profile in terms of achievement measured on standardized tests. In geopolitical knowledge, which includes economics, history, and geography, males enjoyed a slight advantage when mean scores were considered. This finding has been consistent over time (ETS 1997, pp. 12–15).

Fourth grade Hispanic and African American girls score higher than boys in history, and African American girls retain their advantage in history and geography through grade 8. These advantages are wiped out by grade 12 for all young women, when they fall behind young men (AAUW 1999, p. 43).

In contrast, the most recent Civics Assessment report card of the National Assessment of Educational Progress (NAEP) indicated no statistical difference between males' and females' scores normatively. That represents a distinct difference from test scores reported 15 years ago that found males outscoring females on political knowledge (Hahn and Bernard-Powers 1985, p. 281; NAEP 1998).

The parity that young women and young men enjoy in NAEP Civics results and the evident disparities in geographic knowledge, historical knowledge, and economic knowledge represent only one dimension of gender issues in social studies. The content of the curriculum is another important consideration.

In 1985 and 1986, 300,000 grade 8 students in California were tested under the California Assessment Program (CAP). On the history/social science test, boys did better on 467 of the questions, while girls scored higher on 253. Whereas "Boys did better on questions related to war, historical documents (such as the Declaration of Independence, the Constitution, the Bill of Rights), and questions involving geography or chronology. . . . Girls did better on questions related to interpretation of slogans, quotations (except those associated with war), women's rights, or questions in which the focus of the question was a woman (Kneedler 1988). This research suggests that there are gender differences in the perceived salience of topics.

Similarly, Hahn reported in her study of "Gender and Political Learning" (1996) that young men seemed noticeably interested in national and international news, with no comparable evidence for young women, whereas young women were particularly interested in controversial issues that were domestic in nature, such as abortion, animal rights, school prayer, and the death penalty. I am not making an argument here for essentialism, but I am acknowledging the potential significance of topics in social studies curricula.

The most extensively documented inequity in social studies is the underrepresentation and stereotyping of females in social studies textbooks. Despite the virtual revolution in scholarship germane to ethnic, family, social, and women's histories, textbooks continue to lag behind what is possible. While AAUW's 1999 study reported that textbooks are more balanced now than they were in 1992, it is evident to me that the limitations on role models for young men and young women of all races and ethnic groups are sustained in textbooks. As Vicki Ruiz notes in her recent history of Mexican American women in the last century, "Their stories . . . have remained in the shadows" (Ruiz 1998, xiii; AAUW 1999).

Hahn's study of "Gender and Political Learning" corroborates these phenomena in her content analysis of civics textbooks. She reported that "the historic chapters named 3 male philosophers, 2 male kings, 13 'founding fathers,' 18 male presidents, 6 male vice presidents, 3 male chief justices and 6 males who were the focus of landmark Supreme Court Cases, among others" (Hahn 1996, p. 27). According to Hahn, the shortcomings of the textbook were not balanced or countered by the teachers. "Students were not asked to consider the roles of women in government, nor were they provided with many role models of politically active women" (Hahn 1996, p. 28).

All students need to see the connections between the curriculum they experience and their own lives. Social studies curricula are a particularly vital place for providing connections and creating possibilities for leadership and community growth. The more evidence students have that they can be leaders in their communities, the more likely it is that communities will be enriched by their presence. This is particularly true for the more disenfranchised—African American males, Latinos, and Latinas.

Reading/Writing and Language Arts

Reading and writing are areas that have been reported on extensively in relation to gender. Gender differences favoring girls and young women have been reported in NAEP results for almost 30 years (NAEP 1997). White, Hispanic, and African American females demonstrate consistently strong abilities to read and interpret texts, compared to their masculine counterparts. This finding holds true for Great Britain as well as the United States (White, 1996).

There has been considerable concern directed at the low performance of minority youths in reading. An unpacking of the aggregate statistic finds that 45% of white 17-year-olds are "adept" in reading, according to the NAEP 1996 test results, which means they can find, summarize, and analyze complicated information (NAEP 1997, p. 130). In contrast, only 16 to 20% of Black and Hispanic 17-year-olds are adept readers. The correlation between reading skills and African American or Hispanic identity seems clear: I surmise in the absence of data from standardized testing sources that a sizable group of young men of color fall in the lowest percentiles in reading. They also occupy a high percentage of spaces in special education classes.

Dropout rates for Black and Hispanic males are reported to be generally higher than for females of all races and ethnic groups, and this may be related to reading and the extent to which the needs of this population are not being met. Data collection and analysis that combine gender, ethnicity, and reading abilities are critical for illuminating these important issues.

Literature texts in classrooms and writing assignments constitute a significant part of the reading, language arts curriculum in all grades. As Mem Fox, a children's book author, has eloquently argued, books continue to present stereotyped views of male and female that limit students' potential. Authors such as Mem Fox have made significant strides for readers in presenting characters who experience and demonstrate a full range of human emotions and dreams—the Straight Line Wonder and Leo Lipinski are examples. These male characters were modeled after Fox's nephew Andrew, who wanted to be a dancer but was heavily discouraged by family and society. Straight Line went on to a career in dancing, and Leo Linpinski chose painting over high finance (Fox 1993, p. 84). In the words of Fox, "My old men are allowed to weep . . . ; my pirates cry; my baby-sitters are leather-wearing teenage boys with punk hair; my heroes in love don't live and love happily ever after; and my male adventurers are led to success by stronger women, without being demeaned by the experience" (p. 85).

The books our students read play a major role in the elementary school curriculum, where the foundations of reading are established. Stories and narratives about real people in their lives, where courage is not confined to war and monumental acts but to the multiple ways that children and adults have of acting courageously in their families, schools, and communities, are a critical part of the curriculum of the new century (Rogers 1993). These stories need to be related to the lives of our multiethnic, multilingual student populations and made comprehensible to them.

Math, Science, and Technology

Science educators are perennially concerned about national levels of achievement in science, and the most recent international study supports the concern. The United States was above average in the Third International Mathematics and Science Study (TIMSS) at the fourth grade, but substantially lower than the international average by the twelfth grade (AAUW 1999, pp. 42–43). This decrease mirrors the performance of young women, compared to young men. The gender gap between performance in both math and science increases over time, favoring males, and the gap is largest at the highest levels of achievement.

However, the overall gender gap in math and science has decreased over time in both the United States and in Great Britain. According to the most recent AAUW study, "the most measurable . . . success" has been in mathematics and science, as evidenced by test scores and course enrollments—excluding computer science (AAUW 1999, p. 13). For example, 1977 NAEP data indicated that only one-third of the females "demonstrated the ability to analyze scientific material and data" (NAEP 1985, pp. 30–31). Two decades later, 44% percent of female 17-year-olds can analyze scientific material and data (NAEP 1997, p.142). Increased attention to specific populations can result in learning and achievement. Thus, specific efforts of organizations such as the National Science Foundation are especially important to gender equity in math and science.

When young women indicate what they plan to study in college, persistent gender differences surface. More women select psychology, sociology, education, health services, and language as fields of choice. More young men select engineering, math and computer science, architecture, and physical science. Females and minorities continue to self-select out of fields that have advanced mathematics prerequisites.

Computer science is recognized as a significant area of competency for students in the 21st century. The potential of computer education for reorganizing educational settings makes computer competency an important issue. Moreover, technology is an increasingly important dimension of the workplace. Student use of computers at schools is gender fair, according to statistics included in the Statistical Abstract of the United States. In 1993, 56.5% of males and 60.5% of females were using computers in schools. The "digital divide" is more evident when comparing households with incomes of $5,000 to $9,999, where 55% of students in grades 1 to 8 use computers at school, compared to 75.6% in households with incomes from $50,000 to $74,000 (Bureau of the Census 1998, p.180).

However, there are other indicators that suggest a gender divide in computer use. Although using computers as communication tools is becoming increasingly common (e.g., online conversations between students doing homework), using computers to learn sophisticated applications and graphics is more prevalent among young men. A College Board survey of college-bound seniors indicated that males were far more likely to choose using personal computers as an activity or educational choice (ETS 1997, p. 17). "Computer science and applications electives attract very few girls, and, in 1996, females comprised only 17% of Advanced Placement computer science test takers" (AAUW 1999, p. 123).

The links between school performance and the job market represent part of the unfinished business of education. Statistics still indicate that women earn only 75 cents to each dollar that men make. Researchers in Great Britain who recently studied the gender gap in schooling found that while substantial gains had been made in reducing the gender gap in the areas of math and science, career and occupational choices remained conventional and stereotyped (Arnot, David, and Weiner 1999, p. 24). A study by Gilson corroborates this particular gap for young women. While female students may do well in mathematics according to their grades, their perception of their mathematics abilities does not match, nor do their aspirations (Gilson 1999).

In technology, there is compelling evidence of new labor market segmentation. Computer "jocks," hackers, and millionaires who do start-up companies are in the first tier, and women and minorities who do skilled labor occupy the second tier.

These findings in performance differences for males and females in math, science, and computers suggest the need for change in several areas.

Teacher training needs to include information about contexts that foster equal participation for males, females, and minorities in all three of these areas. Continued support for elementary science teachers, who find time and resources at a premium, is critical. Interdisciplinary teaching that incorporates teaching reading with science and social studies will increase the number of minutes that young women and minorities are provided with instruction. After-school programs and special programs, such as the Equals project at the Lawrence Hall of Science in Berkeley, California, can provide out-of-school time for hands-on work in science, mathematics, and computing, thereby developing students' confidence in their abilities and increasing their interest in careers (Skolnick, Langbort, and Day 1982).

Classroom Organization and School Climate

Another topic for consideration in the discussion of gender effects in school is what I will characterize as classroom organization and school climate. Classroom interaction can be a source of learning as well as a source of distress. When Caille Millner, an African American undergraduate, moved from San Jose, California, to Cambridge, Massachusetts, she kept a journal that she shared with subscribers to the Pacific News Service. Her observations about gender effects in classrooms at Harvard corroborated previous findings about classroom interactions and gender. She wrote: "I never realized just how true the studies are about gender divisions in the classroom until I entered a co-ed classroom after four years' absence. Men truly do dominate, even when they are in the minority" (Millner 1997, p. B-7).

Group work based on theory guiding daily practice holds great promise for maximizing learning and harnessing the effects of gender, ethnicity, and race in the classroom. By providing training for group roles, very specific feedback on demonstrated student strengths, and modeling for equal treatment for all persons, we can increase learning in math and science, group problem solving, and prosocial behavior for every student—including young men.

The program for Complex Instruction at Stanford University in California is an example of a program that trains educators to use instruction that is designed to be gender friendly as well as racially, ethnically, and linguistically friendly (Cohen 1988). The program is predicated on the belief that students learn effectively when they are talking and interacting with each other and with learning materials. Learning opportunities, such as taking a leadership role in a group discussion, can be learned and the effects of privilege and dominance by any group can be mitigated by assigning roles, providing training for the roles, and building powerful instruction around roles and explicit cooperative norms.

Research on complex instruction classrooms that focused on gender effects found a substantial difference in the perception of girls as leaders.

Whereas 94% of votes were cast for boys as leaders in a previous study (1983), 54% of 290 votes were cast for boys and 46% for girls in this more recent study of Complex Instruction outcomes (Leal-Idrogo 1997). Clearly, girls and boys are able to perceive girls as leaders when the classroom models gender equity.

Barrie Thorne has researched and written about cross-sex groupings in elementary schools, finding that some contexts in schools are more conducive to cross-sex interaction than others (Thorne 1990). Recognizing the complex choreography with open, flexible lenses and strategies provides the hope that our very diverse populations will be able to succeed in schools and may also change the structures and beliefs of schools.

Harassment, or bullying, is a topic that has gained attention in the last decade. The success of young people in school is clearly related to how safe they feel in school. Yet there is evidence that a high percentage of students in the United States experience sexual harassment on a regular basis. According to an AAUW study published in 1995, 86% of girls and 71% of boys experienced some form of harassment at school (Donhoff 1995). As indicated in a study of bullying in Great Britain, the effects of bullying can lead to students leaving school (Cullingford and Morrison 1995). Teachers' reticence to intervene in the underworld of hallways and playgrounds represents a serious statement to bullied or harassed students.

Athletics

Sports is an aspect of the curriculum where participation rates for young women have increased dramatically since Title IX was passed in 1972. It is one of the success stories of the 20th century, in the sense that many more girls and young women participate in school sports programs than was true in 1971. One out of three female students participated in school sports in 1997, whereas one out of 27 young women participated in school sports in 1971 (AAUW 1999, p. 96). Moreover, the participation rate of particular populations has increased along with the population as a whole: young black women are participating at the same rate as young white women. On the other hand, women's sports lag behind men's in important ways. According to the Women's Sports Foundation, only 37% of collegiate scholarship dollars are awarded to women athletes, and 27% of college sport operating budgets go toward recruiting female athletes (Women's Sports Foundation 1998).

Research cited in the AAUW study of 1999 indicates that playing in sports holds secondary gains for young women in general achievement and self-esteem (exclusive of African American females, for whom self-esteem is not a salient school issue). Women's sports programs need to be strengthened by financial support, and girls need role models and good skill building in the early elementary years.

Newcomers

David Corson, a researcher in Ontario, Canada, has written about the connections of ideas, beliefs, values, and knowledge that immigrants share. He characterizes these connections as ligatures. He observes in a chapter on "Girls From Immigrant Cultures" that immigrant girls find that the special ligatures they share with the other girls from similar backgrounds are missing from the public symbols and practices of schools. In their place are few opportunities to build close ties with nonimmigrant girls and boys (Corson 1993, 1998).

Patterns of speech or discourse are central to classroom life. Corson finds that discourse styles from traditional cultures are likely to influence the speech and interaction patterns in classrooms. This means that men and boys dominate the public speech opportunities, using a competitive mode of speech, much the same as Caille Millner observed at Harvard. In Corson's words, "during and after the middle childhood years, schools give more recognition to the competitive discursive practices that most boys learn to use early in their lives. As a consequence, girls from immigrant backgrounds who are already affected by being culturally different are doubly disadvantaged by the gendered practices" (Corson 1998, p. 89).

Conclusion

Our work in sex equity in the 1960s and 1970s raised questions and built a scaffolding from which we continue to profit. The problem of equal access to opportunities and education for young women and young men of all races and ethnic groups has not been totally redressed, but we now have more than 25 years of experience in policy work and research to inform us. In the last two decades especially, research and scholarship in the content areas as well as in pedagogy, classroom management, achievement motivation, extracurricular programs, and testing have led us to an understanding of the complexity of gendered systems.

The gendered experiences of particular populations have to be appreciated for their differences as well as commonalties. African American males experience classrooms differently in many ways from African American females, Asian males and females, and European American males and females. Gender is an omnipresent reality that rarely stands alone. An appreciation of salience, context, negotiation, and a healthy skepticism of any easy prescription for progress will sustain us. Our diverse and gendered student population provides the motivation and the modeling for us to move into the 21st century. Support for research, preservice teacher preparation and teacher development, and an assertive data analysis program that involves gender issues is critical. These are the minimal tools needed to provide a gender-fair education in this new century.

References

American Association of University Women. (1992). *How schools shortchange girls.* Washington, DC: AAUW Educational Foundation and National Education Association.

American Association of University Women, American Institutes for Research. (1999). *Gender gaps: Where schools still fail our children.* New York: Marlowe.

Anyon, J. (1983). Intersections of gender and class: Accommodation and resistance by working-class and affluent females to contradictory sex-role ideologies. In S. Walker and L. Barton (Eds.), *Gender, class, and education* (p. 33). Sussex: Falmer.

Arnot, M., David, M., and Weiner, G. (1999). *Closing the gender gap: Postwar education and social change.* Cambridge, England: Polity.

Arnot, M., and Weiner, K. (1993). *Feminism and social justice in education.* Philadelphia: Falmer.

Biklen, S., and Pollard, D. (1993). *Gender and education* (pp. 2–9). Chicago: National Society for the Study of Education.

Bureau of the Census. (1998). *Statistical Abstract of the United States.* Washington: Government Printing Office.

Cohen, E. (1988). *Designing groupwork: Strategies for the heterogenous classroom.* New York: Teachers College Press.

Cole, M., and Griffin, P. (Eds.). (1987). *Contextual factors in education.* Madison: Wisconsin Center for Education Research.

Corson, D. (1998). *Changing education for diversity.* Philadelphia: Open University Press.

Corson, D. (1993). *Language, minority education and gender.* Philadelphia: Multilingual Matters Ltd.; and Toronto: Ontario Institute for Studies in Education.

Cullingford, C., and Morrison, J. (1995). Bullying as a formative influence: The relationship between the experience of school and criminality. *British Educational Research Journal, 2*(5). Reprinted in M. Arnot, M. David, and G. Weiner (Eds.), 1999, pp. 547–560.

Donhoff, K. (1995). Sexual harassment among students can lead to learning disruption. *CTA Action* (May), p. 11.

Educational Testing Service. (1997). *The ETS gender study: How males and females perform in educational settings* (pp. 5–27). Princeton: ETS.

Fox, M. (1993). Men who weep, boys who dance: The gender agenda between the lines in children's literature. *Language Arts, 70* (February), 84–88.

Gilson, J. (1999). Factors contributing to the achievement and positive attitudes of females in mathematics: A study of middle-school students. Unpublished paper presented at the American Education Research on Women in Education meeting, New York.

Hahn, C. (1996). Gender and political learning, *Theory and Research in Social Education, 24*(1), 8–35.

Hahn, C., and Bernard-Powers, J. (1985). Sex equity in the social studies. In S. Klein (Ed.), *Handbook for achieving sex equity in education* (p. 281). Baltimore: Johns Hopkins University Press.

Kerber, L. (1988). "Why should girls be learn'd and wise?": Two centuries of higher education for women as seen through the unfinished work of Alice Mary

Baldwin. In J. M. Faragher and F. Howe (Eds.), *Women and higher education in American history* (p. 19). New York: W. W. Norton.

Kneedler, P. (1988). Differences between boys and girls on California's new state-wide assessments in history–social science. Paper presented at the California Council for the Social Studies, March 1988.

Leal-Idrogo, A. (1997). The effect of gender on interaction, friendship, and leadership in elementary school classrooms. In E. G. Cohan and R. Lotan (Eds.), *Working for equity in heterogeneous classrooms* (pp. 92–102). New York: Teachers College Press.

Millner, C. (1997, December 2). Black student's introduction to Harvard. *San Francisco Examiner*, B-7.

National Assessment of Educational Progress. (1985). The reading report card. Princeton, NJ: Educational Testing Service.

National Assessment of Educational Progress. (1985). The science report card. Princeton, NJ: Educational Testing Service.

National Assessment of Educational Progress. (1997). "1996 trends in academic progress (p. 130, table 112)." Washington, DC: U.S. Department of Education, Office of Educational Research and Improvement.

National Assessment of Educational Progress. (1998). Civics assessment report card, highlights. http://NCES.ed.gov/NationsReportCard/civics/civics.asp

Peterson, V. S., and Runyan, A. S. (1999). *Global gender issues*. Boulder, CO: Westview Press.

Pipher, M. (1994). *Reviving Ophelia*. New York: Ballantine Books.

Porritt, A. (1911). The feminization of our schools and its political consequences. *Educational Review, 41*, 441–448.

Rogers, A. (1993). Voice, play, and a practice of ordinary courage in girls' and women's lives. *Harvard Educational Review, 63*(3), 265–294.

Rosser, P. (1989). *The SAT gender gap: Identifying the causes*. Washington, DC: Center for Womem Policy Studies.

Ruiz, V. (1998). *From out of the shadows*. New York: Oxford University Press.

Skolnick, J., Langbort, C., and Day, L. (1982). How to encourage girls in math and science. Palo Alto, CA: Dale Seymour.

Thorne, B. (1990). Children and gender: Constructions of difference. In D. Rhode (Ed.), *Theoretical perspectives on sexual difference* (pp. 100–114). New Haven: Yale University Press.

United Nations. (1995). *The world's women 1995: Trends and statistics*. New York: United Nations. Reprinted in V. S. Peterson and A. S. Runyan, 1999, *Global gender issues*. Westview.

Willingham, W., and Cole, N. (1997). *Gender and fair assessment*. Mahwah, NJ: Lawrence Erlbaum.

Weiner, G. (1999). Closing the gender gap: Cause for celebration or anxiety? *Education Journal* (November 1999), pp. 32–33.

White, J. (1996). Research on English and the teaching of girls. In P. Murphy and C. Gipps (Eds.), *Equity in the classroom: Towards effective pedagogy for girls and boys* (p. 99). London: Falmer.

Women's Sports Foundation. (1999). Fair Play? [Brochure].

chapter **7**

Addressing the Academic Needs of Immigrant Students: Issues and Trends in Immigrant Education

Dilys Schoorman

Immigration to the United States has contributed to dramatic and ongoing shifts in the nation's social and political landscape over the past 100 years. The century ended in a manner similar to how it began: on the brink of yet another reconfiguration of what Portes and Rumbaut (1990) termed this "permanently unfinished society" of immigrants. In 1996, there were 24.6 million immigrants in the United States, comprising approximately 9.3% of the total population (U.S. Census Bureau 1998). This figure refers to those who were born in nations outside the United States who did not have a U.S.-born parent.

It is estimated that the immigrant population will continue to grow at the rate of approximately one million each year and that currently one in every five children enrolled in school is an immigrant. This diversity holds both promise and challenge. Immigrants bring to the community new knowledge bases, experiences, and perspectives, providing local residents with a taste of the "outside world" with no need for travel. Immigrants tend to invest highly in efforts to better themselves and to ensure their family's success in their new homeland. As such, they tend to be hard-working and uncomplaining students and employees. Nevertheless, immigration has presented challenges to host communities and local institutions that need to adapt to the changing demographics of their constituents. Areas with high populations of immigrants have had to institute support systems to address immigrants' unfamiliarity with the dominant language and culture so they might have access to education, health care, and employment. Ultimately, the social integration of immigrants often depends on how well educators and other community leaders respond to this diversity.

The purpose of this chapter is to provide insight to this promise and challenge through a discussion of (a) the current social, political and legal context of immigration in the United States, (b) diverse philosophical approaches to the social integration of immigrants, (c) multiple factors that impact the adaptation of immigrants, and (d) strategies that could be undertaken within educational communities to better address the needs of immigrant students.

Current Context of Immigrant Education

The most recent influx of immigrants to the United States began in the 1980s. It was during this decade that 34.3% of the current total immigrant population arrived; a further 25% arrived in the 1990s. The immigrants entering during these decades were predominantly of Latin American and Asian origin, with Mexico accounting for the highest population from a single nation. The cultural background of this population represents a marked contrast from immigrants of the first half of the 20th century, who were predominantly of European descent. Although immigrants of all periods endure many common challenges, the more recent immigrants have had an additional difficulty "fitting in" because they often looked different from the mainstream population. As such, their immigration experiences did not fit into the traditional "model" of assimilation which, based on European immigrant experiences in the first half of the century, emerged as the dominant paradigm of immigrant social integration.

Immigrants have tended to settle close to their ports of entry. Therefore, immigrant communities in the United States are predominantly clustered in six states: California (8 million immigrants amounting to 25.1% of the total state population in 1996), New York (3.2 million amounting to 17.7% of the population), Florida (15.2%), Texas (11.1%), New Jersey (14.6%), and Illinois (under 10%; specific figures unavailable). Each of these six states were home to at least a million immigrants. Other states where immigrants account for at least 10% of the population include Hawaii (16.6%), Nevada (11.4%), Arizona (10.9%), and Rhode Island (10.4%) (U.S. Census Bureau 1998).

Who Is an Immigrant?

Legally, an immigrant is someone who is admitted for legal and permanent residence in the United States. Socially, the term "immigrant" is applied to a broader category of persons which also includes refugees (who might not have been granted permanent residency yet), migrant workers, and undocumented persons (those who entered the country without visas or those whose visas have expired). Also among the foreign-born in the United States are those who are classified as "nonimmigrants." Included in this category are international students and scholars who are in the United States as "sojourners" (those who intend to return to their country after they complete their study or work), and temporary workers who arrive in the United States for brief periods of work each year (e.g., Jamaicans who work in the sugarcane fields in Florida). Many of the issues discussed in this chapter pertain to all of these groups of people. In specific focus are the concerns that pertain primarily to immigrants and their children, first- and second-generation immigrants, those who were born in a country outside the United States, or those whose parents are foreign born.

Despite the traditional notion of the "huddled masses" sailing to Ellis Island or contemporary media images of desperate boat people or illegal border crossers that typify immigrants, they constitute an economically and socially diverse group of people that includes labor migrants, professionals, entrepreneurs, refugees, and asylees. They represent the most educated (Asian Indians and Taiwanese) and least educated groups (Mexicans and Salvadoreans) in the United States, as well as the groups with the highest (Laotians and Cambodians) and lowest (Filipinos) poverty rates.

Responses to Immigrants

Public policy concerning immigrants in the United States represents an ongoing struggle between liberalism and conservatism. Legislation that exemplified openness to immigration were the Immigration and Nationality Act Amendments of 1965 and the Immigration Reform and Control Act of 1986. The 1965 Act greatly expanded opportunities for immigration by eliminating the nation-based quotas designed to curtail immigration through the Immigration Act of 1924 and the Immigration and Nationality Act of 1952. The 1924 Act followed efforts in 1917 to restrict immigration by making English a criterion for admission to the United States. Immigration opportunities were further increased by legislation in 1986 that granted legal status to many illegal residents and created greater opportunity for agricultural workers to obtain legal residency.

Several features of educational policy also have been favorable to immigrants. The 1974 *Lau v. Nichols* ruling stated that instruction provided in a language that a student did not understand amounted to a violation of a student's access to equal educational opportunity. The exponential growth of English as a Second Language programs and multicultural and bilingual teaching training efforts have afforded immigrant students a more hospitable climate for academic success. Broader societal acceptance of diversity has alleviated some of the immigrants' struggle for social integration.

Nevertheless, these responses have also been accompanied by an increase of what many view as mean-spirited attacks on immigrant and immigrant-specific concerns. These were exemplified in California initiatives such as Proposition 187, which sought to exclude children of undocumented immigrants from public education and other social services, and Proposition 227, which banned the use of non-English languages in the California school system. The backlash against immigration is prevalent in many communities that have experienced increased diversity. Media portrayals of immigrants as "illegal," and community fears of losing one's sense of "tradition" or "identity," tend to obfuscate the positive impact of immigration on the nation. On average, immigrants pay $1,800 more in taxes than they receive in benefits, contribute to social security, and cannot enter the country legally without demonstrating financial support. Furthermore, U.S. employers and consumers benefit from the cheap labor of immigrants, who sometimes work under dangerous and exploitative conditions in occupations that few native Americans will accept (White House 1998; Schwartz 1996).

The variety of responses to immigrants often have made schools an arena of struggle between forces of marginalization and inclusion. On one hand, there are many who resist any efforts to educate "those" children, consider it a waste to expend money on "others," and insist that immigrants "fit in" to U.S. mainstream culture without "burdening" the system for additional support. On the other hand, there are those who argue that "We, the descendants of those who passed through the portals of Ellis Island must not lock the door behind us. . . . We should treat immigrants as we would have wanted our own grandparents to be treated. . . . We have responsibilities to welcome our newest immigrants (and) to vigorously enforce laws against discrimination" (White House 1998). The dynamics of this struggle have been further affected by the fact that many first generation immigrants have now recently begun to vote and have more impact on policy making.

Nevertheless, even among educators who value cultural pluralism and inclusiveness, the ability to successfully educate immigrant children lies in their ability to clarify their own philosophical approaches. Successful educators of immigrant students need to understand the social integration of immigrants, their awareness and understanding of the sociocultural context in which their students live, and how to help their students successfully negotiate the challenges they typically encounter.

Approaches to the Social Integration of Immigrants

Immigration in the late 19th and early 20th centuries was understood and framed in the context of assimilation. Traditional notions of assimilation entailed that immigrants gave up their cultural identities, including native language proficiency, as they gradually "fit in" to dominant U.S.

culture. The experiences of early immigrants were explained in terms of straight-line assimilation. Straight-line assimilation was based on the assumption that acculturation (the process of acquiring sufficient knowledge of the new culture to survive) was an incremental process, and as immigrants spent more time in the country, they (or their descendants) would become incorporated, structurally and culturally, into "mainstream" U.S. culture.

The assumptions of straight-line assimilation have since been challenged. Alternate views of the immigrant experience have been framed by concepts such as "segmented assimilation" (Portes and Zhou 1999) and "selective assimilation" (Rong and Preissle 1998). Others have dropped the term assimilation in favor of the idea of "additive acculturation" (Gibson 1995) and "adaptation." Segmented assimilation underscores that all immigrants groups do not become incorporated into the American mainstream. Instead, many achieve stable economic status while retaining strong native ethnic identities or have relatively little contact with mainstream cultures. Others who live in racially structured communities assimilate toward the relevant underclass, where they tend to remain for generations. Selective assimilation addresses the fact that immigrants could "selectively" adapt by becoming more "Americanized" in some aspects of their lives (e.g., more fluent in American English) but retain cultural traits in other aspects (e.g., being bilingual, attitudes towards dating, the type of food consumed) regardless of the time spent in the United States.

The notions of additive acculturation, or adaptation, suggest that the immigration experience could lead to cultural enrichment for the immigrant. As Gibson (1998) notes about additive acculturation, "The acquisition of knowledge and skills in the new culture and language are viewed as an additional set of tools to be incorporated into the child's cultural repertoire rather than as a rejection of old traits" (p. 5). The term adaptation is frequently used to emphasize the reciprocal influence between immigrant groups and their host communities. Concepts such as assimilation and acculturation tend to draw attention to the newcomers' willingness and abilities to integrate into the new culture. However, a view of newcomers' experiences as adaptation emphasizes that the successful social and cultural incorporation depends, in large part, on the response of the community to the immigrant groups.

Diverse theoretical perspectives not only describe the reality of the immigrant experience but also tend to reflect their authors' prescriptions for what that experience should be. The perspective of this chapter is that the immigration experience is ideally viewed as a process of adaptation which incorporates the notion of additive acculturation. Immigrants do not have to lose their native identity in order to succeed, and the role of the community is recognized as a crucial facet of successful social and cultural integration.

Factors That Impact Adaptation

The reality of the immigration experience is that the process of "becoming American" while maintaining one's cultural identity is, for many, an arduous struggle. This struggle is created and mediated by diverse individual, familial, cultural, social, and institutional factors.

Individual and Family Factors

Several factors that pertain to individual and family characteristics have been known to affect the cross-cultural adaptation of immigrants. These include: time spent in the United States, age, socioeconomic status, educational and professional background of adults, and individual and family educational aspirations.

Time Spent in the Host Country

It is generally true that the longer immigrants spend in the host culture, the more they (or their descendants) are likely to successfully adapt to life in that culture. Similarly, the longer immigrant students spend in U.S. schools, the more likely they are to succeed academically. Time allows students to become accustomed to the educational practices in the new culture and is especially salient in improving reading scores.

However, academic achievement does not always increase uniformly with time spent in the United States. Contrary to the straight-line assimilation perspective, there has been an observable decline in academic achievement between first- and second-generation immigrants in certain groups. This "second generation decline" (Gans 1992) has been attributed to the negative effects of Americanization; students, no longer perceiving their education as the primary means for success in the new country, become less academically motivated. As Olsen (1997) observes, even among first generation immigrant students, many give up on their educational aspirations when they perceive that their schools (often in less affluent districts) are ill-equipped to provide them the competitiveness for college entrance or professional success.

Age

Closely related to the time spent in the United States is the age of the immigrant on arrival. Rumbaut (1995), echoing the general consensus among researchers, found that older age among immigrant students is strongly and negatively associated with grade point average and math and reading scores. While this observation is congruent with the commonsense perspective that the younger child growing up in the new culture is more likely to succeed than a newcomer who is older, there are other mitigating factors to explain this relationship. First, more academic support services tend to be available to immigrant students in elementary schools than in middle or high schools. Such support services are crucial to a student's adaptation. Second, adolescents tend to experience added social pressures of "fitting in" than do their elementary counterparts. These social pressures sometimes lead to an abandonment of academic focus, making the adaptation of older newcomers much more complex. Third, many older children enter U.S. schools with interrupted or limited schooling experiences. These students typically have more difficulty in school than do younger students for whom the implications of such interruptions are not as far reaching. Nevertheless, Rumbaut also points out that the age of the student and the time spent in the United States need to be considered as separate but interrelated factors. Although the older students tended to experience more difficulty with their education, younger students tended to lose their drive to do well academically as they spent more time in the United States.

According to the U.S. Census Bureau (1993), immigrants were generally older than the native-born population. The median age for immigrants in 1990 was 37 years, representing a drastic drop from 52 in 1970. What this means for children is that although they might be technically the "second generation" because they were born in the United States, they are, in effect, what Rumbaut (1995) terms the "1.5 generation." This term attempts to capture the unique experiences of children whose parents have not become accustomed to life in the United States, even as the children are growing into the mainstream culture.

Socioeconomic Status

There is much diversity in socioeconomic class among immigrants in the United States. While some immigrant groups enjoy high levels of professional success, home ownership, and access to private schools, others face significant economic hardship. According to the 1996 U.S. census, 22.2% of immigrants lived below the poverty level and 55% earned under $20,000 annually. Although socioeconomic status has an impact on the academic achievement of immigrant students, net income alone is not a predictor of achievement. Many immigrant students in poverty have high levels of academic achievement (Gibson 1987; Rumbaut 1995; Suarez-Orozco 1987). Furthermore, factors related to socioeconomic status, such as their parents' participation in the labor force and the type of work they do, have an impact on students' education.

For instance, many immigrant families in poverty are manual laborers who work under harsh conditions and are often forced to move to areas where there is work. This is most frequently observed among migrant workers, many of whom are of Mexican or Central American origin. These moves interrupt children's schooling and supportive social networks. Often, children are pulled out of school to help parents picking fruit in the orchards. In a study of Nicaraguan high schoolers, Suarez-

Orosco (1987) found that two-thirds of the sample worked 15 to 30 hours while attending school full time, in order to help support their family in the United States or overseas.

Another facet of socioeconomic class is the educational level of immigrant students' families. Many of those in the professional class immigrated to the United States with high levels of formal education. In 1990 over 60% of immigrants from India and Taiwan, between 33% to 50% of immigrants from the Philippines, Japan, South Korea, and China, and approximately 50% from African nations had college degrees. In contrast, only 3.5% of Mexican immigrants (the lowest proportion of any ethnic group in the United States) and 4% to 5% of Cambodians and Laotian refugees had a college education. Children whose parents have a formal education are more likely to have been educated in their homeland. As noted by McDonnell and Hill (1993), students who have attended school full time prior to immigration tend to perform better than U.S. students, especially in the areas of science and math.

However, the lack of parental education is not necessarily a "handicap" to students. In the case of the Nicaraguan students, Suarez-Orosco found that only 6% of their mothers and 8% of their fathers had completed college, while 57% and 78% of their mothers had not completed elementary and secondary education respectively. Among their fathers, 39% and 55% had not completed elementary and secondary education. Nevertheless, 50% of these students were on the honor roll and 10% were accepted into college.

Educational Aspirations of Students and Their Families

As suggested in the previous section, what has proved more salient to immigrant children's academic achievement than parental educational level has been their parents' (and family's) educational aspirations. Studies have found that immigrant students and their parents have higher educational aspirations than do natives of the same cultural group (Kao and Tienda 1995; Schwartz 1996; Vernez and Abrahamse 1996). Many immigrant students view their education as the primary mode for attaining the "American Dream" that their families pursued in their decision to leave their home country and settle in the United States. Students' aspirations are motivated by the sacrifices that their parents have made to offer them a better life and opportunities, and by a sense of duty that compels them to fulfill their family's expectations of them.

Many students tend to exhibit what Rumbaut (1995) refers to as the "immigrant ethos": a high motivation to succeed academically, which alone accounts for their otherwise inexplicable ability to overcome many of the challenges they face. Rumbaut found that the Asians in his study demonstrated this "ethos," not only by their in-school performance, but also by spending more hours on their homework and less time watching television. An example are the Vietnamese, who have excelled academically even though many of their parents were not literate. Their academic progress is especially commendable because many of their families arrived as refugees in very desperate economic and psychological straits. Educational aspirations of Vietnamese students have been positively affected by family size. As Rumbaut reports, "the largest families were well organized as "mini school systems," with older siblings tutoring the younger ones (often giving them harder practice tests than the ones they got in school) even in the absence of any direct parental involvement in the school or in homework (p. 51).

Cultural Factors

Ethnic Identity

In a study of students of diverse cultural backgrounds, Phelan, Davidson, and Yu (1998) found that students who were academically successful were those whose home culture and school culture were similar, or where such differences were surmountable. Students for whom the cultural difference between home and school were insurmountable experienced greater academic problems and adaptation difficulties. The implication of this finding is not that cultural difference is an obstacle to adaptation; rather, cultural difference could be either an asset or a hindrance, depending on the particular context. Consequently, the traditional notion that "Americanization" is essential to success (academic, social, and economic) no longer holds true. In fact, studies have demonstrated that increased "Americanization" of students has led to decreased academic achievement (Gans 1992; Olsen 1997; Rumbaut 1995).

For some groups, their ability to retain their cultural identity has facilitated their academic success. This is particularly observable among many Asian groups, for whom the desire to maintain cultural traditions is strongly linked with academic success. For instance, Punjabi Sikhs in U.S. schools experience extreme pressure from their families to maintain their cultural traditions by not participating in typical U.S. practices of engaging in extracurricular activities, dating, dancing, leaving home at 18, or making decisions without parental consent. Although these restrictions have led to tensions within families and limited social interactions with their peers, they have also helped students to stay focused on their schoolwork. To this end, their parents have supported additive acculturation by also encouraging them to become proficient in English and the ways of the dominant culture, and to learn useful skills from their teachers in order to help them deal successfully with the mainstream culture (Gibson 1987, 1995, 1998).

Proficiency in English

English language fluency is arguably the most significant factor in an immigrant student's ability to do well in U.S. schools. Immigrants who are fluent in English, or who have had prior exposure to the language, have significantly different (and more successful) adaptation experiences than their counterparts with limited or no proficiency. As reported by Nieto (2000), in 1996 there were 3,184,696 students classified as having limited English proficiency. This represents an increase by 5% from the previous year. Limited English Proficient (LEP) students represented about 7.3% of all public school students. According to statistics issued in 1993, approximately 80% of newcomers speak a language other than English at home, compared with 8% of the native-born population (U.S. Census Bureau). Rong and Preissle (1998) note that of all foreign born children, 45% speak Spanish, 23% speak an Asian language, and 12% speak a non-English European language. Although native language fluency is often a critical component of their ethnic identity, for many immigrant students, learning English becomes their first priority in the United States. Fueled partly by their inability to understand teachers and peers, or to express themselves, many students develop a preference for English over their native language (Dugger 1998).

The pressure for immigrant students to learn English extends beyond academics. Many students end up being their family's only social connection to the English-speaking world. It is not uncommon for students to be pulled out of school to serve as translators for their parents as they try to open bank accounts or visit the doctor. These additional responsibilities have also led to additional family tensions. Many parents worry about "losing control" of their children because they have had to depend linguistically on the younger generation.

Within the school, the lack of English language proficiency further inhibits students' social interactions, and as Olsen (1995) observed, students engage in self-silencing in the classroom because of their perceived weaknesses in the language. However, limited English proficiency or bilingualism are not precursors to academic failure among immigrant students. Rumbaut (1995) found that non-English-speaking immigrant minorities outperformed their English-only co-ethnics as well as majority white students. All students who were bilingual with fluent English proficiency (FEP) had a lower dropout rate than their English-only co-ethnics. Nevertheless, the challenges of limited English proficiency are illustrated in the fact that FEP students outperformed their LEP co-ethnics and had a lower dropout rate.

Conditions for Leaving

Immigration implies the presence of choice and a conscious decision on the part of immigrants to leave their country. However, given the conditions under which many immigrants have entered the United States, the extent to which they had a choice to leave their homeland is questionable. Ogbu's (1999) notions of voluntary and involuntary groups can be extended to the understanding of the diverse conditions under which immigration is undertaken. For some, the "pull" factors of the U.S. economy, education, or lifestyle are the primary motivators for immigration. Termed voluntary immigrants by Rong and Preissle (1998), these individuals have a viable choice of immigrating or remaining in their homelands. Such immigrants are more likely to approach their lives and schooling in the United States with greater confidence and with the perception that they have control over their futures. They also tend to be educated, professionals, and often enjoyed considerable power and status in their home country.

At the other extreme are the involuntary immigrants, for whom the "push" factors (conditions within their country that motivated them to leave) were more salient in their decision to immigrate. They tend to be those who were oppressed by economic and social barriers in their own countries and sought relief from such conditions as a matter of survival. These immigrants often undergo immense hardship and danger to get to the United States. While many of these immigrants are grateful and relieved to be in the United States and their experiences are shaped by such feelings, others suffer significant trauma and have trouble reorienting themselves to school following psychologically challenging experiences. For instance, Guatemalans, escaping genocide in their country, arrived in the United States primarily on foot. It was estimated that approximately 150,000 to 200,000 Guatemalan children had lost one or both parents to massacres in the Guatemalan Civil War (Ashabrenner and Conklin 1986). The Hmong immigrated to the United States under similarly challenging circumstances. Both of these populations have been prone to post-traumatic stress disorder (Cerhan 1990; Padilla and Duran 1995). As Olsen (1988) points out, these children tend to be at high risk for problems in school, including failure and dropping out.

Community Factors

The dynamics of the community into which immigrants enter play a significant role in shaping the experiences of newcomers. The first waves of immigrants from any nation experience greater difficulty adapting. Subsequent waves benefit from the presence of support networks of the previous generations. Such networks could be formal or informal. Formal support networks are exemplified by the Migrant Resource Center of Indiantown, Florida (see Ashabrenner and Conklin 1986), which worked in collaboration with the local schools, churches, and other volunteer agencies to provide a diverse range of community services. These include explanations of cross-cultural differences, legal issues, tutoring of school children, clothing give-aways, and providing door-to-door counseling in multiple languages. The absence of such community services, especially in areas with smaller populations of immigrants, make survival in the first few years even more arduous.

Informal social support networks can be seen in the Haitian community of Miami (Stepick 1998). It has become customary for Haitian households to host transients who have just arrived until they find employment and are financially more independent. It is also expected that new immigrants will do the same for other waves of immigrants. Such social networks provide cultural, social, and financial support to newcomers. They are instrumental in disseminating information about employment, providing help with child care, transportation, preparation of food, and establishing informal credit associations.

While such social networks are often the basis for social mobility, they also could serve to insulate immigrants from mainstream U.S. culture. This is evident in ethnic enclaves such as the Chinatowns of California and New York. Such social arrangements often lead to urban ghettoization. This may perpetuate ongoing cycles of poverty, exploitation, and abuse, especially for immigrants who are undocumented (see also Waters and Eschbach 1999). Although the ethnic enclave gives newcomers an alternate reference group to which they could adapt or assimilate, it becomes problematic when communities are characterized by racial stratification. As Olsen (1997) points out, for many immigrants adaptation has resulted in "taking one's place on the racial map of the United States" (p. 11). This pattern can lead to segmented assimilation, where immigrants assimilate toward a marginalized underclass. In other cases, an attempt not to be identified with African Americans in such stratification has led to hostility between Caribbean immigrants and African Americans.

Educational Factors

Undoubtedly, the ultimate success of immigrant students in the United States depends primarily on the quality of their educational experiences. Unfortunately, many students are faced with a learning environment characterized by "overcrowded, understaffed classes in overcrowded, understaffed, poor inner-city schools, . . . a school atmosphere of drugs, violence, low expectations, bitter teachers (who were often very afraid of their students), the seductive offers of more acculturated peers to join the street culture . . . and the need to work to help the family" (Suarez-Orosco 1987, p. 290). Several factors are crucial to surmounting the many challenges that immigrant students face. These include the school's overall philosophy toward diversity, the quality of their teachers, the type of instructional programs and support services offered, and the overall social climate experienced by immigrant students. The successful implementation of these factors will be discussed in more detail in the final section of this chapter.

Educational Philosophy Toward Diversity

In a study of schools in three states, Dentler and Hafner (1997) noted that schools that best served immigrant students were those whose administrators viewed the increasing diversity of their population in positive and proactive terms. As Olneck (1995) observes, the traditional educational response to immigrant students has been to "Americanize" them. Strategies for such Americanization have varied, depending on local school cultures. For some students, this goal has been reached through a de-emphasis on cultural differences, and sometimes at the cost of cultural identity, where this identity has been detrimentally viewed. In such schools, students have been encouraged to give up their culture and were banned from speaking their first language (National Association for the Education of Young Children 1996). In other schools, a focus on culture and culture-based needs has characterized immigrant education. For students in such schools, additive acculturation (rather than assimilation) has been the means to academic success (see also Gibson 1998; Goode, Schneider, and Blanc 1992). Dentler and Hafner (1997) underscore the importance of adaptation—the need for schools and communities to make some changes in standard operating procedures so as to better address the needs of students, even as students are expected to acculturate.

Teacher Quality

The characteristics of teachers who are instrumental in the academic success of immigrant students include having high expectations of all students and the ability to address the individual (and culture-based) needs of students as they progress academically. These abilities are usually based on a teacher's rich cross-cultural knowledge and his or her commitment to learn and do more for all groups of students. Such teachers typically go "beyond the call of duty" by conducting tutoring sessions after school hours, providing coaching for standardized tests such as the SAT and ACT, directing extracurricular activities, and advising students. An example of such an outstanding teacher was described by Freedman (1990) in *Small Victories*.

Unfortunately, not all immigrant students encounter such teachers. Many teachers fall prey to stereotypes that are often linked to low academic expectations and the tendency to place students in remedial tracks. In a study of Mexican American students, Romo and Falbo found that "many of them dropped out because they correctly perceived that the education they were getting was at such a low level that it would not give them the kind of life they wanted after graduation. None of the students dropped out because they felt the classes were too difficult, but because of boredom or lack of motivation" (in Nieto 2000, p. 223). One of the more promising students in this study was informed by a teacher, "Well, you're

not college material." Gibson (1998) noted that teachers' negative attitudes about the use of Spanish by students adversely affected their attitudes about school and contributed to adversarial and oppositional
relationships with their teachers.

A noted exception to such negative expectations is the "model minority" stereotype associated with Asian students, who are expected to achieve
at high standards with relative ease. As Nieto (2000) points out, this stereotype is widely resented by Asians and Asian Americans because it ignores
the diversity among Asians, places immense pressure on students to live up
to this stereotype, and causes hostility between Asians and other immigrant
groups. This myth tends to discredit the legitimate demands for social justice by other groups, and assuages the guilt of some schools and communities that do little for Asian immigrants because of the perception that they
can take care of themselves and do not need any help.

Another teacher-related issue that many immigrant students face is that
many teachers do not have adequate knowledge about the cultural backgrounds of their students and how to address this diversity in their teaching.
This is further exacerbated by the growing cultural gap between the increasingly diverse student population and a teaching faculty that is increasingly
Euro-American. The lack of knowledge may lead to a lack of understanding
and negative consequences. Cofer (1990) recounts being beaten on the head
by a teacher who misunderstood her silence for disrespect when she could
not understand English and was unable to respond to the teacher. It is
important for all teachers to understand that education in a new culture is
wearisome. As Igoa (1995) observes, "A recurring theme regarding the inner
world of the immigrant child is a feeling of exhaustion, not only from the
sounds of a new language but also from the continual parade of strange
sights and events in a new culture" (p. 50).

Teachers, especially those who work in inner-city environments, also
experience burnout or an increasingly ingrained sense of despair and frustration because of the tremendous challenges that they often have to face
alone and with minimal institutional support. Furthermore, many teachers
recognize that there are problems within their own schools but have little
knowledge or resources to address them. While a few students succeed
despite many educational challenges, ethnographies and case studies of
immigrant education (e.g., Freedman 1990; Igoa 1995; Nieto 2000; Olsen
1997, 1988) indicate that most immigrant students achieve academic success
because of the tireless efforts and dedication of their teachers.

Instructional Support Systems
Despite the best efforts of individual teachers, academic success for immigrant students cannot be facilitated without institution-wide instructional
support systems. The most common are those linked with language. Some
examples of these are classes in English offered to speakers of other lan-

guages, "sheltered" classes for recent immigrants, or the presence of languages facilitators at the school. However, the presence of English language support programs alone do not always indicate positive responses. It is important to ensure that students are not permanently tracked into ESOL classes. Nieto (2000) reported a case where counselors retained students in ESOL classes because of the lack of space in mainstream classrooms.

Support systems pertaining to tutoring, home-school communication, and health services are also crucial for overall educational success. The availability of such services in languages with which students are comfortable is even more helpful. The need for psychological and mental health services has been underscored by Padilla and Duran (1995), who note that immigrant students experience more sources of stress than their native-born colleagues. These include the stress related to their immigration status and accompanying culture shock, culture change associated with the process of acculturation and their minority status in the community. They also highlight the dismal failure of most school systems to provide such help because of the lack of bilingual psychologists and counselors and the high professional-student ratio. In a survey conducted in California, Padilla and Duran found that only 15% of school psychologists and 7% of academic counselors were bilingual, and the bilingual professional-student ratio ranged from 1:1000 to 1:3500.

Institutional support for immigrant students' needs is also demonstrated through faculty development efforts. Schools that were proactive in addressing the needs of immigrant students invested time and money to provide teachers with workshops and in-service training on issues central to immigrant education. As the findings of Dentler and Hafner (1997) indicate, the schools in which immigrants had recorded increased academic achievement were characterized by more support services than were at the schools with no increase or a decline in immigrants' academic achievement.

School Climate

A significant challenge encountered by immigrants in education is a school climate that is hostile toward newcomers and unaccepting of their differences. As Gibson (1998) reports about the experiences of Punjabi Indians, "They were told directly by White classmates and indirectly by their teachers that they stank. They were accused of being illegals. They were verbally and physically abused by White students, who refused to sit by them in class or on school buses, threw food at them when they walked through the central quad, crowded in front of them in lines, told them to go back to India, even spat at them, stuck them with hairpins, and worse" (p. 5).

Olsen (1997), in her ethnography *Made in America: Immigrant Students in Our Public Schools,* provides a detailed description of the cultural segregation within a school, where particular locations in the school were seen as the "territory" of certain cultures. Crossing of these domains was difficult, and such border crossers were seen as "wannabees" and faced rejection from their co-ethnics as well as the general student population. Segregation was further exacerbated because of academic tracks that were simultaneously racial tracks. A Mexican student who was placed in the advanced track described her social isolation from other immigrants: "It's like, are you supposed to be in this class? . . . They had never seen a Latin person in their classes and they couldn't believe it" (p. 86).

Hostilities exist between old and new immigrants as well. According to Olsen, "The rage at newcomers for 'still believing' is one of the dynamics that serves to wear down immigrant students" (p. 80). This rage is exemplified by a student who observed: "Sometimes I see them [immigrants] with their backpacks and their books, studying so hard that I want to knock them in the face. What makes them think that studying so hard is going to do them a damn bit of good? They try so hard it makes me sick. School hasn't done a thing for many of us" (p. 80).

The previous discussion of the factors that affect immigrant children's adaptation in the United States was intended to serve two purposes. First, it was designed to identify the wide variety of challenges that immigrant students face as they adapt to their new homeland and its system of education. Second, it was presented to underscore that while many of these factors affect their progress in school, the direction and nature of such an impact is often unpredictable. As a result, one might observe that despite the tremendous challenges faced by immigrant students, they are often able to do well in school. This discussion also challenges the conventional theories that immigrant students (or other ethnic minorities) will not do well in school because of "cultural deprivation" or "cultural deficits," since immigrant students who perform well in school differ significantly from their "mainstream" counterparts.

Academic Achievement of Immigrants

Statistics in 1990 revealed comparable rates of school enrollment for foreign-born students (93%) and for those who were native born (94.5%). According to Schwartz (1996), immigrant youths were as likely as natives to graduate from high school within four years of their sophomore year. Kao and Tienda (1995) found that immigrant students or students with immigrant parents have higher educational aspirations, earn higher grades, and receive higher math scores than children of native-born parents. Comparisons within higher education reveal that foreign-born persons 25 years or older are just as likely as the rest of the population to have a college degree (23.5% vs. 23.6%). According to Vernes and Abrahamse (1996), immigrants were more likely to be enrolled in academic tracks in preparation for college entrance and tended to have more positive attitudes about schooling and higher expectations for going to college than their native-born counterparts. Furthermore, many teachers thought immigrant students were more respectful, eager to learn, and consequently, easier to teach (Gibson 1998; Suarez-Orosco 1987).

However, these facts mask the diversity among immigrant groups, who account for the highest and the lowest educated groups in the nation. Disaggregation of enrollment statistics reveals disparities between foreign and native born, as well as among various foreign-born groups. For instance, among those 14 to 18 years of age, 68% of the foreign born had completed eight years of schooling compared to 75% of the native born, and 31% of 18-year-old foreign-born students had completed 12 years of school compared to 43% of their native-born counterparts (Rong and Preissle 1998). Yet within those age groups, completion rates ranged from 81% for Koreans to 63% for Mexicans who had completed eight years of school. The variance among those who had completed 12 years of schooling ranged from 65% for English-speaking immigrants, 62% for Asian Indians, to 18% for Mexican immigrants.

Strategies for Engaging in Successful Immigrant Education

School Culture and Attitude to Diversity

Central to addressing the academic needs of immigrant students is the institutional culture and the overall attitude toward diversity. According to Dentler and Hafner (1997), schools that have been successful in integrating immigrants were those whose key stakeholders viewed their increasing immigrant population as an opportunity rather than a problem. Such schools also tended to be proactive in addressing the needs of these students, and teachers demonstrated a "can do" attitude. According to Olsen (1995), such schools had leadership and personnel who took time for discussion and planning for diversity, were comfortable with discussing opposing perspectives, were risk takers, and maintained open channels of communication between the school and students' homes. In these schools, time and money were invested in professional development of teachers, school personnel were representative of diverse cultural backgrounds, and there was a keen monitoring of current research in teaching policy and practice.

Language

The issue of language is so inextricably related to the immigrant experience that educational responses to immigrant education have been targeted primarily (and in some cases solely) on the teaching of English. Perhaps the most common response has been the teaching of English as a second language. These classes are introduced in a variety of formats. These include "pull out" programs, in which immigrant students are pulled out of their regular class for a limited time each day to work on their language skills, or "sheltered" classes, in which immigrant students are grouped together for instruction. These classes offer students a "comfort zone" within which to work on their language skills, gain individual attention, and interact with peers who are going through similar experiences. Such classes also offer the opportunity for students to come to terms with culture shock, learn about the customs, expectations, and realities of life in their new society, and rapidly master communicative competence in English. However, such approaches to language instruction frequently undermine or ignore the potential of the students' first language. As Valenzuela (1997) argues, "Rather than building on students' cultural and linguistic knowledge and heritage to create bicultural and bilingually competent youth in an additive manner, schools subtract these identifications from youth to their social and academic detriment" (p. 326).

Dentler and Hafner (1997) observed that the schools that reported greater academic gains among their immigrant student populations were those that addressed language-based needs primarily through bilingual programs which built on the students' first language. There are two general approaches to bilingual education: the transitional and maintenance models. Transitional bilingual education programs offer students instruction in their native language and English until they are able to make the transition into an English-only class. Maintenance bilingual programs are offered throughout the student's education and are designed to facilitate bilingual literacy.

Several problems are associated with the implementation of bilingual education. These include the lack of qualified teachers, low-incidence populations (too few students to warrant a bilingual program), and the prevalent notion that education in the native language is a deterrent to speedy mastery of English. This was exemplified by the passage of Proposition 227 in California, where the use of a non-English language by the teachers was banned although school districts were permitted to ask to continue bilingual instruction. For these reasons, the teaching of English as a second language remains the dominant response to the needs of language minority students.

Also prevalent among schools is the use of language facilitators. These staff members are fluent in non-English languages and can act as liaisons between immigrant students and their teachers. Frequently, however, it is their bilingual peers who serve as translators for new arrivals in the school system.

Curriculum

The educational needs of immigrant students can also be met by the adaptation of curricular material to reflect cultural relevance. This entails the inclusion of subject matter pertinent to the students' background—as is currently being implemented in Palm Beach County,

Florida, with the inclusion of units on Haitian culture (Dozier 1999)—as well as the adaptation of content to better address the experiential knowledge base of students.

For example, a preservice teacher who volunteered at an after-care program observed the curricular enigma presented to a kindergartner, a recent immigrant from Haiti. The child's homework was to write the initial of the words depicted in a series of pictures on a worksheet, in order to discover a message spelled by the initials. The child wrote the letter *B* next to what she thought was a bottle. When encouraged to think of what was in the bottle, she wrote *W* for water. The answer should have been *I* for ink; the child was looking at a picture of a bottle of ink, which she (and probably many of her U.S.-born friends) had never seen before. She encountered the same difficulty with a picture of an igloo, which she could not identify. In this case, the child was unable to complete her assignment. She could not identify the initial letter of each word because the pictures were alien to her experiences.

Simple modifications can be made to the mainstream curriculum to establish relevance for immigrant students. For instance, when encouraging students to read or write in English, it would be more appropriate to have them work on topics with which they can relate. A child from Guatemala who is struggling to read in English is more likely to do better with a book about making new friends, or one about his or her native land, than with a book about making a snowman, an experience alien to his or her cultural experiences. Oakes and Lipton (1999) describe the relevance to a Mexican child of a social studies lesson on the Pilgrims, who were described as "the first immigrants." Freedman (1990) describes the success of a teacher of English who was able to link her lessons with the needs and interests of her immigrant students. She had students write a journal entry titled "Who am I?" that was gradually developed into an autobiography. This gave her insight into her students' lives. She also asked students to write an essay that they would submit with their college applications. For the school paper, which she edited, she encouraged them to write about drugs, gang violence, and gentrification. More specific examples of the adaptation of curriculum to better address the needs of diverse student populations can be found in the work of Grant and Sleeter (1998), Davidman and Davidman (1997), and Tiedt and Tiedt (1999).

Immigrants and their teachers at the high school level encounter an additional dilemma. For many immigrant students, their principal classes are designed to improve their English. Although these classes are important, it is also crucial to ensure that they are provided the opportunity to take classes that prepare them for college entrance. As noted previously in this chapter, the adaptation of curriculum for immigrant students should be designed to facilitate their success in school. Establishing cultural relevance should not be confused with lowered standards or diminished expectations.

Instruction

In a review of the instructional quality of teachers of immigrant students, Dentler and Hafner (1997) identified the following as exemplary instructional practices: teaching basic and advanced skills through meaningful tasks, encouraging active student participation, validating multicultural values and practices, making connections with students' experiences, and using manipulatives, realia, and alternative modes to teach concepts. These teachers were in touch with students' cultural values. They minimized lectures and encouraged students to ask questions and to challenge them. They used experiential and theme-based approaches. While these instructional approaches are appropriate for all students, their use among immigrant students is particularly salient in order to overcome entrenched patterns of inappropriate instruction.

Teachers tend to have low expectations of immigrant students, particularly those who are not fluent in English or who are of non-Asian backgrounds. It is also important that teachers actively encourage students to participate in class discussions, because immigrant students often engage in self-silencing due to their weak command of the English language. In such contexts, it is also crucial to create a classroom atmosphere in which diverse accents, constructions, and varying levels of fluency are accepted without derision. Teachers can model openness to such diversity by making a genuine attempt to pronounce students' names correctly (in contrast to the traditional practice of assigning immigrant students Anglicized names), and demonstrating basic (but nonstereotypical) knowledge about their countries and cultures of origin.

Instructional style is an important complement to the curriculum. As Freedman (1990) noted in his observations of a high school English teacher, it is a teacher's energetic instructional approach, designed to draw on students' interests in order to make them active and enthusiastic learners, coupled with an indefatigable commitment to the success of all students, that paves the way to academic success.

Academic Support Services

Academic support services are central to the success of immigrant students. Many programs facilitated through initiatives such as Title VII, Chapter 1, Even Start, and Bright Start have provided greater acculturation to the U.S. system of education for young students. However, in the face of diminishing federal support for programs that target immigrant children, local efforts have to develop alternate programs.

Many urban areas now have several after-care programs designed to offer children tutorial services and homework help. These programs are typically run by volunteers in the community and serve both immigrant and nonimmigrant populations. The need for additional tutorial services and preparation for taking standardized tests and English language classes has been felt in many communities with immigrant populations. Such programs, when offered, are often given before or after school through voluntary efforts of community members or teachers and the philanthropic gestures of community organizations.

Career counseling is another crucial area of academic support needed by immigrant students. Unaware of the requirements of the U.S. education system, students need direct and explicit advice on the types of classes they should be taking to be eligible for college entrance. Others, often lured by the lucrative appeal of the street culture, or whose role models are found in the lower rungs of the labor force, need to be counseled on the range of professional opportunities available to them. Students also need to be made aware of the nonacademic criteria to be fulfilled for college entrance. For instance, many students have worked hard toward gaining college entrance only to learn that their applications were denied because their immigration status was out of compliance. All of these services, before, during and after school hours, are integral to addressing the many challenges that immigrant students face in U.S. schools.

Community-Based Support

School districts in which immigrant students have made good academic progress typically have a network of community programs designed to address the noncurricular needs of immigrants. Such programs are typified by Migrant Resource Centers, which offer help to new immigrant families by providing native language explanations and information central to their acculturation in the United States. They sponsor clothing and food drives and serve as a liaison between the school and the families to address academic concerns. Community-based responses also include the provision of language and life-skills classes for adult members of the community, affordable preschool, afterschool and summer programs, and counseling to address issues of culture shock and acculturation. In some communities, social workers collaborate with educators to visit homes where the lack of telephones or limited English proficiency among parents hinders home/school communication.

In addition to these social services, many communities have set up health clinics to provide free health care and immunizations. Where possible, these health clinics are also staffed by multilingual personnel, especially those familiar with the cultural and linguistic traditions of the dominant groups of the community. Some school districts in California have begun to implement school-based health centers based on the California state statute 620, the Healthy Start Initiative. These services also extend to mental health care.

The need for mental health care and psychological services has been often overlooked and underestimated. Such services have been particularly important for those who have had to leave their country under extremely traumatic conditions. Nevertheless, there is a significant need for counseling among immigrants, which arises from the cross-cultural conflicts that occur within families as children become more "Americanized," or as a result of the rejection felt by newcomers. Despite the obvious need for such services to be provided in the language best understood by the clients, Padilla and Duran (1995) note that few professionals are bilingual, and this competency is not yet required for certification purposes. They also advocate the need for greater coordination between school and community support agencies such as mental health clinics (to reduce prolonged waiting periods), churches, and ethnic community centers in addressing the needs of students in a linguistically and culturally relevant manner.

Conclusion

The ideas presented in this chapter underscore that the desired responses to meet the needs of immigrant students involve a community-wide, multifaceted effort. One might argue that few communities can offer such a comprehensive approach to help immigrants adapt. Many communities are too impoverished to afford even a few of these support services. Lack of funding, together with inadequate human resources, local politics, anti-immigrant attitudes, and educators' busy schedules often explain the failure to implement such strategies.

As the numbers of immigrants continue to grow in the 21st century, the likelihood that all educators will encounter immigrant students in their classes is extremely high. Immigration is not a new phenomenon in the United States. As educators and citizens, we have over a century of experience with immigrants on which to draw. The discussion of factors central to immigrants' adaptation demonstrates that adaptation is a complex process. How communities and schools address the increasing diversity of their populations will ultimately determine the stability of those communities in the future.

References

Ashabrenner, B., and Conklin, P. (1986). *Children of the Maya*. New York: Dodd, Mead.

Cerhan, J. U. (1990). The Hmong in the United States: An overview of mental health professionals. *Journal of Counseling and Development, 69*, 88–92.

Cofer, J. O. (1990). *Silent dancing: A partial remembrance of a Puerto Rican childhood*. Houston: Arte Publico Press.

Davidman, L., and Davidman, P. T. (1997). *Teaching with a multicultural perspective: A practical guide*. White Plains, NY: Longman.

Dentler, R. A., and Hafner, A. L. (1997). *Hosting newcomers: Structuring educational opportunities for immigrant children*. New York: Teachers College Press.

Dozier, M. (1999). Schools take steps toward Haiti's past. *Sun Sentinel*, October 31, B1–2.

Dugger, C. W. (1998). Among young of immigrants, outlook arises. *New York Times*, March 21, A1.

Freedman, S. (1990). *Small victories: The real world of a teacher, her students and their high school*. New York: Harper Perennial.

Gans, H. (1992). Second-generation decline: Scenarios for the economic and ethnic futures of the post–1965 American immigrants. *Ethnic and racial studies, 15*, 173–192.

Gibson, M. (1987). The school performance of immigrant minorities: A comparative view. *Anthropology and Education Quarterly, 18*(4), 262–275.

Gibson, M. (1995). Additive acculturation as a strategy for school improvement. In R. Rumbaut and W. Cornelius (Eds.), *California's immigrant children: Theory, research and implications for educational policy* (pp. 77–106). San Diego: Center for U.S.-Mexican Studies.

Gibson, M. (1998). Promoting academic success among immigrant students: Is acculturation the issue? *Educational Policy, 12*(6), 615–633. (Page reference in text is based on electronic version of journal.)

Goode, J. G., Schneider, J. A., and Blanc, S. (1992). Transcending boundaries and closing ranks: How schools shape interrelations. In L. Lamphere (Ed.), *Structuring diversity: Ethnographic perspectives on the new immigration* (pp. 173–213). Chicago: University of Chicago Press.

Grant, C., and Sleeter, C. (1998). *Turning on learning: Five approaches for multicultural teaching plans for race, class, gender, and disability* (2nd ed.). Upper Saddle River, NJ: Merrill.

Igoa, C. (1995). *The inner world of the immigrant child*. New York: St. Martin's Press.

Kao, G., and Tienda, M. (1995). Optimism and achievement: The educational performance of immigrant youth. *Social Science Quarterly, 76*(1), 1–19.

National Association for the Education of Young Children (1996). NAEYC position statement: Responding to linguistic and cultural diversity—Recommendations for effective early childhood education. Young Children (January), pp. 4–12.

McDonnell, L. M., and Hill, P. T. (1993). Newcomers in American schools: Meeting the educational needs of immigrant youth. Santa Monica, CA: Rand.

Nieto, S. (2000). *Affirming Diversity: The sociopolitical context of multicultural education* (3rd ed.). New York: Longman.

Oakes, J. and Lipton, M. (1999). *Teaching to change the world*. Boston: McGraw-Hill College.

Ogbu, J. (1999). Minority status and literacy in comparative perspective. In N. R. Yetman (Ed.), *Majority and minority: The dynamics of race and ethnicity in American life* (6th ed.) (pp. 363–375). Boston: Allyn and Bacon.

Olneck, M. (1995). Immigrants and education. In J. Banks and C. M. Banks (Eds.), *Handbook of research on multicultural education* (pp. 310–327). New York: Macmillan.

Olsen, L. (1988). *Crossing the school house border: Immigrant children and California schools*. San Francisco: California Tomorrow.

Olsen, L. (1995). School restructuring and the needs of immigrant students. In R. Rumbaut and W. Cornelius (Eds.), *California's immigrant children: Theory, research and implications for educational policy* (pp. 207–232). San Diego: Center for U.S.-Mexican Studies.

Olsen, L. (1997). *Made in America: Immigrant students in our public schools*. New York: New Press.

Padilla, A. M., and Duran, D. (1995). The psychological dimension in understanding immigrant students. In In R. Rumbaut and W. Cornelius (Eds.), *California's immigrant children: Theory, research and implications for educational policy* (pp. 131–160). San Diego: Center for U.S.-Mexican Studies.

Phelan, P., Davidson, A. L., and Yu, H. C. (1998). *Adolescents' worlds: Negotiating family, peers and school*. New York: Teachers College Press.

Portes, A., and Rumbaut, R. (1990). *Immigrant America: A portrait*. Berkeley, CA: University of California Press.

Portes, A., and Zhou, M. (1999). The new second generation: Segmented assimilation and its variants. In N. R. Yetman (Ed.), *Majority and minority: The dynamics of race and ethnicity in American life* (6th ed.) (pp. 348–362). Boston: Allyn and Bacon.

Rong, X. L., and Preissle, J. (1998). *Educating immigrant students: What we need to know to meet the challenges*. Thousand Oaks, CA: Corwin Press.

Rumbaut, R. (1995). The new Californians: Comparative research findings on the educational progress of immigrant children. In R. Rumbaut and W. Cornelius (Eds.), *California's immigrant children: Theory, research and implications for educational policy* (pp. 18–70). San Diego: Center for U.S.-Mexican Studies.

Schwartz, W. (1996). Immigrants and their educational achievement: Some facts and findings. ERIC Digest, 116. Washington, DC: Office of Educational Research and Improvement.

Stepick, A. (1998). *Pride against prejudice: Haitians in the United States*. New Immigrant Series. Boston: Allyn and Bacon.

Suarez-Orozco, M. (1987). 'Becoming Somebody' Central American immigrants in U.S. inner-city schools. *Anthropology and Education Quarterly, 18*(4), 287–299.

Tiedt, P. L., and Tiedt, I. M. (1999). *Multicultural teaching: A handbook of activities, information and resources* (5th ed.). Boston: Allyn and Bacon.

U.S. Census Bureau. (1993). We the American: Foreign Born. Washington, DC: U.S. Department of Commerce.

U.S. Census Bureau. (1998). The foreign-born population. The Official Statistics. Washington, DC: U.S. Department of Commerce.

Valenzuela, A. (1997). Mexican American youth and the politics of caring. In E. Long (Ed.), *From sociology to cultural studies: New perspectives* (pp. 322–350). Cambridge, MA: Blackwell.

Vernes, G., and Abrahamse, A. (1996). *How immigrants fare in U.S. education*. Santa Monica, CA: Rand.

Waters, M. C., and Eschbach, K. (1999). Immigration and ethnic and racial inequality. In N. R. Yetman (Ed.), *Majority and minority: The dynamics of race and ethnicity in American life* (6th ed.) (pp. 312–326). Boston: Allyn and Bacon.

White House. (1998). Remarks by President Clinton at Portland State University Commencement, June 13, 1998.

chapter **8**

Connecting Multicultural and Special Education

Christine E. Sleeter and Rodolfo Puente

The identity of the university will be framed by substantive commitment to multilingual, multicultural, gender-equitable learning.

This sentence is found in the first paragraph of the Vision Statement of a university in California. Students of color, students whose first language is not English, and women students can see their concerns represented in that statement. Where are students with disabilities in the vision of universities or school districts? Is disability connected with multicultural education? If so, how? We decided to explore this question, both by examining the literature and by interviewing students on a university campus.

Multicultural Education and Disability in the Literature

Both multicultural education literature and disability literature address how to make schools and classrooms more responsive to and supportive of a diversity of children, but the fields tend not to work together. Most of the literature about multicultural education does not address disability. When disability appears, it generally does so as one of several forms of difference, commonly in a separate chapter in an edited volume (e.g., Banks and Banks 1997; Gollnick and Chinn 1997). Connections between multicultural education and disability tend to be made around a few issues. Cultural and language bias in assessment for special education is one important issue. For example, Gutierrez-Clellen and colleagues (1995) examined differences in narrative styles between Spanish-speaking and English-speaking children and argued that diagnosis for learning disorders needs to be culturally sensitive. Discussions of prejudice and stereotyping in the multicultural education literature occasionally address stereotypes about people with disabilities. For example, Gleason (1991) argued that children often develop negative attitudes toward culturally diverse and exceptional peers, and these attitudes evolve into stereotypic thinking, which leads to prejudice and discrimination. Lyter-Mickelberg and Connor-Kuntz (1995) applied this analysis to physical education classes and offered suggestions for teachers. Inclusion of diverse groups in curriculum is yet another topic under which multicultural education and disability are sometimes connected. For example, Grant and Sleeter (1997) presented lesson plans for multicultural education, some of which include content about disability.

As a field, multicultural education gives most attention to ethnicity and race, and connections with disability have grown largely out of the problem of overrepresentation of students of color in special education. An area in which multicultural education offers a good deal of insight is how culture connects with learning, and how schooling can serve students of color more effectively. At the beginning of the 21st century, children of color and children from low-income homes still struggle to survive in mainstream schools. For example, African American students are still subject to differential treatment (Irvine 1991). Teaching processes in mainstream schools too often ignore the impact culture has on language, learning, and thinking (Cummins 1984; Poplin 1988; Tharp 1989). Instructors too often are not sufficiently prepared to deal with students who are not White or who are gifted. We know, for example, that when learners are given the opportunity to negotiate their cultural backgrounds, interests, and cognitive skills, they are more likely to experience academic success (Franklin 1992; Figley 1985; Fleming et al. 1999). As a student of color, one of us (Puente) attended U.S. schools from kindergarten through high school. When his parents migrated to Mexico for the Christmas vacations, he attended schools in Mexico. As a student in the Mexican schools, he had an opportunity to learn in his way and was given many options as to how to learn. Consequently, he was extremely successful. Having teachers or professors of color who can serve as role models and who understand how to teach culturally diverse students is rewarding for them. Unfortunately, the scarcity of educators of color heightens the need for cultural sensitivity by school personnel and aggravates the problem of overrepresentation in special education (Gay 1989).

Overrepresentation of students of color is a fairly prominent issue in the special education literature. African American students, for example, continue to be substantially overrepresented in classes for mental retardation and serious emotional disturbance, while underrepresented in gifted and talented classes (Artiles 1998; Artiles and Trent 1994). Many researchers continue to stress how important it is not to ignore the impact of culture and linguistics on learning (Almanza and Mosley 1980; Clark-Johnson 1988; Cummins 1984; Franklin 1992) and on assessment (Scruggs and Mastropieri 1995). For example, culturally sensitive instructional practices help African American learners with disabilities (Franklin 1992). An often invisible group is the growing Hispanic population and the increasing number of Hispanic students with disabilities. A special issue of *Exceptional Children*, published in 1989, was devoted to this group. There, Fradd and Correa (1989) argued that revitalization and reform are needed in special education to fit the needs of the Hispanic students and their families. Various programs such as English as a Second Language (ESL), bilingual education, and English for speakers of other languages (ESOL) help Spanish-speaking children bridge the gap between English and Spanish (Fradd and Correa 1989).

Because so many students of color are in special education, and most teachers are White, teacher education is receiving increased attention. Most special education teachers continue to plan their teaching around students' disabilities, with little consideration to students' cultural and linguistic backgrounds (Almanza and Mosley 1980; Clark-Johnson 1988; Cummins 1984; and Franklin 1992). Without adequate training, special education teachers are not able to maintain complementary learning environments to meet the needs of students of color (Almanza and Mosley 1980; Gay 1989; Smith 1988). As the schools become more culturally diverse, and as collaboration across disciplines and roles becomes more necessary, teachers need much more cultural sensitivity in order to assess and work fairly with children (Artiles and Trent 1997; Fradd and Weismantel 1989; McConnell and Townsend 1997; Harris 1996; Jairrels 1999; Kea and Utley 1998; Obiakor and Utley 1997; Salend and Dorney 1997; Valles 1998). Webb-Johnson and colleagues (1998) argue that, while conceptually sound models for preparing teachers for multicultural student populations appear in the literature, fairly little actual use of them appears to be made in teacher preparation programs. This is a huge problem, because preservice teachers continue to display lack of awareness of issues related to race and culture. A special issue of *Remedial and Special Education* (Jan./Feb. 1998, Vol. 19, Issue 1) examines this problem.

Foster and Iannaccone (1994) analyzed 16 special education textbooks for their multicultural content. While all 16 mentioned multicultural factors, only five included substantial multicultural content. They found that "The most extensive body of multicultural content ... was educationally related. Information consistently addressed the area of nondiscriminatory educational assessment, landmark court decisions, and corresponding implications for educational and instructional decisions, including special education placement and service provision." Legal issues related to intelligence testing and overrepresentation of students of color in special education recurred throughout the texts. Overall, however, they found that textbook authors "have not employed a comprehensive model of multicultural special education," which has led to a fragmented and limited addition of multicultural issues to special education concerns.

As the above illustrates, the way multicultural education and disability are connected is mainly around the presence of children of color in special education. This connection, when not carefully examined, is likely to support a deficiency orientation to diversity because of special education's roots in the medical model (Pugach and Seidl 1996). Artiles (1998) argued that debates about overrepresentation reflect larger issues of how people understand and think about human differences. Which differences count, and how differences are viewed and evaluated, are large ethical and sociocultural issues that require researchers to broaden their conceptual paradigms. Artiles and Trent (1994) concluded that,

> instead of examining the issues and problems in special education from a historical perspective, we have continued to overemphasize a pathological ethos that has caused us to define efficacy based on setting versus quality of services. From a social perspective, we have continued to develop educational structures without examining and considering how the belief systems, biases, prejudices, and socioeconomic inequities that have existed for centuries in the American society would be played out and perpetuated in our nation's schools—microcosms of the larger society.

Pugach and Seidl (1996) maintained that the use of a cultural lens to make judgments about students will lead to better teaching and reverse the tendency to place students who do not succeed in mainstream schools into special education. Similarly, Meyer, Harry, and Sapon-Shevin (1997) critiqued the medical model that underlies special education and the manner in which culturally diverse parents are excluded from much substantive decision making about education. They argued that the special education system, by institutionalizing "pull-out" solutions to differences among children, has solidified racial and ethnic biases in education. They advocated making schools and classrooms more responsive to and supportive of a wide diversity among children.

Disability itself, when framed through the lens of special education, tends to be equated with deficiency. Connecting multicultural education and disability can help to reframe the paradigm used to judge what counts as normal and how education should function to support a wide diversity of students, by offering analytic constructs that contradict the deficiency paradigm: culture, identity, and discrimination (see Charlton 1998). For example, conceptual connections between pedagogy, culture, language, power, and disability are made strongly in *Critical Pedagogy in Deaf Educa-*

tion (Nover and Andrews 1998), which uses a bilingual/bicultural model in staff development for deaf education. Nover and Andrews argue that deaf education should use principles of bilingual education for teaching American Sign Language, and also teach deaf culture and examine issues of "oppression, audism, and hearization" (p. 4).

In this study, we were interested in finding out what university students think of connections between multicultural education and disability. In a university context that has frequent and explicit discussions of multiculturalism, how is disability discussed and understood? Do students see connections between these forms of difference? If so, how do they connect them? The following case illustrates these questions.

Method

This study was conducted at a university in California between August and November 1999. The university has considerable explicit discussion of multiculturalism on campus, but far less explicit discussion of disability. The participants were six undergraduate students from that university. Two of the participants were males and four were females. One student had a physical disability, one was deaf; other respondents did not specifically tell us whether or not they had a disability. To obtain a participant pool, we contacted the coordinator of disability services on campus for help identifying students. She suggested that we place an ad in the school's e-mail accounts, which staff, faculty, and students access daily. Our original plan was to interview each student, which later proved inefficient due to constant schedule conflicts, so we offered the option of conducting the interviews over e-mail. All but one of the interviews were conducted over e-mail. For some students with disabilities (such as a deaf student), this option facilitated participation.

We asked students how well the campus addresses disability issues, how well it addresses multicultural issues, and what connections they saw between the two. We were also interested in finding out what students saw as the best sources of information for learning about disability.

Results

When asked how well the campus addresses disability issues, students gave a mixed report, and negative remarks outweighed the positive ones. Four out of six students claimed to encounter negative experiences on campus. The campus that these students attend is fairly new, with renovations being done to its buildings. According to students, the campus is not meeting the ADA (Americans with Disabilities Act) regulations. Two students said that landscaping is a problem, and some of the buildings around campus are hard to access for students with wheelchairs or walking problems. For example one student said, "I am also disappointed I cannot access rooms of my friends in the upper floor of the dorms." Furthermore, some students who are assigned note takers felt the note takers were not completing their task. In addition, some students felt that they were not equally being heard, so their concerns and needs were not being met.

Although most of the students we interviewed criticized the disability services offered at their campus, the same students described the campus as somewhat responsive to their needs. For example, one student stated that her access to classrooms and interpreters was great, as well as the transportation services she receives on campus. Other students said the campus is giving them an opportunity to speak their concerns. For example, one student stated that it took an effort of four students to make the campus grant students with disabilities priority registration. The students' need should have been obvious, but it wasn't being met, so students pressed the university until there was a policy change.

When asked how well the campus addressed multicultural issues, one student indicated that the campus was addressing these issues well and the other five gave mixed responses. Two students described this as a diverse campus in which there is a lot of talk about multiculturalism but not enough movement. For example, one student stated, "In theory, very well. In practice, very poorly." Another student felt that the staff and faculty take this issue to heart, and consequently, rallies and talks are held to try to solve multicultural issues. Yet another student commented, "I am not sure what the definition is when used in so many contexts that appear to be contradictory. I think it has become a powerful buzzword without a lot of meaning here on campus."

Students had different examples of what is being done poorly. One student commented, "I don't see representation of all groups," and another said that issues were too dominated by Whites and Hispanics: "No thought is given to other groups, or the disabled which cross all groups." Yet another stated that, "This campus is not aware of students needs from different ethnicity" and went on to say that the campus assumes one way of succeeding in college: "the old boys' way." When asked why they felt the campus addresses the issues this way, students commented that there is no template, except to do what is required. One student commented: "This campus is this way, because it is part of another structure. It is part of a ... system built to serve those in power, ... 'rich white men.'"

When asked if they saw any connections between multiculturalism and disability, five out of six said that the issues are connected, and the sixth agreed they are for "a person from a particular culture with a disability." Four participants stated that they see both these groups as being minorities, and two felt that both groups have faced hardships. One participant stated that, "If we look back into history, we can see atrocities that have happened to people who were 'different.'" One pointed out that the words "multicultural" and "disabilities" are both broad words used to categorize a bunch of people with different needs. Another said that, "Multiculturalism should include disability because we are the cross-group minority that interconnects with everyone. At the same time we are taken the least seriously because we are then forced to align with the group with which we identify, instead of together, in order to try to affect the politics here."

A Deaf participant explained that, "As a Deaf person that uses American Sign Language, I see myself as a member of a linguistic minority group and not as a disabled person." Another participant commented that it is of a greater advantage to be "multicultural" than to be someone with a disability, and that studies have shown that students who are bicultural, bilingual, or multicultural have demonstrated high academic levels and self-esteem.

When asked about the best sources of information for learning about people with disabilities, five out of the six participants stated that the best way to learn is to get to know a person who possesses a disability. The sixth felt word of mouth is best. One student added that the Internet is one of the most advanced and critical ways to learn about people with disabilities and any other subject one might want to study or research. Another felt that having a strong student disabilities center would be vital to assist students with disabilities as well as helping people without disabilities to understand them. Still another student felt that being exposed to students with disabilities, while performing service learning, gave her a little more insight about what it is like to have a disability.

Participants had a few ideas about good sources for learning about disability issues. One felt a positive tool to learn about disabilities is recent research and literature. She recommended the Americans with Disabilities Act as a good tool to describe what disability is and what falls under it. Two participants felt strongly that awareness is also a good teaching tool for disability issues, and that workshops and classes would help expand the knowledge of disability issues. One participant advocated teaching students, faculty, and staff so that they can be sensitive to people who possess disabilities.

All six participants stated that people with disabilities should not be discriminated against just because they have a special need and might need special tools to do their work. According to a Deaf participant, "All people deserve equality, and fairness." Two participants thought it was really important to listen and be sensitive to the needs of people with disabilities. According to one, "Disability doesn't make me a lesser person, it just changes my strengths and weaknesses to what isn't the norm." One participant felt that putting someone without a disability into the shoes of someone with a disability would give that individual a hands-on experience. One participant stated that people with disabilities don't ask for too much; all they ask for is for people to "Be aware, listen, learn, then do, and be sure to pay attention, especially to those who need your help."

Discussion

Multicultural education and disability generally are not addressed in the same bodies of literature, even though the fields are concerned with many similar issues, such as access to education, representation in curriculum, language, fairness in testing, and teacher preparation for diverse learners. The main area of convergence in the literature concerns students of color in special education, and the problem of overrepresentation of students of color. A few scholars have suggested that this problem reflects wider issues, particularly the normalization of a narrow conception of intelligence, of what schools should teach, and of how students and parents should relate to school (Artiles and Trent 1994; Meyer, Harry, and Sapon-Shevin 1997; Pugach and Seidl 1996). These wider issues tend to be addressed in the literature on multicultural education more so than the literature on special education.

The principal aim of the earlier case study was to examine how students see connections between multicultural education and disability, in an environment in which equity issues were openly acknowledged and discussed. Students interviewed tended to see more parallel between multicultural education and disability than the literature reflects. Further, our interviews found that students saw both disability and multicultural education as requiring institutional reform to meet needs of diverse students. From the students' perspectives, students do not need to be "fixed" to fit institutions, but rather, institutions need more flexibility and responsiveness to their students.

Most of the students felt that a connection between multiculturalism and disability exists. Both categories fall under the definition of minority and both have faced difficulties in the past. Both know what their own needs are, but both have to fight for those needs despite institutional rhetoric. Needs related to access and representation are not automatically met. Students with disabilities come from all races but often are not seen as equal because they sometimes need extra assistance or tools to complete their tasks.

Students had mixed reports about how well disability issues were handled around campus, but their criticisms outweighed the praises. They felt that the campus failed to provide the services they needed, although it responded when there was an expressed student concern. Students with disabilities wanted to be seen as equal; they felt they are just as good as anyone else and should not be seen as "less" because they needed special tools to complete tasks. They were not always given an opportunity to express themselves and, at times, felt their needs to be somewhat invisible. They felt that much more attention went toward multicultural issues than toward disability issues. Respondents observed that people with disabilities were smaller in number than were students of color, and many people do not wish to be identified by a disability.

Despite multiculturalism having more visibility on campus, students felt that these issues received more talk than action. Students found multiculturalism to be addressed well in some respects (such as in the curriculum) but also felt that the campus would only do what was required without continuously being pressed to do more. Students wanted more access, representation of diverse groups and diverse needs, and more people to know about issues of diversity.

The literature in special education addresses disability mainly through the eyes of professionals who do not have a disability themselves. In contrast, much of the literature in multicultural education addresses race and ethnicity through the eyes of people of color. In other words, the multicultural education literature is more reflective of "insider" perspectives of historically marginalized groups than is the special education literature. As a result, the multicultural education literature tends to highlight cultural strengths children bring, arguing that schools need to be reformed around these strengths; a focus on remediation of students' deficiencies is more common in the special education literature.

Students with disabilities ("the insiders") know what their needs, as well as their strengths, are. They are willing to work with school and university personnel to strengthen existing programs and services and to invent new ways to meet their needs. Students with disabilities should be involved in the implementation of new services, since they are the ones who will benefit from the services. Further, according to students interviewed, people can learn about disabilities in different ways, which parallel the ways that people learn about diverse racial and ethnic groups. The best way to learn about disabilities is to know a person who has a disability. Increasingly, the Internet offers helpful sites, such as the Association on Higher Education and Disability (http://www.ahead.org/pub.htm) and the National Institute on Disability Rehabilitation and Research (http://www.ed.gov/offices/OSERS/NIDRR/index.html).

Conclusion

From students' perspectives, educational institutions need to become more responsive to the strengths, aspirations, and needs of students. Categories like "multicultural" and "multilingual" might draw attention to some of these needs and might provide a way of talking about them. But students cannot be left out of the conversation. They are the ones who know what works for them. When a school or university addresses multicultural education issues, students with disabilities want their needs to be visible as well. Many of the things they advocate are similar to those addressed by multicultural education. Students see parallels between these two areas, even if the published literature tends not to. As professional educators work to figure out how to make schools work better for culturally different students, we urge them to involve students with disabilities in that work.

References

Almanza, H. P., and Mosley, W. J. (1980). Curriculum adaption and modifications for culturally diverse handicapped children. *Exceptional Children, 46,* 608–614.

Artiles, A. J. (1998). The dilemma of difference: Enriching the disproportionality discourse with theory and context. *Journal of Special Education, 32*(1), 32–36.

Artiles, A. J., and Trent, S. C. (1994). Overrepresentation of minority students in special education: A continuing debate. *Journal of Special Education, 27*(4), 410–437.

Artiles, A. J., and Trent, S. C. (1997). Forging a research program on multicultural preservice teacher education: A proposed analytic scheme. In J. W. Lloyd, E. Kameenui, and D. Chard (Eds.), *Educating students with disabilities* (pp. 275–304). Hillsdale, NJ: Erlbaum.

Banks, J. A., and Banks, C. M. (Eds.). (1997). *Multicultural education: Issues and perspectives* (3rd ed.). Needham Heights, MA: Allyn and Bacon.

Charlton, J. I. (1998). *Nothing about us without us: Disability, oppression and empowerment.* Berkeley: University of California Press.

Clark-Johnson, G. (1988). Special focus: Black children. *Teaching Exceptional Children, 20*(4), 46–47.

Cummins, J. (1984). *Bilingual and special education: Issues in assessment and pedagogy.* San Diego: College-Hills Press.

Figley, G. E. (1985). Determinants of attitudes toward physical education. *Journal of Teaching in Physical Education, 4,* 229–240.

Fleming, D. S., Mitchell, M., Gorecki, J. J., and Coleman, M. M. (1999). Students change and so do good programs: Addressing the interest of multicultural secondary students. *The Journal of Physical Education, Recreation and Dance, 20*(2), 79.

Foster, H. L., and Iannaccone, C. J. (1994). Multicultural content in special education introductory textbooks. *Journal of Special Education, 28*(1), 77–92.

Fradd, S. H., and Correa, V.I. (1989). Hispanic students at risk: Do we abdicate or advocate? *Exceptional Children, 56*(2), 105–110.

Fradd, S. H., and Weismantel, M. J. (1989). Precedents, prototypes, and parables: The use of narratives for training teachers to work with limited English proficient and handicapped students. *Journal of Special Education, 13*(2), 159–171.

Franklin, M. E. (1992). Culturally sensitive instructional practices for African American learners with disabilities. *Exceptional Children, 59*(2), 115–122.

Gay, G. (1989). Ethnic minorities and educational equality. In Banks and Banks (pp. 167–188).

Gleason, J. J. (1991). Multicultural and exceptional student education: Separate but equal? *Preventing School Failure, 36*(1), 47–49.

Gollnick, D., and Chinn, P. C. (1997). *Multicultural education in a pluralistic society* (5th ed.). Columbus, OH: Prentice-Hall.

Grant, C.A., and Sleeter, C. E. (1997). *Turning on Learning* (2nd ed.). Columbus: Merrill/Macmillan.

Gutierrez-Clellen, V. F., et al. (1995). Accommodating cultural differences in narrative style: A multicultural perspective. *Topics in Language Disorders, 15*(4), 54–67.

Harris, K. C. (1996). Collaboration within a multicultural society. *Remedial and Special Education, 17*(6), 355–362.

Irvine, J. J. (1991). *Black students and school failure.* New York: Praeger.

Jairrels, V. (1999). Cultural diversity: Implications for collaboration. *Intervention in School and Clinic, 34*(4),236–238.

Kea, C. D., and Utley, C. A. (1998). To teach me is to know me. *Journal of Special Education, 32*(1), 44–47.

Lyter-Mickelberg, P., and Connor-Kuntz, F. (1995). How to stop stereotyping students. *Strategies, 8*(6), 16–21.

McConnell, M. E., and Townsend, B. L. (1997). How do you keep going? *Intervention in School and Clinic, 33*(20), 125–127.

Meyer, L., Harry, B., and Sapon-Shevin, M. (1997). School inclusion and multicultural issues in special education. In Banks and Banks (pp. 334–360).

Nover, S. M., and Andrews, J. F. (1998). *Critical pedagogy in deaf education: Bilingual methodology and staff development.* Santa Fe: New Mexico School for the Deaf.

Obiakor, F. E., and Utley, C. A. (1997)..Rethinking preservice preparation for teachers in the learning disabilities field: Workable multicultural strategies. *Learning Disabilities Research and Practice, 12*(2), 100–106.

Poplin, M. S. (1988). Holistic/constructivist principles of the teaching/learning process: Implications for the field of learning disabilities. *Journal of Learning Disabilities, 21*(7), 401–416.

Pugach, M. C., and Seidl, B. L. (1996). Deconstructing the diversity-disability connection. *Contemporary Education, 68*(1), 5–8.

Salend, S. J., and Dorney, J. A. (1997). The roles of bilingual special educators in creating inclusive classrooms. *Remedial and Special Education, 18*(1), 54–64.

Scruggs, T. E., and Mastropieri, M. A. (1995). Assessment of students with learning disabilties: Current issues and future directions. *Diagnostique, 20*(1–4), 17–31.

Smith, M. K. (1988). Effects of children's social class, race and gender on teacher expectations for children's academic performance: A study in an urban setting. In C. Heid (Ed.), *Multicultural education: Knowledge and perceptions* (pp. 101–117). Bloomington/Indianapolis: Indiana University, Center for Urban and Multicultural Education.

Tharp, R. G. (1989). Psychocultural variables and constants: Effects on teaching and learning in schools. *American Psychologist, 44*(2), 349–359.

Valles, E. (1998). The disproportionate representation of minority students in special education: Responding to the problem. *Journal of Special Education, 32*(1), 52–54.

Webb-Johnson, G., Artiles, A. J., Trent, S. C., Jackson, C. W., and Velox, A. (1998). The status of research on multicultural education in teacher education and special education. *Remedial and Special Education, 19*(1), 7–15.

chapter **9**

Assessment and Diversity

Patsy Ceros-Livingston

Assessment and diversity go together hand in glove. There is tremendous diversity in types of assessment procedures used in education. The real issue is assessment for what? That is, the purpose of the assessment. Assessment for whom? The people for whom the assessment is intended. Assessment when? The time of the assessment.

These questions are some of the many that are posed when the classroom teacher begins to recognize the necessity of ascertaining whether students have achieved the objectives of the unit or course. The focus of this chapter will be on the relationships among teaching, assessment, and student diversity in the classroom.

Classroom assessment is sometimes viewed as a simple task that teachers perform. However, upon closer consideration, the reader will find that it is not simple to implement and will take a great deal of energy and planning to carry it out appropriately.

Instructional Model

Teachers at all levels of education recognize the necessity of planning prior to teaching. A critical issue is: "What should be the focus of the planning?" Most schools tell teachers that they must construct teaching objectives. However, many teachers do not know how to construct measurable objectives or do not fully understand the importance of having objectives prior to the actual teaching. The following steps should be pursued to achieve appropriate instruction and assessment.

First, the objectives are constructed. Second, the objectives are taught. Third, the students are assessed to see if the objectives have been achieved. This instructional model ties the teaching process to the assessment process. Many authors in the fields of measurement and evaluation have discussed the need to tie the assessment of student achievement to the teaching process in a direct manner (Abebe and Sands 1993). Some authors have developed certain labels to make this point. For example, terms like "integration of testing and instruction" (Nitko 1989), "instructional alignment" (Cohen and Hyman 1991), and "measurement driven instruction" (Popham 1987) all allude to the necessity to relate teaching and assessment (Abebe and Sands 1993). This also implies that the assessment process is fluid rather than static. That is, assessment procedures change based on instructional objectives as well as the results obtained from the assessment. For example, if the results from an assessment indicate that none of the students have achieved the measured objectives, then it is clear that the objectives were not taught, or at least not taught in the manner that they were being assessed. Viewing objectives, teaching, and assessment as one integrated model leads to many different approaches that teachers may use for the teaching and assessment of diverse groups of students.

Construction of Objectives

There are two major types of objectives: general objectives and specific objectives. A general objective should be broad enough so that more than one specific objective could fit underneath it. A specific objective should be general enough so that more than one test item could be constructed to measure the achievement of the objective. All objectives begin with a third-person verb. The test items are constructed based on the specific objective or learning outcome. Numerous taxonomies of educational objectives may be used. Bloom's *Taxonomy of Educational Objectives* is particularly helpful in this regard. An example of these types of objectives follows.

General Objective: Knows basic math functions

Specific Objectives: Labels math functions

Selects math functions

Notice that the objectives are in terms of student performance and not teacher performance. They are not in terms of what the teacher does, but what students are able to do. The point here is not to teach how to write appropriate objectives, but to understand that teachers must have appropriate objectives in order to teach effectively. One of the major problems in classrooms today is that teachers attempt to teach without having measurable objectives; as a result, teaching is not sufficiently focused and relevant. If teachers don't have the appropriate objectives, students will not learn. This is especially true of students who come from culturally different backgrounds. The more precise the teaching, the higher the probability that students will learn.

The specific objective verb tells the teacher the type of test item that needs to be constructed to measure a specific learning outcome. The earlier example specifically tells the teacher that items requiring the students to "label" parts of charts or graphs are the types of items that should be used. The second specific objective states the student "selects"; therefore, test items must be those in which the student must select from given information (i.e., multiple choice, true-false, and matching items).

The teacher's objectives set the stage for what is to be taught as well as what is to be assessed. This structure of teaching can guide assessment.

Teaching the Objectives

The second major step in the instructional process is to *teach* the objectives. Amazingly, some teachers teach all sorts of information but forget or refuse to teach the specific objectives that they have constructed. Part of the problem may be that the objectives have been written in an unteachable form.

Psychological variables sometimes enter into the teaching process, which may hinder the teaching of the objectives. For example, some teachers are afraid that students may know as much as they do and their level of self-esteem becomes involved in the teaching process. Sometimes, these teachers refuse to teach content they have not mastered. They may talk too fast, or not answer questions raised by students. These behaviors make it clear to students that their teachers are not well prepared. When these behaviors are present, they will negatively impact the teacher-learner process with all students, but particularly with those from cultures different from the mainstream culture.

It is important to note that the level at which the content is taught should be the level at which it is assessed. That is, if the content is taught at the application level, then it should be assessed at the application level and not at a higher level of Bloom's Taxonomy of Educational Objectives (1956).

Assessment of the Objectives

Appropriate assessment of student achievement is one of the most important tasks, if not the most important task, of the teacher. Many states have written laws with regard to teacher accountability. State and nationally constructed standardized tests are used to assess whether students have been performing at appropriate levels. For the classroom teacher, the task is formidable. The teacher should assess the objectives which have been taught and grades *should be based on no other factors.* Obviously, the teacher will be unable to assess all of the objectives that have been taught via paper/pencil instruments. However, content that has not been taught should not be on an examination from which a grade will be obtained. This is a blunt but true statement.

When teachers have not constructed appropriate assessment instruments, they cannot ascertain if their students achieved the objectives. Also, teachers may construct an item for which there is no answer. When asked why it is included on the test, the teacher may say, "I wanted to see what they would do with it." This is a *creative exercise and not a test item.* Does this mean that no unanswerable questions should be discussed in class? No, but why attempt to grade the ungradable? If teachers teach what they want students to know, then there is a higher probability that students from many different backgrounds will know what is expected.

When classroom tests contain items that have not been specifically taught, they mitigate particularly against low-income students or those not from the mainstream culture. These students often lack the life experiences that allow many of their mainstream peers to ascertain the correct answer.

Personality variables of the teacher may enter into the assessment process. The reader may have had the experience of entering a classroom only to be told by the teacher, "No one makes an A in my class." It is sad that students generally do not raise their hands and ask, "Which objectives are not going to be taught but will be tested in order for students to be unable to earn the grade of A?" Another example concerns teachers who give a test that most of the students fail. In this case, teachers must address the root of the problem: either the material was not taught, or the assessment instrument was not tied to what was taught. Teachers concerned about the painful consequences often decide to "curve the grades." This is unethical, since curved grades do not represent actual achievement on the part of students. This practice has contributed significantly to the issue of grade inflation. This also contributes to the problem of students saying they cannot do well on standardized tests but have all A's in their courses with content similar to what is contained in the standardized tests.

Two major concepts in measurement and evaluation are *validity* and *reliability.* Validity is whether or not the results of a test measure the purpose for which it was constructed. In short, are the results of the test valid? Reliability is a measure of consistency of results. Test results may be reliable but invalid. For example, a test could be constructed properly and administered properly. However, the test uses unfamiliar language and everyone fails. The same test could be administered the next day with the same results. The test results would be consistent (reliable) but invalid.

Factors That Lower the Validity of Test Results

Following are some of the factors in assessment (Linn and Gronlund 2000) that may lower the validity of test results.

1. *Unclear directions.* Directions that do not clearly specify how and where the student is to respond and how to record the responses may reduce the validity. Some assessments have omitted directions all together. For example, many students have had the experience of receiving a paper-and-pencil test that simply says "multiple choice" without any other instructions. Unclear directions will especially impinge on students for whom English is a second language. Students from cultures other than the majority culture may have little experience with fixed-choice assessment instruments such as multiple choice, matching, and true-false. It may also be beneficial to teach these students test-taking behaviors, since these may be lacking.

2. *Vocabulary and sentence structure that are too difficult.* Students from other cultures who speak English as their second language are apt to have significant difficulty if this factor is present. A good rule of thumb is to use the language in the classroom (and define it) when constructing the assessment instrument. Often, reading comprehension will distort the results of assessment.

3. *Ambiguity.* Ambiguous statements lead to incorrect answers and also distort the results of the assessment. This is especially true with students who are from linguistic or cultural backgrounds different from the majority culture.

4. *Inadequate time.* Time limits that do not permit students to think about the content and its application can reduce the validity of the interpretations made from an assessment. Unfortunately, many test makers assume that "faster is better" when, in reality, speed is not the factor that is being measured. Obviously, there are situations where speed is necessary. However, to measure achievement of students, speed is not usually a critical factor. This factor tends to significantly affect students from diverse cultures. For example, students for whom English is not their first language often have to translate from English to their first language and then reverse the process to answer an item on a test.

5. *Test items and learning outcomes that don't match.* Attempting to measure higher levels of the taxonomy such as synthesis or evaluation with items that measure factual recall will lower the validity of the test results.

6. *Poorly constructed test items.* There are rules for the construction of test items, and when these rules are not followed, the expected results don't occur. Errors in test construction are a major factor leading to invalid test results. Some universities do not require that prospective teachers successfully complete a course in measurement and evalua-

tion prior to teaching students. Almost no universities require their professors to document their background in tests and measurement. Unfortunately, students from diverse cultures are especially affected by having to attempt to understand poorly constructed test items.

7. *Overemphasis on knowledge levels and little emphasis on higher levels of the taxonomy.* Often, factual recall items are used rather than application, synthesis, and evaluation items. Another major problem is that some teachers misunderstand what an essay item is and how it must be constructed. If the item is not measuring the ability of the student to organize and integrate the material, it is not an essay item, but is likely a short-answer item. A common mistake that some teachers make is thinking that any item to which the students must write an answer is an essay item.

8. *Tests that are too short.* Any test is only a sample of behavior and many other items could be used that measure the same domain of material. However, when too few items compose a test instrument, the possibility of an unrepresentative sample is raised and the validity of the test results will be in question.

9. *Improper arrangement of test items.* All of the same types of test items should be presented together. For example, one should not have a true-false item followed by a multiple-choice item and then another true-false item. Second, the items should be arranged (as much as possible) from easy to difficult so that students don't immediately exhibit test anxiety or other motivational problems.

   It is a poor practice to administer the same test to the same class with the items for part of the class in one order and the items for another part of the same class in another order. This assumes that there are no order effects. One would have to compute the appropriate correlations to ascertain if the two forms were equivalent prior to assuming equivalence. Students who received the more difficult items first may respond differently than those students who received the easier items first. This is also true if two different forms of the test were administered.

10. *Identifiable pattern of answers.* One should not use an identifiable pattern of answers, since the students will be able to obtain the correct answer by guessing rather than through achievement.

Mistakes in Constructing Tests

Teachers may make some of the following mistakes in constructing classroom tests.

1. *Waiting until the end of the unit to construct test items.* Teachers will make fewer mistakes if test items are constructed immediately after the objectives have been taught. The greater the length of time

between the teaching of the objective and the construction of the test items, the higher the probability of the teacher forgetting how the objective was taught. Assessment is a major part of the learning process and should not be treated as an afterthought.

2. *Using unedited test items that come with the book.* Many authors of text-books do not know how to construct test items. Remember, the test item must be based on what *you* taught and how *you* taught it.

3. *Giving too much emphasis to some areas and not enough to others.* This mistake is more likely to occur if specific objectives are not followed. Sometimes teachers construct items that are easy to construct rather than items that measure the objective correctly. The emphasis and the amount of time the teacher spends on teaching the objective should guide the number and type of test items used on a test. A table of specifications is a test blueprint that specifies what proportion of test items deal with each content area and each objective. The table indicates the emphasis given during instruction by indicating the number of items that will test the content and objectives. This will aid in making sure the test is representative of what was taught. Table 9.1 is an example of a table of specifications for a unit on item construction.

4. *Using words or phrases that tend to be gender, racially, or ethnically biased.* This practice may lead to emotional reactions by students being tested. It is a good idea to share a copy of the assessment instrument with colleagues to make sure that these types of biases are not present. These types of errors may certainly interfere with the test-taking behavior of students from diverse cultures.

5. *Teaching and assessing different domains or levels of a taxonomy.* When the assessment does not measure the content at the same level that it was taught, error is introduced. For example, if objectives are taught at the application level, they must be measured at the same level on the assessment instrument.

Table 9.1
Specifications for a Unit on Test Item Construction

| | Instructional Objectives | | | |
Content Area	Knows Terms	Understands Advantages and Disadvantages	Constructs Items	Total Number
True-False	2	3	3	8
Short Answer	1	2	3	6
Multiple-Choice	5	3	3	11
Matching	2	3	3	8
Essay	2	3	3	8
Interpretive Exercise	3	3	3	9
Total	15	17	18	50

Standardized Tests

Standardized tests are instruments designed by test specialists and administered, scored, and interpreted under standard conditions (Ceros-Livingston 1995). A standardized test is constructed for a particular purpose or purposes. Unfortunately, people often make too much or too little out of standardized test results. Because standardized tests are often viewed as having greater "objectivity" than teacher-made tests, the results of standardized tests are often given credence they were not designed to deliver.

As the accountability movement strengthens in this nation's school districts, care must be taken not to place undue weight on any single measure of achievement or aptitude. This includes standardized tests. Teachers need to understand the principles of tests and measurement so they may advocate appropriate measures for themselves and their students. The following errors frequently happen at the school and school district level when administering and interpreting standardized tests:

1. *Choosing an inappropriate standardized test with a norm group that is different from the students who are to take the test.* If the students who are to be tested are from diverse populations, or students of color, then those students must be represented in the norm group. The way to ascertain who is represented in the norm group is to read the manual of the test. The demographics of the school district must be similar to those of the norm group. Some of these demographic characteristics are race, ethnicity, gender, age, income, and geography.

2. *Attempting to use a test for purposes other than its intended ones.* A good example of this error is to decide to use standardized test scores from students to measure a teacher's effectiveness. Unless the test manual states that the test measures teacher effectiveness and shows data tied to teacher effectiveness, then the standardized test is being used inappropriately. Another example is to treat standardized tests as if they are equivalent and measure the same thing. For example, one test that measures reading comprehension is not equivalent to another test that measures reading comprehension unless the appropriate research has been conducted to show that equivalence.

3. *Treating the results from standardized tests as unchanging.* All tests are samples of behavior, and all tests have error built into them. This includes both teacher-made tests and standardized tests. An example of this type of error is found in the area of intellectual assessment. Teachers or parents may state that "a student has an IQ of 135." This statement implies that (1) IQ scores don't change, (2) that all IQ scores on all intellectual assessment instruments are the same, and (3) that an IQ score means that the student will do well in all areas. Different intellectual assessment instruments measure different variables and are not interchangeable.

When teaching students from different cultures, the teacher must be aware that an intellectual assessment instrument that has both a verbal and performance component might be a better choice. That is, the student who speaks a language other than English may do well on the performance section but poorly on the verbal section, due to the language barrier. After the student becomes more proficient in the English language, he or she should be retested. Again, *test results change!*

4. *Misinterpreting standardized test scores.* One must interpret a score based on the purpose of the test and the data presented at a particular time, in a specified place, for a specified purpose. The results are interpreted in terms of the norm group for that test. Mistakes have occurred, such as using a standardized test to place pupils in classes for mentally handicapped students. Educators often misinterpret test results from minority students and students from diverse cultures. Years ago, a significant number of minority students were overrepresented in classes for mentally handicapped students. It was found that the standardized test being used for placement had no minority students represented in the norm group (Guthrie 1976). (The IQ score is not among the most important data that may be obtained from test results. It is far more important to ascertain the strengths and weaknesses that the student's performance depicts.)

Test Bias

Anderson, Stiggins, and Gordon (1980, p.16) stated that a test is biased if "individuals from different groups who are equally able do not have equal probabilities of success." There are many factors involved in test bias with regard to the construction, administration, and interpretation of tests. For example, there are examiner effects. Some research has indicated that performance on tests is increased when the examiner and the student are of the same race (Abramson 1969) while other authors disagree with this conclusion (Graziano, Farca, and Levy 1982). Sattler (1979) pointed out that in 24 out of 28 studies reviewed with regard to the effects of examiner race on test results, the race of the examiner had no significant effect. It has also been reported that students perform better when they have good rapport with the examiner (Fuchs and Fuchs 1986). This certainly is important when students of diverse backgrounds are involved.

The necessity of the examiner (or teacher) to know and understand cultural differences is paramount in assessment. Cultural and linguistic factors are two contextual variables that influence the assessment process. Banks (1994, pp. 300-301) relates that culture acts as a filter through which a person understands what behavior is expected to function in a particular society. However, knowledge and language are learned as a result of experiences gained in a culturally specific environment. Cultural and linguistic differences found among students may be unknown to the examiner, or different from the experiences of the examiner (Hernandez 1994). For example, in some cultures it is considered impolite to ask questions. Obviously, many test instruments require answers to questions. Therefore, students may be less than forthcoming when asked questions, especially if the questions are asked orally. Another area of concern is proximity of the examiner and the examinee. There are cultural differences with regard to space and the sharing of space in interpersonal contact.

Hernandez (1994) proposed five strategies that may reduce test bias. These include increased knowledge/awareness of cultural and linguistic background, determination of level of acculturation, controlling cultural variables, determining the language to be used in testing, and the use of interpreters. These strategies were presented primarily to assist speech language pathologists who administer tests.

Some research studies have reported that teacher expectations regarding students' intellectual functioning have increased actual test scores (Rosenthal and Jacobson 1968). However, some writers have felt that these data were overinterpreted and that the statistical results were not valid (Snow 1969; Elashoff and Snow 1971; Thorndike 1968).

There are diverse opinions with regard to the usefulness of using standardized tests with students of color. No consensus can be found in the research literature. However, there have been many significant cases with regard to this issue. Table 9.2 depicts examples of several major court cases regarding the placement of students of color in special education classes or academic tracks. These court cases not only indicate the problems of assessing children from diverse cultures, but underscore the necessity of having representative norm groups for score comparisons. Another factor that may be seen from Table 9.2 is that court decisions change with time and may be reversed.

One major California case, *Larry P. v. Wilson Riles* (1979), dealt with an African American child being tested and placed in special education classes. (See Table 9.2.) The Federal District Court for the Northern District of California first ruled on this case in 1972. It found that Larry had been incorrectly labeled as EMR (educable mentally retarded) and his right to equal educational opportunity was violated. As a consequence of this finding, the school district was prohibited from using IQ tests for EMR placement decisions. Subsequently, the California Department of Education called for a temporary moratorium on IQ testing until another court ruling on the validity of the tests could be obtained. The same case returned to the original court again in order to obtain a ruling on test validity for African American children. Both sides in the dispute prepared significant arguments. The State of California called many well-known experts on IQ tests. They presented extensive evidence that well-known tests such as the Stanford-Binet and the Wechsler Intelligence Scale for Children (W.I.S.C.) were not biased against African Americans. Although the tests

Table 9.2
Some major Court cases Regarding Assessment and Diversity

Case	Issue	Outcomes Involving Assessment
Brown V. Board of Education (1954)	School segregation.	Segregation denied equal protection; testimony by psychologists suggested that African American children would be made to feel inferior if segregated.
Stell v. Savannah– Chatam County Board of Education (1963). Reversed in 1964.	African American children did not have ability to be in classrooms with White students.	Psychology testimony indicated that the median IQ for African American children was 81 in contrast to a median IQ for White children of 101. The validity of the test scores was never mentioned. Court agreed that the district should not desegregate. This outcome was reversed.
Hobson v. Hansen (1967)	The use of standardized group ability tests to place students in honors, regular, general, and basic tracks.	Ruled against the use of a tracking system when tracking was based on group ability tests.
Diana v. State Board of Education (1970)	Over-representation of bilingual children in EMR classes based on scores on the Wechsler Intelligence Scale for Children (WISC) or the Stanford-Binet test. These tests were standardized on Whites only.	The California State Board of Education decided to adopt special rules for the testing of Mexican American and Chinese American children. New tests would be developed that reflected Mexican American culture and were normed on Mexican American children.
Larry P. v. Wilson Riles (1972, 1979, 1986)	Placement of African American children in EMR classes by scores on IQ tests.	Federal district court Judge Robert Peckham opined that a school district had incorrectly labeled Larry as EMR and violated his right to an equal educational opportunity. In the 1979 case, the ruling led to a permanent abolition of the use of IQ testing to place African American children in EMR classes in California. A 1986 ruling of this case extended the ban of intelligence testing for placement of minority students in special education programs.
Crawford et al. (1992)	Parent request for African American child to be tested for special education.	Court issued order lifting the earlier prohibition on IQ tests for African American students for placement in special education.

were not originally normed for African American populations, studies had shown that they were equally valid for Black and White children. However, the issue was raised that if the tests were not biased, why did Larry and others receive higher scores when retested by Black psychologists? The defense argued that standard testing procedures were not followed by the Black psychologists and that IQ test scores did not change when standardized testing procedures were followed.

The plaintiffs' side of the case also had distinguished experts. Their attorneys argued that all humans are born with equal potential and that any test that assigns disproportionate numbers of children of one race to an EMR category is racist and discriminatory. They argued that historically more powerful social groups used tests such as IQ tests to discriminate against less powerful social groups, that the district had intended to discriminate against Black children, and that the tests were used to keep Blacks in dead-end classes for the mentally retarded. This insured African Americans would not receive the appropriate training in order to move up in the social strata. The plaintiffs said that EMR labeling had devastating social consequences for children because they lost confidence and self-esteem. The label became a self-fulfilling prophecy, since the labeling could cause children to behave as though they were mentally retarded.

Later court cases involving testing became concerned with affirmative action programs in universities. In the case of *Regents of the University of California v. Bakke* (1978), a White engineer was denied admission to the University of California medical school although his scores on the MCAT test and grade point average were higher than those of some minority students admitted to the program. Under the affirmative action program in place at the University of California, the cutoff scores used for admission for nonminority students were higher than those for minority students. The attorneys for the defense argued that the tests were not valid for minority students. The plaintiffs argued that the tests were equally meaningful for both groups. The Court did not specifically address the use of the test but did rule that Bakke would be admitted on the basis that he had been denied due process. The Court implied that using different cutoff scores was not appropriate but said that race could be considered in selection procedures. In 1995, the Regents of the University of California voted to end affirmative action programs within the university. They also decided that race, *per se*, could not be used in hiring or admission decisions. The ultimate impact of these decisions and the results of a referendum to end affirmative action are not final, but preliminary data showed a marked decrease in minority enrollment at institutions such as the University of California at Berkeley.

A 1995 case before the United States Supreme Court, *Adarand Constructors, Inc. v. Pena, Secretary of Transportation et al.*, decreased the legal basis for affirmative action. Adarand Construction Company bid on a subcontract from the national government. Prior to 1995, financial incentives were given by the national government to contractors who hired subcontractors of small businesses controlled by financially disadvantaged individuals. The Adarand Company submitted the lowest bid to complete some construction work. However, it was denied the job which was given to some companies owned by minority groups. The Court ruled that the equal protection clause of the 14th amendment was violated and Adarand had been denied its due process. This case had an immediate impact on federal programs that awarded contracts under special preference programs.

The ultimate impact of these types of decisions by the courts is yet to be determined. However, the governor of the State of Florida is planning to establish bidding procedures for state contracts without regard to race or gender (Bush 1999). The possibility that future litigation will challenge this bidding procedure for obtaining state government contracts is high.

Literally hundreds of court cases are related to assessment issues. The possibility of bias exists in the use of test results, in the construction of test instruments, and in the interpretation of the relationship between external criteria and test results. What can be culled from all of these data for use by the classroom teacher is that assessment procedures are going to be emphasized more and court decisions will continue to provide precedent-setting rulings that will impact classrooms and school districts. Most assessment procedures have both advantages and disadvantages. The more a teacher knows about students' cultural, linguistic, socioeconomic, and educational background, as well as measurement and evaluation issues, the more likely the assessments used in the classroom will be beneficial to the learning process.

Standards Model

Society at large, educators, and politicians continue to give strong allegiance to the testing of students to ascertain achievement. Janda (1998) points out some information and makes several predictions with regard to future assessment of students. At the national level, the standards model is being supported by large groups of educators and politicians. A national standards movement—Goals 2000—is being advanced. Its proponents suggest that new tests must be constructed to measure the outcomes of programs based on these standards.

Governors in various states have attempted to get on the bandwagon of educational excellence. For example, the governor of Virginia received legislative approval to budget $12 million for the first two years of a program to construct and administer new achievement tests in the public schools of that state. The purpose of this effort was to assess higher academic standards set by the state (Bowers 1996). The governor of Florida has seen fit to follow the example of Virginia. He has proposed "The Bush/Brogan A+ Plan for Education" (Bush/Brogan 1999). The FCAT (Florida Comprehensive Assessment Test) has been constructed and is being administered throughout the state. Although no validity or reliability data regarding the results from this instrument have been published in major research journals, significant decisions such as retention of students, termination of teachers, awarding of financial resources or student vouchers for private schools, and the alphabetical grading of schools are influenced by overall FCAT scores.

A term that has become popular and relates to the standards model is "authentic assessment" (Wiggins 1993). Authentic assessment is said to have three qualities: it is based on multiple indicators of performance, it is criterion referenced, and human judgment is involved (Elliott 1991). Authentic assessment primarily involves performance tasks and portfolios. A portfolio is a collection of student products such as papers, math solutions, and artwork. An example of authentic assessment involving a performance task would be students conducting science experiments. Some states have adopted this approach (Kannapel 1996). In contrast, some people do not agree with authentic assessment (Brooks and Pakes 1993), and they have pointed out that there has been no consensus regarding the setting of the performance standards. Terwilliger (1996) suggested that proponents of authentic assessment have not dealt with the issues of reliability or validity and have been in favor of techniques of unknown quality. However, the standards movement is gaining momentum. For example, the SAT has included some open-ended math problems.

Janda (1998) suggested that it is impossible to set appropriate criteria for performance without having any knowledge of normative performance. He said, "How can one decide, for instance, what ninth graders should know about algebra without collecting information about what ninth graders have mastered in the past?" What constitutes the criterion?

Assessment Issues in the Future

How can teachers expect models of assessment of student achievement to evolve? The answer to this question depends on the respondent. Some major themes seem to be emerging that will impact teaching and assessment in the classroom:

1. *Minimum-competency testing will be expanded.* Although most of these tests are based on minimum levels of accomplishment, tests will be expanded into more content areas, and higher levels of competency will be expected. These instruments will continue to be administered to both teachers and students. ESOL or bilinqual programs will have to be adapted to prepare students who speak other languages for these assessment instruments.

2. *Use of computers will increase.* More advanced computer programs will be developed to assist students to learn material and to assess students' levels of achievement. Computer networks in homes, schools, and universities will assist in monitoring students' progress across time. More programs will be available in which immediate translations from one language to another will be used.

3. *Use of content standards and performance standards will increase.* Professional associations will continue to develop content-specific standards that will be disseminated nationally and internationally. Assessments will be derived from the content standards. Student achievement of the objectives that flow from the standards will be closely monitored.

4. *Accountability standards will be more stringent.* Rewards and punishments will become even more prominent as the consequences of assessment increase. Sanctions such as closing schools, changing teaching and administrative staffs, and withholding monetary resources will continue to be prevalent.

5. *Teachers without measurement and assessment skills will be disadvantaged.* Technology and knowledge of teaching and assessment will continue to hold center stage as global communication systems improve. Teachers will be more aware of the relationship between the achievement of their students and that of students in other countries. Competitive and cooperative values will be incorporated in educational systems in the United States as well as those of other nations.

6. *Teachers without an understanding of individual differences will be disadvantaged.* Lack of knowledge of student diversity and its relationship to learning and achievement will significantly handicap employment prospects for teacher candidates.

7. *Information from varied tests and assessment techniques will be used by teachers.* Teams of teachers will work cooperatively to build appropriate objectives, teaching plans, and assessment instruments to measure learning. Elementary students will have many different teachers assessing their progress. It is possible that several teachers with different cultural backgrounds and specialties will be teaching in the same elementary classroom.

8. *There will be a greater move toward a national and international curriculum.* Pressures to produce graduates who perform at world standards will greatly influence the curriculum in U.S. schools. A common international computer language may further standardize global communications.

9. *Fairness and privacy will continue to be major issues in assessment.* All types of assessment will be looked at carefully. If the results from these instruments or activities cannot show that they predict appropriate criteria for admission to college, job success, and teacher effectiveness,

they will be replaced. Any assessment model that relegates students of lower socioeconomic background into segregated programs is bound to come under scrutiny.

Conclusion

Classroom teachers should remember their importance in the teaching-learning process and the relationship of assessment to teaching. No one assessment procedure is sufficient. Many different objectives that are taught must be individually assessed. Teachers prepare students not only to participate in society, but also to change it. Knowledge is power. Never be afraid to teach too much. Never be afraid to open every possible door of opportunity for all students you teach. Never be afraid to confront ignorance and make every attempt to destroy it. Appreciate and use the diversity represented by your students.

Successful teaching leads to successful learning, which leads to positive self-esteem and achievement—and it all has to be assessed.

References

Abebe, S., and Sands, B. (1993*). Testing and instruction: Partners in educational excellence* (Report No. RIENOV93).

Abramson, T. (1969). The influence of examiner race on first-grade and kindergarten subjects' Peabody Picture Vocabulary Test scores. *Journal of Educational Measurement, 6*(2), 412–426.

Adarand Constructors, Inc. v. Pena, Secretary of Transportation et al., 115 U.S. 2097 (1995).

Anderson, B. L., Stiggins, R. J., and Gordon, D. W. (1980). *Educational testing facts and issues: A layperson's guide to testing in the Schools.* Portland, OR: Northwest Regional Educational Laboratory and California State Department of Education (contract #400-79-0079).

Banks, J. (1994) *Multiethnic Education Theory and Practice* (3rd). Needham Heights, MA: Allyn and Bacon.

Bloom, B. S., et al. (Eds.). (1956). *Taxonomy of educational objectives: Handbook I, cognitive domain.* New York: D. McKay.

Bowers, M. (1996). Educators to decide who'll write state tests. *Virginian-Pilot,* October 10, p. B3.

Brooks, T. E., and Pakes, S. J. (1993). Policy, national testing, and the Psychological Corporation. *Measurement and Evaluation in Counseling and Development, 26,* 54–58.

Brown v. Board of Education, 347 U.S. 483 (1954), 349 U.S. 294 (1955).

Bush, J. (1999). Executive order regarding diversity. Exec. Order No.99–281. http://www.state.fl.us/eog/executive_orders/1999/November /eo99 281.html. (November 9).

Bush/Brogan A+ Plan for Education. (1999). http://fcn.state.fl.us/eog/aplus-plan/A+_plan/A+_plan_revised.html. (June 1).

Ceros-Livingston, P.A. (1995). *Measurement and evaluation for professional teachers: A learning perspective for educators* (4th ed.). Minnesota: Burgess International Group.

Cohen, S. A., and Hyman, J. S. (1991). Can fantasies become facts? *Educational Measurement: Issues and Practice, 10*(1), 20–23.

Diana V. State Board of Education, C.A. No. C–70 37 RFP (N.D.Cal., filed Feb. 3, 1970).

Elashoff, J., and Snow, R. E. (Eds.). (1971). *Pygmalion revisited*. Worthington, OH: C. A. Jones.

Elliott, S. M. (1991). Authentic assessment: An introduction to a neobehavioral approach to classroom assessment. *School Psychology Quarterly, 6*, 273–278.

Fuchs, D., and Fuchs, L. S. (1986). Test procedure bias: A meta-analysis of examiner familiarity effects. *Review of Educational Research, 56*, 243–262.

Graziano, W. G., Farca, P. E., and Levy, J. C. (1982). Race of examiner effects and the validity of intelligence tests. *Review of Educational Research, 52*, 469–497.

Guthrie, R. V. (1976). *Even the rat was white: A historical view of psychology*. New York: Harper and Row.

Hernandez, R. D. (1994). Reducing bias in the assessment of culturally and linguistically diverse populations. *Journal of Educational Issues of Language Minority Students, 14*, Boise State University, Boise, ID 83725.

Hobson v. Hansel, 269F. Supp. 401 (D.D.C.1967).

Janda, L. H. (1998). *Psychological testing: Theory and applications*. Needham Heights, MA: Allyn and Bacon.

Kannapel, P. J. (1996). *"I don't give a hoot if somebody is going to pay me $3600": Local school district reactions to Kentucky's high stakes accountability program*. Eric Document Reproductive Services No.: ED397135.

Larry P. v. Wilson Riles, 343 F. Supp. 1306 (N.D. Cal. 1972), affd 502 F. 2D 963 (9th Cir. 1979).

Linn, R. L., and Gronlund, N. E. (2000). *Measurement and assessment in teaching* (8th ed.). New Jersey: Prentice-Hall.

Nitko, A. J. (1989). Designing tests that are integrated with instruction. In R. L. Linn (Ed.), *Educational measurement* (3rd ed.) (pp. 447–474). London: Collier Macmillan.

Popham, W. J. (1987). The merits of measurement-driven instruction. *Phi Delta Kappan, 68*, 679–682.

Regents of the University of California v. Bakke, 438 U.S. 265, 17 Fair Empl. Prac. Cas. (BNA) 1000 (1978).

Rosenthal, R., and Jacobson, L. (1968). *Pygmalion in the classroom*. New York: Holt, Rinehart and Winston.

Sattler, J. M. (1979). Intelligence tests on trial; *Larry P. et al. V. Wilson Riles et al.* Paper presented at the meeting of the Western Psychological Association, San Diego, April.

Snow, R. E. (1969). Review of *Pygmalion in the Classroom* by R. Rosenthal and L. Jacobson. *Contemporary Psychology, 14*, 197–199.

Stell v. Savannah-Chatham County Board of Education, 210 F. Supp. 667 (S.D. Ga. 1963), rev'd 333 F.2d 55 (5thCir. 1964), cert. denied, 379 U.S.933 (1964).

Terwilliger, J. S. (1996). *Semantics, psychometrics, and assessment reform: A close look at "authentic" tests*. Eric Document Reproduction Service No. ED397123.

Wiggins, G. P. (1993). *Assessing student performance: Exploring the purpose and limits of testing*. San Francisco: Jossey-Bass.

chapter 10

Teaching Multicultural Education From a Foundations Perspective

Angela Rhone

A number of educational theorists who previously examined the philosophy and goals of multicultural education in a democratic society now question the rationale for developing a new paradigm that speaks not only to ethnic minority groups but also to reform of the total school environment (e.g., Banks 1991, 1993, 1994, 1996; Sleeter and Grant 1999). It is Rodriguez's (1997) belief that in order to endorse these multicultural goals, one would have to "understand and appreciate the differences that exist among the nation's citizens" (p. 7). His perspective encompasses one of the fundamental objectives of multicultural education: understanding history and culture while simultaneously appreciating those differences. Because of these connections, multicultural education should incorporate the study of the history and philosophy of education in the United States.

Multicultural education still faces some struggles to avoid mischaracterization. Banks (1994a) and Sleeter and Grant (1999) have argued that one of the failures of multicultural education is that it is viewed only as education for women and for minority groups such as African Americans and Hispanics. With this in mind, it is not surprising that any attempt to use this reform movement to effect changes in the curriculum has led to misunderstanding in and out of the educational environment.

This chapter describes how a course was developed to teach prospective educators. This course embraced the foundations of education combined with the philosophy and goals of multicultural education. Its focus was three-fold: (a) It assumed that multicultural education should be taught in such a way that prospective teachers would understand its aims, goals, and philosophies. To achieve this, a historical foundations perspective of education, along with the theories of multicultural education, was provided. (b) It assumed that prospective educators should be able to see that the significance of this critical pedagogy is rooted in an attempt to identify and to correct education practices that have been tradition in American education. (c) It assumed that prospective educators engaged in studying multicultural education should not only have a theoretical framework in race, class, and gender, but also should be encouraged to understand the historical significance of these topics in light of events that have shaped this nation.

Goals of Multicultural Education

Multicultural education is a reform movement that is attempting to address major inequities that have existed in school practices and curricula over time. Bennett (1995) stated that "multicultural education is an approach to teaching and learning that is based upon democratic values and beliefs, and seeks to foster cultural pluralism within culturally diverse societies and an interdependent world" (p. 13). Inherent in this new paradigm are the assumptions that educational institutions should embody fundamental values that adhere to macrocultural ideologies of justice, liberation, equality, and freedom. It is important to realize that multicultural education does not attempt to omit the accomplishments of Europeans or Euro-Americans, but seeks to expand the paradigm to include cultural and ethnic groups who have been historically omitted or underrepresented in the curriculum.

Grant and Sleeter (1998) maintain that based on the ideals of equal opportunity and cultural pluralism, multicultural education includes the following goals:

1. To promote an understanding and appreciation of cultural diversity in the United States.
2. To promote alternative choices for people, with full affirmation of their race, gender, disability, language, sexual orientation, and social class background.
3. To help all children achieve academic success.
4. To promote awareness of social issues involving the unequal distribution of power and privilege that limits the opportunity of those not in the dominant group. (pp. 163–164)

While these goals appear to be easy goals to pursue, they left many school teachers seeing few connections between the purpose of multicultural education and historical issues, such as justice and liberation, which are deeply embedded in the American past. Moreover, for educators studying multicultural education foundations and philosophy, contemporary goals seem disconnected without a strong sense of the history of American education instruction. In teaching multicultural education, the author has created a model that is deeply rooted in a foundations perspective. Banks (1994b) noted that despite attempts made in schools to apply multicultural education to the curriculum, many schools and university practitioners have a limited conception of multicultural education and view it primarily as curriculum reform that involves changing or restructuring the curriculum to include content about ethnic groups, women, and other cultural groups (p. 4).

Case Study: The Author's Development of a Multicultural Perspective

In a departure from traditional third-person exposition, the author will provide a brief first-person account of the forces that shaped her own development and understanding of multicultural education.

I grew up in Jamaica. My education reflected traditional schooling influenced by the British system through the end of my secondary school experience. There were no critical questions to ponder. The British model of education gave me no ideas about critical analysis of history, justice, and inequality. Just as my education did not critically appraise the existing social order, I felt no need to assess it. I had no clear view of what Jamaican culture was: its roots, its history, its politics, or its relationship to other nations. Moreover, I did not link the power relations in Jamaican society to education and social class. Because of this lack of history and connection, certain assumptions were common. Jamaica was considered to have no race problems. All individuals were thought to have equal status. Those who did not make it were viewed as lazy and not willing to work.

As an immigrant who earned a B.A. and an M.A. in English Education from universities in the United States, I received no theoretical structure that offered to help me comprehend the complexity of class, power relations, and race in American society or the world at large. After completing my master's degree, I returned to Jamaica and taught at a teachers' college for three years. It was during the political and social upheaval in Jamaica that I began to connect the power relations in that society to the existing class structure.

Although I lacked full understanding of these issues, I began to comprehend that history, power, violence, poverty, and the hierarchical structures of society are all connected. These factors are usually played down in the educational system. If power relations are not incorporated into democratic education, the public will not understand the struggles that occur in every society. I began to see that small countries were inextricably bound to dominant countries whose hold over them is usually centered around economic dependence, not economic empowerment. I learned that it was those in power who decided what was to be taught. I was not living in a democratic society where things were as equal as I thought. I was in a society that placed wealth in the hands of only a few individuals.

Courses taken in the United States on the history and philosophy of education forced me to reexamine my concept of society and provided me with insights into how individuals should be educated to create a more just society. Friere's work (1970) allowed me to link knowledge with the distribution of wealth and one's place in society. It became important for me to investigate the following critical issues: (a) the importance of having a critical, historical knowledge about one's society; (b) the role of the schools in perpetuating the ideologies of those in power; (c) the school's relation to the workplace in society; (d) the education of immigrants and minority groups; (e) the preparation of new teachers; and (f) the failure of the curriculum to connect history with current problems and events.

Because I had a limited theoretical understanding from which to look at social class and the construction of knowledge, my early education did not stimulate my thinking to connect, understand, or question my class position in society. With an understanding of education and class structures and their connection to the power structures in society, I was able to see my own shortcomings, despite coming from a middle-class environment.

My understanding of race was furthered teaching African American studies at the University of North Carolina at Greensboro from 1989 to 1995. I came from a society that chose to study England and English culture rather than Africa and African culture. Over time, teaching about race allowed me to explore the ideologies of racism and sexism in the United States as well as in the rest of the world.

After achieving the doctoral degree, I continued to teach the philosophy and foundations of multicultural education to prospective teachers. This teaching is committed to engaging students in their education and challenging them to think critically about their history, nation, and world. This type of education is centered on democratic principles and the social and historical foundations of the United States. As cited in Pietig (1997), Dewey said that "Prospective teachers must have a thorough grounding in social and psychological foundations to give them critical perspectives on education so that they might remedy deficiencies in the school curriculum." Further, Dewey's overall plan for teacher education included: (a) the school as a social and political institution; and (b) the historical development of ideas concerning education" (pp. 177–184).

In looking at these two points, Pietig (1997) and Purpel (1989) argued the importance of studying history. Specifically, Purpel noted this connection between knowing history and liberation:

A critical consciousness of history actually can be more liberating for it enables us to remember that there are origins and beginnings to the present and that their origins are worked in human events. A strong sense of the past gives us the reality that we will eventually create tomorrow's past, the present, and that our response represents not only a commitment on the future but on the past. When we know our past, we can maintain continuously whatever we do, since even drastic change would represent a thoughtful and conscious concern with both past and future. (p. 127)

With a theoretical framework in race, class, gender, the historical foundations of education, and the experience of an immigrant woman of African descent, I have a broder basis of knowledge/experiences to draw on when teaching multicultural education. It is imperative that prospective teachers see the interconnection between historical, social, political, and educational events that have shaped the United States both at home and abroad. In order that future teachers can better understand contemporary practices in American education, I developed a strong foundational emphasis in a multicultural education course. This was rooted in the belief that when teachers understand the historical roots of current ineffective practices, change is more likely to follow.

Teaching Multicultural Education From a Foundations Perspective

A three-semester-hour course composed of six phases was developed at a university in the southeastern United States. Each phase had certain goals to achieve and specific learning activities were assigned. For certain phases, reading assignments are also given.

Drawing on the reconstructivist approach, which argues for a critical appraisal of all elements of society (Armstrong, Henson, and Savage 1997; Myers and Myers 1995), students are encouraged during the semester to become aware and critically analyze the social, political, and historical aspects of education in America. Reed and Bergman (1995) argued that the task of education in this philosophy is two-fold. First, educators must reconstruct the theoretical base of the United States' cultural heritage. Second, they must develop school programs with a clearly thought-out curriculum of social reform to deal with extreme cultural crisis and social disintegration.

Each of the six phases of this multicultural education course encourages students to think critically about problems inherent in American education/society and to propose solutions. The role of the teacher as a "transformative intellectual" is presented. (Giroux 1988). The following description of the six phases of the course will explain how this process developed.

Phase 1: Stereotypes

In Phase 1, students are placed into groups of five for two learning activities. The first learning activity is to list the stereotypes that are common to men and women of various ethnic and cultural groups, gays and lesbians, and the aged. Using African Americans as an example, the students are asked to list stereotypes common to the men and women of that group. After an hour of working together, a member from each group goes to the blackboard and writes what his or her group recorded. This exercise attempts to reach three goals: (1) to have students face the images they know as stereotypes; (2) to see how these stereotypes shape their consciousness; and (3) to understand how these stereotypes affect the school environment. Embedded in the exercise are tensions and struggles that occur when students begin to list the stereotypes. White students often say that they grew up in homes where everyone was considered equal; African American students often comment that they do not feel comfortable writing down stereotypes of their group. Foreign students remark that they are not "American," thus they do not know any stereotypes. All students are challenged to talk with each other until they become more relaxed within their groups. Often, the room fills with laughter and tension. When questioned about this, many students say that this happens because (a) they are nervous to discuss and to write down stereotypes; (b) it is painful; (c) when they bring stereotypes out in public, they realize they are not the only ones who think these things. Allowing students to talk and write openly about stereotypes takes the power of stereotypes away and defuses the anger that normally occurs when they are mentioned.

Additionally, many students complain during this exercise that they have difficulty with listing stereotypes because they fear being labeled "bad" people or being called "racists." In order to help them create the list, students are encouraged to expand upon the following questions:

- What were you taught about this ethnic or cultural group?
- How did these stereotypes originate?
- How have these stereotypes affected you?
- How was history taught to you?
- What do you remember about the contributions of women, Native Americans, and African Americans?
- To what extent are social policies shaped by stereotypes?
- What is lacking when stereotypes about cultural and ethnic groups are perpetuated?

In response to the last question, many students agree that what they lack is sufficient information, content, and historical background. However, many imply that even knowing these three elements, it is hard to change the stereotypes. It is interesting to note here that over the years this course has been taught, the stereotypes expressed by each class remain fundamentally the same.

For their second learning activity, students were asked to list several social, political, economic, and educational events that have shaped the nation over the past 200 years. The goal was to see how much prospective teachers knew about the history of the United States and, more importantly, to develop an understanding of how these events are tied to the history of education in the United States. Having listed the events, students are then asked to describe their effects on society, politics, and education. They are then asked to further link these events to social policies and reform movements in education. Although students can list *Brown v. Board of Education of Topeka* (1954) as one of the important events that shaped education in the United States, most can neither critically analyze how it has impacted their lives, nor can they link it to other social or political events in society.

Most students say they can understand AIDS because AIDS is real. Other historical events appear to be categorized as situations to be memorized, not critically analyzed. Most students suggest that they do not connect with history because the subject is taught in a manner that is isolated from contemporary events. As is evident from these responses, students leave history classes with a concept of history that is not connected to their personal lives.

Phase 2: The Historical Foundations of Education

Phase 1 asked the students to list stereotypes of different ethnic and cultural groups and to try to understand what they have listed in the context of history. For their first learning activity in Phase 2, they are asked to look at the purpose and foundations of education in America. They are specifically asked how different groups of people have been educated over the past 200 years. The goal of this activity is to have the students identify educational reform movements and to note the social, political, and historical factors that shaped these movements. As part of this activity, they are asked to reflect on the following question: "How important was this knowledge to me in light of my gender, racial, and ethnic background?" Given the historical knowledge that most prospective teachers bring to the study of multicultural education, it is important that time be provided for critical connections to be developed between the history of education and the study of contemporary multicultural education.

There are two major goals to a foundations perspective in multicultural education. The first goal is to have students develop an understanding of American education rooted on a basis of history and personal connection. The second dimension is for students to link educational practices with the education of different groups in this society. In order for students to fulfill the first goal, they are asked to read several articles about the history and philosophy of education in America.

The historical component contains the following objectives:

1. To examine the historical, sociological, and philosophical foundations of education in the United States.
2. To critically examine different educational reform movements in the United States.
3. To identify the goals and ideologies of reformers such as Thomas Jefferson, Horace Mann, and John Dewey.
4. To examine the social and political conditions that have shaped educational reform movements over the years.
5. To examine the link between the goals of earlier reform movements in education and the current objectives of multicultural education.
6. To have students research immigration patterns of different European groups who came to the United States.

In analyzing these topics, students are encouraged to look critically at the following:

1. How men, women, and immigrant and minority groups were educated.
2. How educational institutions dealt with the presence of different European immigrant groups who came to the United States.
3. How historical arguments against immigration resemble/differ from arguments posed today.

At this point, students should begin to understand the historical, philosophical, and political framework of American education in light of their own history.

While studying the history of education in the United States, students begin to see that inequities in education existed not only for African Americans, but also for many Europeans. In this phase, students are challenged to look at concepts such as nativism in education, and ethnic and racial prejudice. Students are challenged to look at the anti-Catholic feeling that existed when Irish and other mostly Catholic immigrants came to this country. Many students begin to see a connection between oppressive educational practices in history and inequities that remain in today's schools. Many understand that their own history will impact the students they will be teaching. Some understand why certain groups were or were not excluded from the educational process. All students are challenged to understand that struggles which occurred earlier made it possible for many groups to be educated today. Many African American students are surprised to learn that, at one time, many White ethnic groups were victims of blatant prejudice and nativism. At the end of the first three weeks, some students have begun to connect past practices in American education with current ones, but most have not yet begun to put a human face on this.

Students are asked to research immigration patterns of different European groups who came to the United States from the mid-1800s to the early 1960s. Nieto (1996) has argued the following regarding the history of immigration and its connection to the teaching of multicultural education:

> It has become clear that the immigrant experience is an important point for beginning our journey into multicultural education. This journey needs to begin with teachers who themselves are unaware of or uncomfortable with their own ethnicity. By going through a process of reeducation, about their own background, their families' pain, and their rich legacy of stories, teachers can lay the groundwork for students to reclaim their own histories and voices. (p. 25)

The final activity of Phase 2 is a group presentation. Students research different European ethnic groups (Italians, Poles, Irish, Germans, British, Swedes, and Greeks). Most of the students descend from these groups. The topics they explore are causes of immigration, educational experiences, rates of assimilation and acculturation, ethnocentricism, dropout rates, and the degree of discrimination faced by these groups. Students conduct research and present their findings. Their introduction to the concepts of nativism, the melting pot ideology, and cultural or religious differences found among White ethnic Europeans is provided by reading Banks (1994b). This text discusses the plight of European immigrants to America. The difficulties encountered by European immigrants are very surprising to students. They often believed that stereotypes and prejudices existed only between Blacks and Whites. Banks points out the following regarding European immigrants:

> Most of the European immigrants who came to North America before 1890 were from nations in Northern and Western Europe, such as the United Kingdom, Sweden and Switzerland. Most of the new immigrants from Southern, Central and Eastern Europe were considered a threat to the United States civilization and its democratic tradition. The nativists pointed out that the new immigrants were primarily Catholics, whereas the old immigrants were mainly Protestants. Strong elements of anti-Catholicism became an integral part of the nativists' movement. Because of their Catholicism, cultural differences, and competition for jobs with the old immigrants and Native-born Americans, the new immigrants became the victims of blatant nativism. (p.19)

When learning is shifted from a monocultural perspective to a multicultural one, students are able to understand their own historical roots in the context of a multiethnic and pluralistic society. As they become aware of the nature of their own ethnicity, they begin to see the role of the educational system in promoting Americanization and the extinction of immigrants' cultural beliefs that differed from the mainstream culture. Regarding the process of Americanization, Banks (1994b) states: "Reflecting the prevailing goals of the nation as articulated by its powerful and economic leaders, the schools and colleges promoted and embraced Americanization and blind loyalty to the nation and also showed a distrust for foreigners and immigrant groups during the turn of the century and World War I periods" (p. 22).

Discussion followed as students began to link education to class, race, ethnicity, gender, immigrant status, and their own personal identification. The dialogue centered around such issues as (a) the assimilation of second and third generation White ethnic groups in American society, (b) the role of the school in perpetuating assimilation, (c) the school curriculum and its role in the representation of ethnic minorities, (d) the extent to which schools have addressed the needs of the underclass in American society, and (e) the importance of having critical knowledge about one's society. Students began to grasp and to understand the privileges that some groups are privy to because of their ethnic background, race, class, and gender. They began to understand the factors that promoted cultural assimilation and structural assimilation by the second generation, as well as the circumstances of those who had difficulty in gaining structural assimilation because of color or national origin.

For many students, this is the first opportunity they have had to examine their own ethnicity in a safe environment. At this stage in the course, many who enrolled with the notion that differences existed only between Whites and non-Whites were now aware through their own research, presentations, and readings that the acceptance or rejection of individuals who are different from the mainstream has always been a part of this society. For White students, understanding their own European past and various immigration acts that were passed to exclude some groups and admit others made them realize what many of their ancestors had to give up (e.g., name, culture) to assimilate. Students now grasp their own history, and most connect these concepts of exclusion, discrimination, racism, and sexism to other groups who were excluded on the basis of color. In the case of African Americans and other persons of color, Banks (1994b) notes that:

> Even though society demanded that they assimilate culturally in order to integrate socially, politically, and economically, it was very difficult for them to assimilate because of their skin color. Even when African Americans, Mexican Americans, and Native Americans succeeded in becoming culturally assimilated, they were still structurally isolated and were denied full unqualified entry into the organizations and institutions sanctioned by the larger society. They became, in effect, marginal persons, for they were not accepted totally by their own ethnic group or by the mainstream culture. (p.69)

As the second phase ends, students have acquired a better understanding of the connection among power, education, and the hierarchical structures of society. They begin to understand how these differences have separated the nation not only racially, but also culturally. As the students finish this section, they struggle with these questions: (a) Who is an American? (b) What is American culture? (c) How do people accommodate and assimilate at the same time? (d) Does the school have the right to disregard the home culture of students and replace it with the school's culture? and (e) What would have resulted if strict assimilation had not prevailed in classrooms? Students begin to understand their own history and connect it to the diverse students they will be teaching. Finally, they begin to understand why some reform educational movements failed and why some succeeded.

Phase 3: The History and Goals of Multicultural Education

With a general understanding of the historical foundations of education in America, the students are now prepared to examine the history and goals of multicultural education. Throughout Phase 3, students were asked to look at this question: "As the United States moves into the 21st century, can the goals of multicultural education ameliorate racism, sexism, injustice, crime, and violence against certain groups in society?"

The purpose of Phase 3 is to have the students understand the theory and philosophy of multicultural education. In order to contextualize these new ideas, students study concepts and engage in analytical discussions about the philosophy and goals of multicultural education. However, this phase avoids Freire's (1970) banking concept of education. The banking concept of education maintains that "knowledge is bestowed by those who consider themselves knowledgeable upon [those who] they consider know nothing" (p. 58). In contrast, the course engages students in cointentional learning:

> Teacher and students (leadership and people), co-intent on reality, are both subjects, not only in the task of unveiling that reality, and thereby coming to know it critically, but in the task of recreating that knowledge. As they attain this knowledge of reality through common reflection and action, they discover themselves as its permanent recreators. (Freire 1970, p. 56)

This phase of the course helps students to see how education, knowledge, and cultural capital are influenced by race, class, gender, ethnicity, and immigrant status. The following are five key questions that permeate instruction in Phase 3.

1. Can multicultural education impact the social, political, and economic ills in today's society?

2. If implemented in today's classrooms, can a curriculum in multiculturalism alleviate racial and ethnic injustice in society?

3. Can multicultural education, if implemented, better educate an increasingly diverse student body in this nation?

4. Is multicultural education divisive to society?

5. How far and how well can all people be educated?

Students are asked to ponder each of these questions. They are then asked, "How important is this information to you as a prospective teacher?" For example, one topic that generated much discussion was the level of cross-cultural functioning which Banks (1994b) described. Students were asked to identify which level they thought they had achieved. Additionally, they were asked to describe the levels of cross-cultural functioning they believed their students would have when they came into their classrooms. They were also asked to address this question: If teachers are functioning on Level 1 (low level) and students are functioning on Levels 3 and 4 (higher levels), what difficulties would arise in this scenario?

As students became more committed to cooperative learning and understanding the goals of multicultural education, they also became more aware of the politics of education. They were now more involved in "problem-posing" education, which, according to Freire (1970), is the "essence of consciousness and embodies communication" (p. 66).

Phase 4: Investigating Multicultural Issues at the National and International Level

The main goal of Phase 4 is to have students develop an understanding of how different countries deal with issues of diversity. Students investigate a number of issues in multicultural education at the national and international levels. At the start of the semester, students are given six weeks of preparation to work in their assigned groups. At the end of the six weeks, they present their findings to their peers. Some of these issues include:

- The relevance of multicultural education to the society.
- The acculturation of immigrant students in U.S. schools.
- Infusing multicultural content into a discipline.
- Bilingual education: methods and research.
- Bilingual education: historical perspective.
- Analyzing the role or representation of ethnic groups in the curriculum.
- Cross-national comparisons of education.
- International dimensions of the U.S. public school curriculum.
- Research on the academic achievement of students from different ethnic backgrounds.
- The presentation of African Americans in history textbooks.
- The presentation of women in history textbooks.

This exercise provides students with the opportunity to verify material learned elsewhere in the course through the information presented by their colleagues. This is an important component of instruction, since there is some tendency for students to doubt certain ideas and hearing the same information from their fellow students provides independent verification.

Phase 5: Essays and Examinations

In Phase 5, students write two reflective essays on any of the following topics: (a) English-only laws in the United States; (b) prejudice reduction and the school curriculum; (c) Dewey's ideology of progressive education and Banks's ideology of multicultural education; (d) the history of American education as a framework for understanding multicultural education.

One approach that is helpful for students is to ask them to write their thoughts about many of the issues discussed in class during the term. As they become more critical thinkers, not only do their vocabularies change, but also their critiques are supported by more research. It is evident from these essays that, as students write, they become more analytical in their thinking. Their essays frequently indicate their desire to create multicultural classrooms when they become teachers. At this point, the students are given an examination covering material presented through Phase 5.

Phase 6: Building a Multicultural Education Curriculum

Phase 6 usually takes place during the last two weeks of the semester. The activity is for students to follow a step-by-step procedure to create a multicultural curriculum for their future classrooms. This project has the students working in groups. The goal of this activity is to enable them to connect theory with practice and to synthesize all of the knowledge they have acquired over the semester. Having reviewed the five dimensions of multicultural education developed by Banks (1994b), students are asked to use a thematic or conceptual approach in preparing a curriculum. Each curriculum includes (a) a rationale; (b) the ethnic makeup, grade level, reading level, immigrant status, ratio of boys to girls, and percentage of LEP students in the classroom; (c) the disciplines they plan to teach; and (d) five objectives. Finally, students write ten activities that correlate with their goals and objectives and include a bibliography. The curricula are approximately 15–20 pages long, and students are asked to write a critical evaluation explaining why they believe their curriculum would work in their chosen school setting. Then they are asked to answer the following question: "What resistance would you expect from parents, teachers, superintendents, and the community when you attempt to present this curriculum in your classroom?" Students are also asked to suggest ways in which they would overcome this resistance. On the last day of the class, each group shares its overall experiences in curriculum writing with the other members of the class.

Conclusion

After teaching several multicultural education courses with a historical/foundations perspective, the author has learned that for transformative learning to take place, several elements must be present. Students should develop an understanding of the history of education. Many students take a multicultural education course with the misconception that this subject concerns only people of color. In order to avoid this, they should be allowed to connect past reform movements to contemporary reform movements and learn about their own ethnic group's history as well as confront their biases. Bhola (1988) argues that, for teachers, the most important concept "is learning the fact of our historicity … being a product of historical forces, followed closely by an expanded concept of cultural literacy." Bhola stresses the need for a "critical view of life and society that enables children to understand the functioning of the world system and that of the political economy" (p. 106).

Once students are acquainted with the essentials of the history of American education, they will be able to connect issues and problems in contemporary education with their historical roots. Using comparative analysis, they can analyze multicultural education in other nations, exchange ideas, and critically examine the system of education in the United States. They can also understand the power relations present in creating or altering a curriculum. From this critical reflection, students can begin to look at teaching as a transformative profession.

Providing a historical/foundations perspective in teaching multicultural education allows future teachers to connect not only to themselves and to their nation, but to the global community as well. Understanding the history of education in the United States provides future teachers with a foundation for analyzing equity issues in education today. They begin to realize that students "have not been treated the same" and that the road to equity in education is a long and often difficult one.

References

Armstrong, D., Henson, K., and Savage, T. (1997). *Teaching today: An introduction to education* (5th ed.). Upper Saddle River, NJ: Merrill.

Banks, J. (Ed.). (1991). *Teaching strategies for ethnic studies* (5th ed.). Boston: Allyn and Bacon.

Banks, J., and Banks, C. (Eds.). (1993). *Multicultural education issues and perspectives* (2nd ed.). Boston: Allyn and Bacon.

Banks, J. (Ed.). (1994a). *An introduction to multicultural education*. Boston: Allyn and Bacon.

Banks, J. (Ed.). (1994b) *Multiethnic education: Theory and practice* (3rd ed.). Boston: Allyn and Bacon.

Banks, J. (Ed.). (1996). *Multicultural education, transformative knowledge and action: Historical and contemporary perspectives*. New York: Teacher's College, Columbia University.

Bennett, C. (1995). *Comprehensive multicultural education: Theory and practice* (3rd ed.). Boston: Allyn and Bacon.

Bhola, H. S. (1998). Mediating between policy and pedagogy: A model of multicultural education. *Educational Horizons* (Spring), 104–106.

Freire, P. (1970). *Pedagogy of the oppressed*. New York: Seabury Press.

Giroux, H. (1988). *Teachers as intellectuals: Toward a critical pedagogy of learning.* South Hadley, MA: Bergin and Garvey Publishers.

Grant, C., and Sleeter, C. (1998). *Turning on learning: Five approaches for multicultural teaching plans for race, class, gender, and disability* (2nd ed.). Upper Saddle River, NJ: Merrill.

Myers, C., and Myers, L. (1995). *The professional educator: A new introduction to teaching and schools.* Belmont, CA: Wadsworth.

Nieto, S. (1996). *Affirming diversity: The sociopolitical context of multicultural education* (2nd ed.). New York: Longman.

Pietig, J. (1997). Foundations and teacher: Do we need a metaphor? *Journal of Teacher Education, 48*(3), 177–184.

Purpel, D. (1989). *The moral and spiritual crisis in education: A curriculum for justice and compassion in education.* South Hadley, MA: Bergin and Garvey Publishers.

Reed, A., and Bergemann, V. (1995). *In the classroom: An introduction to education* (2nd ed.). Guilford, CT: Dushkin Publishing Group.

Rodriguez, F. (1997). *Affirming equity: A framework for teachers and schools* (2nd ed.). Dubuque: Kendall/Hunt.

Sleeter, C., and Grant, C. (1999). *Making choices for multicultural education: Five approaches to race, class and gender* (3rd ed.). Upper Saddle River, NJ: Prentice Hall.

chapter 11

We Speak in Many Tongues

Language Diversity and Multicultural Education

Sonia Nieto

The United States is becoming a more multilingual nation than ever, if not in policy, at least in practice. The number of immigrants entering the United States during the 1970s and 1980s was among the largest in history. Between 1981 and 1990 alone, over 7,300,000 people immigrated to the United States legally, increasing immigration by 63% over the previous decade (U.S. Bureau of the Census 1994). The new immigrants of 1990 equaled in numbers those of the peak immigration decade in U.S. history, 1900 to 1910 (Portes and Rumbaut 1996), although the percentage was much smaller (14.7%, compared with 7.9% in 1990). Unlike previous immigrants who were overwhelmingly from Europe, about one-third of the newest immigrants were from Asia and another third from Latin America (U.S. Immigration and Naturalization Service 1995). The growing immigration has resulted in a concomitant increase in the number of people who speak a native language other than English: according to the 1990 Census, almost 32 million people speak a language other than English at home, with almost half of those speaking Spanish. Not coincidentally, the total number of people claiming to speak a language other than English increased from 23 million (11%) in 1980 to almost 32 million (14%) in 1990 (Portes and Rumbaut 1996).

Notwithstanding the widespread perspective that English is the sole language of communication in our society, U.S. classrooms, communities, and workplaces are very linguistically diverse. For example, of the nearly

46,000,000 students in public and private schools in the United States, over 3,000,000 (7.4%) are limited in their English proficiency (Macías 1998). Language minority students are no longer confined to large urban school systems but are also found in small town, suburban, and rural schools throughout the nation. This means that all teachers, not just those who specialize in bilingual and ESL education, need to be prepared to teach students of diverse language backgrounds.

The purpose of this chapter is to propose productive ways that teachers and schools can approach linguistic diversity so that they can teach language minority students to high levels of achievement. Rather than continuing to view linguistic diversity as a problem to be corrected, teachers can learn to think of it as an asset for classrooms and society in general. For that reason, I focus on the importance of native and second language development, and on strategies that all teachers—not simply those who specialize in the education of language minority students—can use to teach them effectively.

Language Diversity and Multicultural Education: Expanding the Framework

To understand language diversity in a comprehensive and positive way, we need to reconceptualize how we view it. This reconceptualization includes:

- perceiving language diversity as a resource rather than as a deficit.
- understanding the key role that language discrimination has played in U.S. educational history.
- placing language diversity within a multicultural education framework and redefining the benefits of linguistic diversity for all students.
- understanding the crucial role of native language development in school achievement.
- making the education of language minority students the responsibility of *all teachers*.

Viewing Bilingualism as a Resource

In the United States, we have generally been socialized to think of language diversity as a negative rather than positive condition (Crawford 1992). Yet in most other countries in the world, bilingualism and multilingualism are the order of the day. The prestige accorded to language diversity is a highly complex issue that depends on many factors: the country in question, the region of the country one resides in, the language variety spoken, where and when one has learned to speak specific languages, and of course, the race, ethnicity, and class of the speaker. Sometimes bilingualism is highly valued. This is usually the case with those who are formally educated and have status and power in society. At other times, bilingualism is seen as a sign of low status. This is usually the case with those who are poor and powerless within their society, even if they happen to speak a multitude of languages (Fairclough 1989; Phillipson 1992; Corson 1993). It is evident that issues of status and power must be taken into account in reconceptualizing language diversity. This means developing an awareness that privilege, ethnocentrism, and racism are at the core of policies and practices that limit the use of languages other than officially recognized high-status languages allowed in schools and in the society in general. When particular languages are prohibited or denigrated, the voices of those who speak them are silenced and rejected as well.

English is the language of power in the United States. For those who speak it as a native language—especially if they are also at least middle class and have access to formal education—monolingualism is an asset. At times, bilingualism is considered an asset, but commonly only in the case of those who are native English speakers and have learned another language as a *second* language. Those who speak a native language associated with low prestige and limited power—especially if they do not speak English well, or speak it with an accent—are often regarded as deficient. The *kind* of accent one has is also critical. Speaking French with a Parisian accent, for example, may be regarded as a mark of high status in some parts of the country, while speaking Canadian French or Haitian Creole usually is not. Likewise, speaking Castilian Spanish is regarded more positively than speaking Latin American or Caribbean Spanish, which are generally viewed in our society as inferior varieties of the Spanish language.

For some people, then, bilingualism is perceived to be a handicap. This is usually the case with Latino, American Indian, Asian, and other Caribbean students, those who are also the majority of the language-minority students in our classrooms. Linguistically, there is nothing wrong with the languages they speak; for purposes of communication, one language is as valid as any other. But socially and politically, the languages spoken by most language minority students in the United States are accorded low status. Students who speak these languages are perceived to have a problem, and the problem is defined as fluency in a language other than English. In this case, the major purpose of education becomes the elimination of all signs of the native language. Even well-meaning educators may perceive their students' fluency in another language as a handicap to their learning English.

Developing an Awareness of Linguicism

U.S. educational history is replete with examples of language discrimination or what Tove Skutnabb-Kangas (1988) has called *linguicism*. Specifically, she defines linguicism as "ideologies and structures that are used to legitimate, effectuate, and reproduce an unequal division of power and resources (both material and nonmaterial) between groups that are defined on the basis of language" (p. 13). Entire communities, starting with American Indian nations and enslaved African Americans, have been denied the use of their native languages for either communication or education. This is evident in policies that forbid the use of other languages in schools as well as in the lack of equal educational opportunity for youngsters who cannot understand the language of instruction (Crawford 1992; Cummins 1996; Spring 1997). While linguicism has been particularly evident in racially and economically oppressed communities, it has not been limited to these groups historically, but has in fact been a widespread policy with all languages other than English in our society. The massive obliteration of the German language is a case in point. German was almost on a par with English as a language of communication during the 18th and 19th centuries, and was one of the most common languages used in bilingual programs during parts of our history. But the use of German as a language of instruction was effectively terminated by xenophobic policies immediately prior to and after World War I (Crawford 1992).

The tremendous pressures to conform to an English-only environment meant that giving up one's native language, although a terrible sacrifice, was accepted as a necessary and inevitable price to pay for the benefits of U.S. citizenship. Educators by and large accepted as one of their primary responsibilities the language assimilation of their students. Even today, it is not uncommon to hear of children punished for speaking their native language, or of notes sent home to parents who barely speak English that ask them not to speak their native language with their children. While today there is more of an awareness of the ethnocentrism of such practices, the fact that they continue to exist is an indication of an ingrained reluctance to perceive language diversity in positive terms. In developing a more accurate understanding of language diversity, it is critical to review how language discrimination has been used to disempower those who speak languages other than English. One implication of this understanding is that language diversity needs to be viewed using the lens of educational equity. That is, it is not simply a question of language difference, but rather of power difference. As such, language diversity is a key part of a multicultural education framework.

The Role of Linguistic Diversity in Multicultural Education

Expanding the framework for language diversity means redefining it as part of multicultural education. Just as race, class, and gender are usually considered integral to multicultural education, language diversity— although it does not fit neatly into any of these categories—should also be taken into account. One of the primary goals of multicultural education is to build on the strengths that students bring to school, but even in multicultural education, language diversity is not always considered an asset.

Currently, the most enlightened and inclusive frameworks for multicultural education consider the significance of language differences (Banks and Banks 1995; Macedo and Bartolomé 1999), but this was not always the case. While it is true that most language minority students in United States schools are also from racial minority and poor backgrounds, language issues cannot be relegated to either racial or class distinctions alone. Language diversity in and of itself needs to be considered an important difference.

The failure of some supporters of multicultural education to seriously consider linguistic diversity, and the inclination of those in bilingual education to view multicultural education simply as a watering down of bilingual and ethnic studies programs, leads to an artificial separation. This separation often results in the perception that multicultural education is for African American and other students of color who speak English, while bilingual education is only for Latino and other students who speak a language other than English as their native language. These perceptions are reinforced by the fact that each of these fields has its own organizations, publications, conferences, political and research agendas, and networks. This kind of specialization is both necessary and desirable because the concerns of each field are sometimes unique. But the implication that bilingual and multicultural education are fundamentally different and unconnected domains denies their common historical roots and complementary goals. As a result, proponents of bilingual and multicultural education sometimes see one another as enemies with distinct objectives and agendas. Ignorance and hostility may arise, with each scrambling for limited resources

Language is one of the most salient aspects of culture. Hence, the education of language minority students is part and parcel of multicultural education. The fields of bilingual and multicultural education are inextricably connected, both historically and functionally. If the languages students speak, with all their attendant social meanings and affirmations, are either negated or relegated to a secondary position in their schooling, the possibility of school failure is increased. Because language and culture are intimately connected, and because both bilingual and multicultural approaches seek to involve and empower the most vulnerable students in our schools, it is essential that their natural links be fostered.

Native Language and School Achievement

Effective teaching is based on the fact that learning builds on prior knowledge and experiences. But in the case of language minority students, we seem to forget this fact as schools regularly rob students of access to their prior learning through languages other than English. That this process contradicts how learning takes place and the crucial role of language is well articulated by Jim Cummins (1996), who maintains that "there is general agreement among cognitive psychologists that we learn by integrating new input into our existing cognitive structures or schemata. Our prior experience provides the foundation for interpreting new information. No learner is a blank slate" (p. 17).

When teachers and schools disregard language minority students' native languages and cultures, it is generally for what they believe to be good reasons. Schools often link students' English-language proficiency with their prospective economic and social mobility: that is, students who speak a language other than English are viewed as "handicapped" and they are urged, through subtle and direct means, to abandon their native language. The schools ask parents to speak English to their children at home, they punish children for using their native language, or they simply withhold education until the children have learned English sufficiently well, usually in the name of protecting students' futures. The negative impact of these strategies on language minority students is incalculable. For instance, in her research concerning factors that promoted or impeded academic success for Mexican-descent students in a California high school, Margaret Gibson (1995) found that the school environment stressed English-language monolingualism as a goal, in the process overlooking the benefits of bilingualism. Rather than focus on the native language abilities of students, teachers encouraged them to speak English as much as possible to the exclusion of Spanish. Gibson defined this perception on the part of teachers as "English only attitudes" (Gibson 1995). David Corson (1993) has suggested that when these kinds of attitudes prevail, students quickly pick up disempowering messages: "The members of some social groups, as a result, come to believe that their educational failure, rather than coming from their lowly esteemed social or cultural status, results from their natural inability: their lack of giftedness" (p. 11).

It is sometimes tempting to point to strategies such as English immersion programs as the solution to the educational problems of language minority students. But the lack of English skills alone cannot explain the poor academic achievement of language minority students. Equating English language acquisition with academic achievement is simplistic at best. For example, a large-scale study of the academic achievement of Mexican American and Puerto Rican students of varying English-language abilities concluded that contrary to the conventional wisdom, Spanish was *not* an impediment to achievement. On the contrary, the researchers found that in some cases, *better English proficiency meant lower academic performance* (Adams et al. 1994). In this case, the researchers theorized that peer pressure mitigated the traditional relationship between English proficiency and academic performance.

In contrast to negative perceptions of bilingualism, a good deal of research confirms the positive influence of knowing another language. Native language maintenance can act as a buffer against academic failure by promoting literacy in children's most developed language. This was the conclusion reached by researchers studying the case of Black English, also called *Ebonics* or *Black dialect*: dialect-speaking four-year olds enrolled in a Head Start program were able to recall more details with greater accuracy when they retold stories in their cultural dialect rather than in standard English (Williams 1991). Lourdes Díaz Soto's (1997) research concerning Hispanic families of young children with low and high academic achievement found that parents of the higher achieving children provided native-language home environments more often than did the parents of the lower achieving youngsters. Likewise, Patricia Gándara (1995), in analyzing the impressive academic achievements of Mexican American adults who grew up in poverty, found that only 16% of them came from homes where English was the primary language. The largest percentage of these successful adults grew up in households where *only* Spanish was spoken, and a remarkable two-thirds of them began school speaking *only* Spanish. A similar finding was reported by Ana Celia Zentella (1997) in a study of Puerto Rican families in El Barrio, a low-income community in New York City. She found that the most successful students were enrolled in bilingual programs and they were also the most fluent bilinguals. Moreover, in their review of several research studies concerning the adaptation and school achievement of immigrants of various backgrounds, Alejandro Portes and Rubén Rumbaut (1996) came to a striking conclusion: *students with limited bilingualism are far more likely to leave school than those fluent in both languages.* Rather than an impediment to academic achievement, bilingualism can actually promote learning.

Conclusions such as these contradict the common advice given to language minority parents to "speak English with your children at home." Challenging the prevailing wisdom of this advice, Virginia Collier (1995) has suggested that speaking English only at home among students who are more proficient in another language can slow down cognitive development because it is only when parents and their children speak the language they know best that they are working at their "level of cognitive maturity" (p. 14). Catherine Snow (1997), another respected researcher in literacy and language acquisition, agrees, stating that "the greatest contribution immigrant parents can make to their children's success is to ensure they maintain fluency and continue to develop the home language" (p. 29).

The major problem facing language minority children has often been articulated as one of not knowing English. But the real problem may be what Luis Moll (1992, p. 20) has labeled the "obsession with speaking English," as if learning English would solve all the other dilemmas faced by language minority students, including poverty, racism, poorly financed schools, and the lack of access to excellent education. Rather than supporting the suppression or elimination of native language use at home and school, the research reviewed here supports developing and maintaining native language literacy. If this is the case, then the language dominance of students is not the real issue; rather, *the way in which teachers and schools view students' language may have an even greater influence on their achievement.*

Articulating the issue of the education of language minority students in this way leads to the conclusion that language diversity must be placed within a *sociopolitical context*. That is, more consequential than language difference itself are questions of how language diversity and language use are perceived by schools, and whether or not modifications are made in the curriculum. The prevailing view that bilingualism is a deficit for language minority students but an asset for students from wealthy and privileged backgrounds has to do *not* with the relative merits of the different languages involved, but with the sociopolitical context of education. For example, it is not unusual to find in the same high school the seemingly incongruous situation of one group of students having their native language wiped out while another group of students struggles to learn a foreign language in a contrived and artificial setting. There are more affirming approaches to teaching language minority students, and they need to be used more widely than is currently the case.

Approaches to Teaching Language Minority Students

In the United States, most of the pedagogical approaches currently used with students who speak a language other than English are compensatory in nature. That is, they are premised on the assumption that language diversity is an illness that needs to be cured. As a result, traditional approaches emphasize using the native language as little as possible, if at all, and then only as a bridge to English. When English is learned sufficiently well, the reasoning goes, the bridge can be burned and the students are well on their way to achieving academic success.

There are several problems with this reasoning. First, a compensatory approach assumes that students are only *lacking* in something, rather than that they also possess certain skills and talents. Instead of perceiving fluency in another language as an asset to be cherished, it is seen as something that needs repair. In many schools, using native language literacy as a basis for English language development is not considered a viable option. As a result, students are expected to start their education all over again. Not only do they flounder in English, but they often forget their native language in the process. Even when language minority students are in bilingual programs where their native language is used as a medium of instruction, they are frequently removed too quickly and end up in special education classes (Cummins 1984).

The most common approaches to teaching language minority students in the past quarter century have been ESL (English as a Second Language) and bilingual education, the latter being far more controversial than the former. In spite of the controversy surrounding it, bilingual education and other programs that support native-language use, even if only as a transition to English, are generally more effective than programs such as ESL alone. This is true not only in terms of learning content in the native language, but in learning English as well. This seeming contradiction can be understood if one considers the fact that students in bilingual programs are provided with continued education in content areas along with structured instruction in English. In addition, these programs build on students' previous literacy so that it becomes what W. E. Lambert (1975) has called an *additive* form of bilingual education. *Subtractive* bilingual education, on the other hand, frequently occurs when one language is substituted for another; as a result, true literacy is not achieved in either. This may happen in programs where the students' native language is eliminated and English grammar, phonics, and other language features are taught out of context with the way in which real day-to-day language is used.

There is a substantial relationship between bilingual education and equity. That is, bilingual education is viewed by many language-minority communities as vital to the educational achievement of their children. Although frequently addressed as simply an issue of language, it can be argued that bilingual education is a civil rights issue because it is the only guarantee that children who do not speak English will be provided education in a language they understand. Without it, millions of children may be doomed to educational underachievement and limited occupational choices in the future.

This connection was recognized by the U.S. Supreme Court in 1974. Plaintiffs representing 1,800 Chinese-speaking students sued the San Francisco Unified School District in 1969 for failing to provide students who did not speak English with an equal chance to learn. They lost their case in San Francisco, but by 1974 they had taken it all the way to the Supreme Court. In the landmark *Lau v. Nichols* case, the Court ruled unanimously that the civil rights of students who did not understand the language of instruction were indeed being violated. The Court stated, in part: "There is no equality of treatment merely by providing students with the same facilities, textbooks, teachers, and curriculum; for students who do not understand English are effectively foreclosed from any meaningful education" (*Lau v. Nichols*, 414, U.S. 563, 1974).

Although the decision did not impose any particular remedy, its results were immediate and extensive. By 1975, the Office for Civil Rights and the Department of Health, Education, and Welfare issued a document called "The *Lau* Remedies," which then served as the basis for providing school systems with guidance in identifying students with a limited proficiency in English, assessing their language abilities, and providing appropriate programs. Bilingual programs have been the common remedy in many school systems.

There are numerous program models and definitions of bilingual education (Ovando and Collier 1998), but in general terms, bilingual education can be defined as *an educational program that involves the use of two languages of instruction at some point in a student's school career*. This definition is broad enough to include many program variations. A primary objective of all bilingual programs is to develop proficiency and literacy in the English language. ESL is an integral and necessary component of all bilingual programs, but when provided in isolation, it is not bilingual education because the child's native language is not used in instruction. While they are learning to communicate in English, students in ESL programs may be languishing in their other subject areas because they do not understand the language of instruction.

Probably the most common model of bilingual education in the United States is the *transitional bilingual education* approach. In this approach, students are taught content area instruction in their native language while also learning English as a second language. As soon as they are thought to be ready to benefit from the monolingual English-language curriculum, they are "exited" or "mainstreamed" out of the program. The rationale behind this model is that native-language services should serve only as a transition to English. Therefore, there is a limit on the time a student may be in a bilingual program, usually three years. *Developmental* or *maintenance bilingual education* is a more comprehensive and long-term model. As in the transitional approach, students receive content area instruction in their native language while learning English as a second language. The difference is that generally no limit is set on the time students can be in the program. The objective is to develop fluency in both languages by using both for instruction.

Two-way bilingual education (Christian 1994) is a program model that integrates students whose native language is English with students for whom English is a second language. Two-way bilingual programs validate both languages of instruction, and their primary goals are to develop bilingual proficiency, academic achievement, and positive cross-cultural attitudes and behaviors among all students. Students in these programs not only learn through two languages, but they also learn to appreciate the language and culture of others, and to empathize with their peers in the difficult process of developing fluency in a language not their own (Christian et al. 1997). This approach lends itself to cooperative learning and peer tutoring, and it holds the promise of expanding our nation's linguistic resources and improving relationships between majority and minority language groups.

What Works With Language Minority Students?

Research concerning the most effective programs for language minority students points to the benefits of native language development. Students generally need between five and seven years to make a successful transition from their native language to English (Cummins 1981; Thomas and Collier 1997). But because bilingual education, and especially native-language instruction, challenges the assimilationist nature of education in our society, it has been the most controversial program. Ironically, when students fail to achieve after being removed from bilingual programs too early, the blame is placed on bilingual programs, rather than on their premature exit from those very programs that could have helped them.

The fact is that bilingual education has generally been found to be more effective than other programs such as ESL alone, even for English language development. This finding has been reiterated in many studies over the years, most recently in a 1998 summary of research conducted by the Center for Research on Education, Diversity, and Excellence (National Association for Bilingual Education 1998). Even in the anti-bilingual climate of California in 1998, surprising results were found: achievement test scores from San Francisco and San Jose found that students who completed bilingual education generally performed better than native English-speaking children in reading, math, language, and spelling (Asimov 1998). Many of the gains were impressive. This situation was reported just one month after the passage of Proposition 227, which virtually outlawed the use of bilingual education in the state.

Research by Wayne Thomas and Virginia Collier (1997) has confirmed once again the benefits of bilingual education. In a comprehensive investigation of the records of 700,000 language minority students in five large school systems from 1982 to 1996, the researchers found that language minority students who received bilingual education finished their schooling with average scores that reached or exceeded the 50th national percentile in all content areas. In contrast, language minority students who received even well-implemented ESL-pullout instruction—a very common program type—typically finished school, if they graduated at all, with average scores between the 10th and 18th national percentiles. Thomas and Collier also found that two-way developmental bilingual education was the most successful program model of all. Unfortunately, this is the least common program model in the United States.

Bilingual programs also may have secondary salutary effects, such as motivating students to remain in school rather than dropping out, making school more meaningful, and in general making the school experience more enjoyable. A related phenomenon is that bilingual education may reinforce close relationships among children and their family members, promoting more communication than would be the case if they were instructed solely in English and lost their native language. This is what Lily Wong Fillmore (1991) found through interviews with immigrant parents when their preschool children were placed in English-only settings. Not only did the children lose their first language, but more significantly, they lost the ability to communicate with their parents and families. In the process, they also lost the academic advantage that fluency and literacy in a language would give them when they begin school.

In my own research with academically successful students (Nieto 2000a), I found that maintaining language and culture were essential in supporting and sustaining academic achievement. In a series of in-depth interviews with linguistically and culturally diverse students, one of the salient features that accounted for school success was a strong-willed determination to hold onto their culture and native language. Although their pride in culture and language was not without conflict, the steadfastness with which they maintained their culture and language in spite of widespread negative messages about them was surprising.

An intriguing conclusion from research on the importance of language and culture on academic achievement is that cultural and linguistic maintenance seem to have a positive impact on academic success. This is obviously not true in all cases, and it cannot be overstated. But the benefits of cultural and linguistic maintenance challenge the "melting pot" ideology that has dominated U.S. schools and society throughout the last century. We can even say that when their language and culture are reinforced both at home and school, students seem to develop less confusion and ambiguity about their ability to learn. Regardless of the sometimes harsh attacks on their culture and language—as is the case in communities that have strident campaigns to pass English-only legislation—students whose language and culture are valued in the school setting pick up affirming messages about their worth. The notion that assimilation is a necessary prerequisite for success in school and society is severely tested by current research.

In spite of the evidence that some form of bilingual education is most effective for teaching language minority students, most students who could benefit are not in such programs. This is due to both political and pragmatic considerations. For one, in many school systems, there are not enough trained teachers for such programs. In addition, the numbers of students who speak the same language is generally too small to require an entire program. Furthermore, the segregation that bilingual education presupposes poses a genuine dilemma. It is also true, however, that every bilingual program has numerous opportunities for integrating students more meaningfully than is currently the case. Moreover, the bilingual program can be more structurally integrated into the school instead of separated in a wing of the building so that teachers from both bilingual and nonbilingual classrooms can work on collaborative projects with their students. This kind of collaboration does not happen often enough. Besides being physically separated from other teachers—often in the basement, an apt metaphor (Nieto 2000b)—bilingual teachers bear the burden of the "bilingual" label in the same way as their students: They may be seen as less intelligent, less academically prepared, and less able than nonbilingual teachers—this in spite of the fact that they are usually fluent in two languages and have a wide range of pedagogical approaches for teaching a diverse student body. Because many bilingual teachers are from the same cultural and linguistic backgrounds as the students they teach, they bring a necessary element of diversity into the school. But many schools have not found a way to benefit from their presence.

Two-way bilingual programs provide another opportunity for integration and enhanced academic achievement for all students. For example, research on a Spanish–English two-way program in Cambridge, Massachusetts, found both groups of children progressing well in all subject matters and neither group declining in its native language development. Researchers also found that children at all grade levels selected their best friend without an ethnic or racial bias, that the self-esteem of children from both groups was enhanced, and that there was much less segregation than before the program—all worthy social and educational goals (Cazabon, Lambert, and Hall 1993). But two-way bilingual education is not always an option. This is because not all languages have the same appeal of Spanish, which is spoken in many places in the world, for English-speaking students and their families.

Other approaches for integrating students of diverse language backgrounds include setting aside times for joint instruction and developing bilingual options in desegregation plans and magnet schools. But much remains to be done in expanding options such as these. Perhaps the most noteworthy change that can take place is a shift in thinking so that bilingual classrooms, teachers, and students are seen as rich resources for nonbilingual classrooms, teachers, and students. When this shift happens, schools will have taken the first step in making bilingualism and even multilingualism central educational goals for all students. This is hardly the case right now. On the contrary, English language acquisition for language minority students is often pursued at the expense of native language development. Even for monolingual English students, the goal of bilingualism is an elusive one because foreign language courses are ineffective in that they are usually delayed until secondary school. But if language diversity were to become an option for all students, the low status and persistent underfunding of bilingual education might be eliminated.

Implications for Teaching Language Minority Students

The dramatic increase in the number of language minority students in our country in the past three decades means that every classroom in every city and town has already been or will soon be affected. The responsibility for educating language minority students can no longer fall only on those teachers who have been trained specifically to provide bilingual education and ESL services; this responsibility needs to be shared by *all* teachers and *all* schools. Yet most teachers have had little training in language acquisition and other language-related issues: even in bilingual classrooms, only 10% of teachers serving English language learners are certified in bilingual education (August and Hakuta 1998).

In what follows, I suggest a number of steps that all educators can take to more effectively educate language minority students. But first let me emphasize that while learning new approaches and techniques may be very helpful, *teaching language minority students successfully means above all changing one's attitudes towards the students, their languages and cultures, and their communities* (Cummins 1996; Nieto 1999). Having said this, however, there are necessary bodies of knowledge and approaches that all teachers need to develop if they are to be successful with the growing number of language minority students in our schools: (1) All teachers need to understand how language is learned. (2) Teachers need to develop an additive perspective concerning bilingualism. (3) Teachers and schools can learn to consciously foster native language literacy.

All Teachers Need to Understand How Language Is Learned

This includes both native and subsequent languages. For example, Stephen Krashen's (1981) theories of second language acquisition and his recommendations that teachers provide students for whom English is a second language with *comprehensible input* by including engaging and contextualized cues in their instruction is useful for all teachers who have language minority students in their classrooms. Likewise, related knowledge in curriculum and instruction, linguistics, sociology, and history are all critical for teachers of language minority students.

The following suggestions should be helpful for all teachers. (For a more detailed discussion, see Nieto, 2000b).

- first and second language acquisition.
- the sociocultural and sociopolitical context of education for language minority students.
- the history of immigration in the United States, with particular attention to language policies and practices throughout that history.
- the history and experiences of specific groups of people, especially those who are residents of the city, town, and state where they are teaching.
- the ability to adapt curriculum for students whose first language is other than English.
- competence in pedagogical approaches suitable for culturally and linguistically heterogeneous classrooms.
- experience with teachers of diverse backgrounds and the ability to develop collaborative relationships with colleagues that promote the learning of language minority students.
- the ability to communicate effectively with parents of diverse language, culture, and social class backgrounds.

Because many teachers have not had access to this kind of knowledge during their teacher preparation, they may need to acquire it on their own. They can do this by attending conferences in literacy, bilingual education, multicultural education, and ESL; participating in professional development opportunities in their district and beyond; subscribing to journals and newsletters in these fields; setting up study groups with colleagues to discuss and practice different strategies; and returning to graduate school to take relevant courses or seek advanced degrees.

Teachers Need to Develop an Additive Perspective Concerning Bilingualism

An additive perspective (Lambert 1975) is radically different from the traditional expectation that immigrants need to exchange their native language for their new language, English. The terrible psychic costs of abandoning one's native language, not to mention the concurrent loss of linguistic resources to the nation, is now being questioned. An additive bilingualism supports the notion that English *plus* other languages can make us stronger individually and as a society.

In their research, María Fránquiz and María de la luz Reyes (1998) set out to answer the question, "If I am not fluent in the languages my students speak, how can I effectively teach English language arts to a linguistically diverse class?" They found that teachers do not have to be fluent in the native languages of their students to support their use in the classroom. Rather, they discovered that encouraging students to use their native languages and cultural knowledge as resources for learning is frequently more important than knowing the students' languages. What does this mean in practice? In their research, Fránquiz and Reyes provide examples of teachers "who are not paralyzed by their own monolingualism" (p. 217). They document, for example, the positive results of teachers' acceptance of a range of language registers and codes, from standard to more colloquial forms of speech, and from monolingual to more mixed language speech. These language forms are often prohibited in classroom discourse, but allowing them to flourish is a way of using students' current knowledge to build future knowledge.

Teachers and Schools Can Learn to Consciously Foster Native Language Literacy

Teachers can actively support the native language literacy of their students by providing them the time and space to work with their peers, or with tutors or mentors, who speak the same native language. In her work with immigrant students, for instance, Cristina Igoa (1995) reserves the last period of the day three times a week for students to listen to stories or to read in their native languages. Because she does not speak all the languages of her students who come from numerous language backgrounds, she recruits college students who are fluent in various languages to help out.

Teachers can also make a commitment to learn at least one of the languages of their students. When they become second language learners, teachers develop a new appreciation for the struggles experienced by language minority students—including exhaustion, frustration, and withdrawal—when they are learning English. This was what happened to Bill Dunn, a doctoral student of mine and a veteran teacher who decided to "come out of the closet as a Spanish speaker" (Nieto 1999). He realized that, after teaching for 20 years in a largely Puerto Rican community, he understood a great deal of Spanish, so he decided to study it formally and to keep a journal of his experiences. Although he had always been a wonderful and caring teacher, putting himself in the place of his students helped him understand a great many things more clearly, from students' grammatical errors in English to their boredom and misbehavior when they could not understand the language of instruction.

The responsibility to create excellent learning environments for language minority students should not rest with individual teachers alone, however. Entire schools can develop such environments. Catherine Minicucci and her associates (1995) analyzed eight exemplary school reform efforts for language minority students and they found that all of the schools shared the following common characteristics, among others:

- They had a schoolwide vision of excellence that incorporated students of limited English proficiency.
- They created a community of learners engaged in active discovery.
- They designed programs to develop both the English and native-language skills of language minority students.
- They made a conscious effort to recruit and hire bilingual staff members.
- They communicated frequently with parents in their native languages.
- They honored the multicultural quality of the student population.

The researchers concluded that the success of schools with these attributes challenges the conventional assumption that students need to learn English *before* they can learn grade-level content in social studies, math, or anything else.

Conclusion

Language is one of the fundamental signs of our humanity. It is "the palette from which people color their lives and culture" (Allman 1990). Although linguistic diversity is a fact of life in American schools and society, many languages are not accorded the respect and visibility they deserve. But given recent trends in immigration, the shrinking of our world, and the subsequent necessity to learn to communicate with larger numbers of people, a reconceptualization of the role of languages other than English in our schools and society is in order. Given this kind of reconceptualization, current school policies and practices need to be reexamined. Those that build on students' diversity need to be strengthened, while those that focus on differences as deficits must be eliminated. This means, at the very least, that bilingual and multicultural programs for all students have to be comprehensively defined, adequately funded, and strongly supported.

The issue of what to do about language minority students goes much deeper than simple language diversity. Above all, it is an issue of educational equity. Whether bilingual education, ESL, or other approaches and support services are offered, they need to be developed with an eye toward promoting, rather than limiting, educational opportunities for all students. Given the increasing number of students who enter schools speaking a native language other than English, it is clear that attending to the unique condition of language minority students is the responsibility of all educators. For students with limited English proficiency, suitable approaches geared to their particular situation are not frills, but basic education. For English monolingual students, too, learning to appreciate and communicate in other languages is a gift to be cherished. When we approach language diversity as a resource that is respected and fostered, all students benefit.

References

Adams, D., Astone, B., Nuñez-Wormack, E., and Smodlaka, I. (1994). Predicting the academic achievement of Puerto Rican and Mexican-American ninth-grade students. *The Urban Review, 26*(1), 1–14.

Allman, W. F. (1990, November 5). The mother tongue. *U.S. News and World Report.*

Asimov, N. (1998, July 7). Bilingual surprise in state testing. *San Francisco Chronicle*, A1.

August, D., and Hakuta, K. (Eds.) (1998). *Educating language-minority children.* Commission on Behavioral and Social Sciences and Education, National Research Council, Institute of Medicine. Washington, DC: National Academy Press.

Banks, J. A., and Banks, C. A. M. (Eds.) (1995). *Handbook of research on multicultural education.* New York: Macmillan.

Cazabon, M., Lambert, W. E., and Hall, G. (1993). *Two-way bilingual education: A progress report on the Amigos Program.* Santa Cruz, CA: National Center for Research in Cultural Diversity and Second Language Learning.

Christian, D. (1994). *Two-way bilingual education: Students learning through two languages.* Santa Cruz, CA: National Center for Research on Cultural Diversity and Second Language Learning.

Christian, D., Montone, C., Lindholm, K. J., and Carranza, I. (1997). *Profiles in two-way immersion education.* McHenry, IL: Delta Systems.

Collier, V. P. (1995). *Promoting academic success for ESL students: Understanding second language acquisition at school.* Elizabeth, NJ: New Jersey Teachers of English to Speakers of Other Languages–Bilingual Educators.

Corson, D. (1993). *Language, minority education and gender: Linking social justice and power.* Clevedon, Eng.: Multilingual Matters.

Crawford, J. (1992). *Hold your tongue: Bilingualism and the politics of "English only."* Reading, MA: Addison-Wesley.

Cummins, J. (1981). The role of primary language development in promoting educational success for language minority students. In Office of Bilingual Bicultural Education, *Schooling and language minority students: A theoretical framework.* Sacramento, CA.: Evaluation, Dissemination, and Assessment Center, California State University, Los Angeles.

Cummins, J. (1984). *Bilingualism and special education.* Clevedon, Eng.: Multilingual Matters.

Cummins, J. (1996). *Negotiating identities: Education for empowerment in a diverse society.* Ontario: California Association for Bilingual Education.

Fairclough, N. (1989). *Language and power.* New York: Longman.

Fránquiz, M. E., and de la luz Reyes, M. (1998). Creating inclusive learning communities through English language arts: From *chanclas* to *canicas. Language Arts, 75*(3), 211–220.

Gándara, P. (1995). *Over the ivy walls: The educational mobility of low-income Chicanos.* Albany: State University of New York Press.

Gibson, M. A. (1995). Perspectives on acculturation and school performance. *Focus on Diversity* (Newsletter of the National Center for Research on Cultural Diversity and Second Language Learning), *5*(3), 8–10.

Igoa, C. (1995). *The inner world of the immigrant child.* New York: St. Martin's.

Krashen, S. (1981). *Second language acquisition and second language learning.* New York: Pergamon.

Lambert, W. E. (1975). Culture and language as factors in learning and education. In A. Wolfgang (Ed.), *Education of immigrant students.* Toronto: OISE.

Lau v. Nichols, 414 U.S. 563 (1974).

Macedo, D., and Bartolomé, L. I. (1999). *Dancing with bigotry: Beyond the politics of difference.* New York: St. Martin's.

Macías, R. R., et al. (1998). *Summary report of the survey of the states' limited English proficient students and available educational programs and services, 1996–97.* Washington, DC: National Clearinghouse of Bilingual Education.

Minicucci, C., Berman, P., McLaughlin, B., McLeod, B., Nelson, B. and Woodworth, K. (1995). School reform and student diversity. *Phi Delta Kappan, 77*(1), 77–80.

Moll, L. C. (1992). Bilingual classroom studies and community analysis: Some recent trends. *Educational Researcher, 21*(2), 20–24.

National Association for Bilingual Education. (1998, May 1). Findings of the Effectiveness of Bilingual Education. *NABE News, 5.*

Nieto, S. (1999). *The light in their eyes: Creating multicultural learning communities.* New York: Teachers College Press.

Nieto, S. (2000a). *Affirming diversity: The sociopolitical context of multicultural education* (3rd ed.). New York: Longman.

Nieto, S. (2000b). Bringing bilingual education out of the basement, and other imperatives for teacher education. In Z. Beykont (Ed.), *Lifting every voice: Pedagogy and politics of bilingual education* (pp. 187–207). Cambridge, MA: Harvard Education Publishing Group.

Ovando, C. J., and Collier, V. P. (1998). *Bilingual and ESL classrooms: Teaching in multicultural context* (2nd ed.). New York: McGraw-Hill..

Phillipson, R. (1992). *Linguistic imperialism.* Oxford, Eng.: Oxford University Press.

Portes, A., and Rumbaut, R. G. (1996). *Immigrant America: A portrait* (2nd ed.). Berkeley: University of California Press.

Skutnabb-Kangas, T. (1988). Multilingualism and the education of minority children. In T. Skutnabb-Kangas and J. Cummins (Eds.), *Minority language: From shame to struggle.* Clevedon, Eng.: Multilingual Matters, pp. 9–44.

Snow, C. (1997). The myths around bilingual education. *NABE News, 21*(2), 29.

Soto, L. D. (1997). *Language, culture, and power: Bilingual families and the struggle for quality education.* Albany: State University of New York Press.

Spring, J. (1997). *Deculturalization and the struggle for equality: A brief history of the education of dominated cultures in the United States* (2nd ed.). New York: McGraw-Hill.

Thomas, W. P., and Collier, V. P. (1997). *School effectiveness for language minority students.* Washington, DC: National Clearinghouse for Bilingual Education.

U.S. Bureau of the Census. (1994). *Statistical abstract of the United States* (114th ed). Washington, DC: U.S. Government Printing Office, p. 11.

U.S. Immigration and Naturalization Service. (1995). *Statistical yearbook of the immigration and naturalization service.* Washington, DC: U.S. Government Printing Office.

Williams, S. W. (1991). Classroom use of African American Language: Educational tool or social weapon? In C. E. Sleeter (Ed.), *Empowerment through multicultural education* (pp. 199–215). Albany: State University of New York Press.

Wong Fillmore, L. (1991). When learning a second language means losing the first. *Early Childhood Research Quarterly, 6,* 323–346.

Zentella, Ana Celia (1997). *Growing up bilingual: Puerto Rican children in New York.* Malden, MA: Blackwell.

chapter 12

Becoming a Cross-Cultural Teacher

Cherry A. McGee Banks

James Baldwin opens his riveting book, *The Price of the Ticket*, with the words, "My soul looks back and wonders how I got over." Baldwin's words reflect the opportunity and the challenge embedded in exploring self. For teachers, exploring self requires that they engage in the difficult process of making explicit how their values, beliefs, and other subjective understandings influence their teaching. Insights gained during the process of exploring self can help teachers gain a more complete understanding of themselves and help them better understand others who are different from them. Those insights and understandings can serve as a foundation for becoming a cross-cultural teacher.

In a pluralistic society, teachers not only need to help students acquire academic skills and subject-matter knowledge, they also need to help students become multiculturally literate. Students who are multiculturally literate have the skills, knowledge, and commitment to participate in personal, social, and civic action to make our society more democratic and just. Multiculturally literate students take their responsibility as citizens in a pluralistic democratic society seriously. They are, for example, able to recognize the complex ways in which structural inequality continues to exist in U.S. society and are prepared to respond to discrimination in U.S. society and in their schools with thoughtful and responsible social action

(Banks and Banks 1989). To help students become multiculturally literate, teachers have to be cross-culturally competent.

In this chapter, I discuss how teachers can begin the process of becoming cross-culturally competent by completing a three-step process at the end of this chapter. I also discuss how their values and communication styles can influence their interactions with others. Teachers are encouraged to critically reflect on their multicultural knowledge and skills and to use insights on their values and beliefs as a concrete departure point for exploring the meaning and power of culture in their lives. Insights revealed during those reflections can help teachers gain a better understanding of how they, in Baldwin's words, "got over." The process can also help teachers recognize the extent to which subjectivities are embedded in their teaching and reveal the extent to which their interactions with students are influenced by their values and beliefs.

The Changing Character of Ethnic Diversity in U.S. Society

Teachers need to be aware of the demographic changes occurring in the United States. The students they teach will live and work in a society that is much more ethnically and racially diverse than that of their parents. They will have more opportunity to interact with people who are ethnically and racially different from themselves. They will also face the challenges of actualizing democratic values in a pluralistic society. Additionally, teachers and students will need to be prepared to respond to the new meanings that will, over time, become associated with race and ethnicity as those concepts become more blurred and complex than they are today.

The ethnic and racial texture of U.S. society is deepening. When the 20th century began, Whites composed 87% of the U.S. population. However, by the end of the century, Whites composed less than 75% of the population. Between 1980 and 1998, the minority population in the United States increased 63% compared to an 8% increase for non-Hispanic Whites. In 1998, the combined population of African Americans, American Indians, Hispanics, and Asian Americans, which was estimated at 74.9 million people, was larger than the population of Great Britain, France, Italy, or Spain. If combined into one country, the population of the four largest minority groups in the United States would represent the 15th largest country in the world. The increase in the number of people of color in the United States represents a significant change in the U.S. population (Pollard and O'Hare 1999).

In addition to a change in the number of minorities in the United States, the make-up of the minority population is also changing. At the beginning of the 20th century, 9 out of every 10 minorities in the United

States were African American. By the end of the century, the Black share of the minority population had dropped to less than one half and was continuing to decline (Pollard and O'Hare 1999). During that same time period, the Hispanic share of the minority population increased. In 1998, Hispanics were the second largest U.S. minority group, with a population of 30 million people. They are expected to exceed African Americans by 2025 (Pollard and O'Hare 1999).

Another change in the make-up of the U.S. population is an increase in the number of interracial people. Even though marriage between people of different races is still an exception, interracial marriage is increasing. Between 1970 and 1998, the number of interracial marriages rose from 300,000 to 1.4 million (U.S. Bureau of the Census 1998). With an increase in interracial marriages there has also been an increase in the number of interracial children. Between 1977 and 1997, the number of babies born to interracial couples increased from less than 2% of the total U.S. births to about 5%. In 1997, interracial births were the third largest racial or ethnic category of U.S. births. In California, the number of interracial births surpassed that of Asian, Black, and American Indian births. Of all the ethnic and racial groups, interracial births were highest for American Indians. Approximately 50% of American Indians born in 1997 were interracial. About 20% of births to Asian women and 5% of births to African American women were interracial (Pollard and O'Hare 1999)

Tremendous diversity also exists within ethnic and racial groups. Differences within ethnic and racial groups are referred to as intragroup differences. Lifestyle, economic well-being, educational achievement, political participation, and other social class differences are frequently masked by race and ethnicity. Intragroup diversity challenges teachers to hold information about cultural factors, learning styles, and other such characteristics tentatively and not assume all members of an ethnic or racial group share a common experience.

Ultimately, teachers have to relate to individuals, not to generalized groups. When too much attention is focused on group norms, there is a risk of losing sight of the individual and viewing the individual as part of a monolithic group. Responding to individual members of an ethnic group based on a composite and often stereotypic picture of the group can lead to misunderstandings. It is unproductive and a misapplication of the concept of culture to assume that all members of a social group are culturally homogeneous. Such assumptions can, for example, cause teachers to perceive students as stereotypic representations of their ethnic group rather than as individuals with unique characteristics. The misuse of the concept of culture generally results from too little rather than too much information about ethnic cultures (Erickson 2000).

A sophisticated understanding of the relationship between individuals and their cultures requires in-depth study of the nature of ethnicity in

American society, the concept of race, and intragroup differences. Teachers who appreciate the limits of cultural knowledge as an explanation of individual behavior are able to increase their cross-cultural effectiveness by linking cultural-group knowledge to information about individual students. In that way, they maintain an awareness of the complexity of ethnic cultures and the diversity within them and the wide range of possible responses and combinations of responses given the personalities and characters of individual group members.

Helping Students Develop Cross-Cultural Competence

Even though the ethnic and racial texture of U.S. society is deepening, and U.S. society has made progress since the civil rights movement in reducing institutionalized discrimination and segregation, prejudice and discrimination continue to be factors in American life (Carnes 1999). Consequently, it is important for teachers to help students explore their attitudes, beliefs, and behaviors toward people who are different from them. All students can benefit from these experiences because prejudice has pronounced effects on prejudiced individuals as well as on its victims.

With intervention, individuals who have weak racial and ethnic biases are more likely to discard their negative beliefs and attitudes than people who have tenacious ones (Stephan 1999). For some people, prejudice has functional significance. Their attitudes and beliefs are often deep and highly resistant to change. Teachers should be aware of three processes that prejudiced individuals use to resist change: selective perception, avoidance, and group support (Allport 1954).

When using *selective perception*, individuals organize their view of the world in ways that reduce the probability that they will encounter information that isn't consistent with their point of view. Prejudiced individuals often use selective perception to dismiss positive information that does not confirm their stereotypic beliefs. Prejudiced individuals also tend to avoid information that contradicts their beliefs.

Avoidance can take many forms. A person who opposes multicultural education programs, for example, may be required to attend a lecture on a topic related to diversity. Even though he attends the lecture, he may refuse to accept the information presented, or may "hear" the speakers make controversial statements that other individuals in the audience do not hear.

Social groups reinforce our values, beliefs, and attitudes. By limiting most of their contacts to persons within their own ethnic and racial group, individuals are often able to avoid changing or examining their biased attitudes and beliefs. Social groups offer emotional support and a feeling of belonging. They can also reinforce beliefs and attitudes about outside ethnic and racial groups.

Once teachers become aware of the processes students use to maintain prejudices, they can select or design appropriate intervention strategies and activities. For some students, this could be the first time they have had an opportunity to thoughtfully reflect on their behaviors and attitudes.

There are a number of prejudice reduction strategies available for teachers to use. For example, teachers can present cases involving prejudiced attitudes and behaviors to students and ask them to discuss and propose solutions to them. Role playing can also be an effective technique for exploring prejudice and discrimination. It can help students gain insight into their personal behaviors and attitudes by providing an opportunity for them to explore the feelings and perspectives of individuals from different ethnic and racial groups. Sensitivity training can also help reduce prejudice if it is directed by a well-trained and skilled leader. This technique involves small-group discussions where members of the group are encouraged to candidly express their feelings and concerns.

Under carefully controlled circumstances, direct contact between members of racial and ethnic groups can help reduce prejudice. Allport (1954) states that three conditions must be met in order for contact between members of racial and ethnic groups to result in a reduction in prejudice. Direct contact should involve members of ethnic or racial groups who are of *equal status*. The contact situations should be *cooperative* not competitive. Lastly, the activities surrounding the groups coming together should be *sanctioned by authorities*.

Values in Teaching

Values are broad attitudes about right and wrong based on ethical ideals and beliefs (Jary and Jary 1991). Though often unnamed as such, they are present in schools and tend to perpetuate existing societal norms (Vogt 1997). Values are reflected in teaching philosophies, pedagogical methods, and conceptions of success and failure. Core classroom values, which frequently reflect teacher values, influence classroom climate as well as determine which behaviors are encouraged and discouraged.

Conflicts can occur in the classroom when there is a mismatch between student and teacher values. John, a second grade student, was sent to the principal's office after he repeatedly refused to call his teacher by her first name. He insisted on calling her Mrs. Jones. His teacher told the principal she had carefully explained to John that all the students at his new school called their teachers by their first names. She grew irritated with him when he refused to do so and sent him to the principal's office. She wasn't sure why John was being disobedient, but he was causing a disturbance in her classroom. The children were laughing at John and he looked as if he was going to cry. When the principal called John's mother, his mother explained that John had been taught to call all adults by their last name. She was surprised and disappointed that children were required to call their teachers by their first name. This is an example of a conflict between student and teacher values that took place in a middle-class, multiethnic school in the Western United States.

To prevent these kinds of conflicts, teachers must be prepared and willing to explore, question, and clarify their own values. In this way, they will be better prepared to identify and work on value conflicts that may occur between them and their students. Effective cross-cultural teachers should be prepared to help students acknowledge their values and live in ways that are congruent with them. Cross-cultural teachers realize that their values are their own and should not necessarily be forced on others.

Cross-Cultural Communication

Cross-cultural communication involves the process of exchanging information between individuals from different social groups who interpret symbols and behavior in similar ways. Cross-cultural communication doesn't just involve verbal communication. Most personal communication is nonverbal. It is estimated that about 65% of all face-to-face communication does not involve speech. Touching, physical space, voice tone and volume, gestures, and use of the eyes are some of the ways people communicate nonverbally. Each nonverbal behavior has specific and often diverse meanings in different cultures. Teachers who are unaware of what is appropriate and normative within other social groups may unwittingly use their own cultural norms as the standard for judging nonverbal behavior in cross-cultural contexts.

Problems can occur in communicating across cultures in the United States because even though Americans from different groups share many similarities in patterns of behavior, they have many subtle differences in the interpretation of behaviors. Lack of attention to nuances in behavior clues may mislead a teacher into believing that she is in complete communication with a student or a parent when she is not. Communication can break down abruptly and misunderstandings can occur when an individual behaves in a way that is quite acceptable in one social group and completely unacceptable in another (Delpit 1995).

It is very difficult for teachers to communicate effectively with students who do not interpret symbols and behaviors in the same way they do. Attempting to bridge the communication gap or to prove that one is culturally literate by using slang or an inaccurate form of a student's language or dialect may be considered patronizing or insulting to students and their parents.

The responsibility for establishing meaningful communication with students lies primarily with the teacher. Teachers cannot assume that just because they feel they are sincere, accepting, and empathetic their students perceive them in the same way. Their attitudes, beliefs, and values should be communicated to students in ways that can be understood within different cultural contexts. To communicate effectively, teachers must understand the dynamics of cross-cultural communication and use their knowledge to help direct their behavior.

Developing Multicultural Competencies

Cross-cultural teachers are multiculturally competent. They are able to work successfully with students from diverse populations and to help students from all groups acquire the skills, knowledge, and attitudes needed to function effectively in a pluralistic society. To become a cross-cultural teacher, teachers must have a clear understanding of how their values, beliefs, and other subjectivities influence their teaching. They also have to master an identifiable body of knowledge, skills, and attitudes that constitute critical attributes of multicultural teaching. Multicultural competencies are most effectively developed through formal instruction, reflection on life experiences, and opportunities to work with students and colleagues from diverse populations. Once the competencies are developed, they must be honed in an ongoing process of reflection, renewal, and growth.

Multicultural competencies do not exist in isolation of subject-matter and pedagogical knowledge. Academic and pedagogical knowledge are required as a foundation for teachers to develop multicultural competencies. Cross-cultural teachers draw on their disciplinary and pedagogical knowledge as they craft ways to frame and link that knowledge to their students' experiences, backgrounds, and interests.

Teachers who are willing to devote the time and energy necessary to reflect on their values and beliefs and acquire new skills, knowledge, and perspectives can increase their multicultural competency. Developing multicultural competency involves three processes: (1) self-examination, (2) insight and planning, and (3) completing and implementing your action plan. (See Figure 12.1.)

The plan of action is a personal one. It varies from individual to individual because each person's plan is based on his or her needs. It is open-ended and allows individuals to enter into the process at a level that is appropriate for them, work at their own speed, and build on their skills and knowledge as they acquire them. The three processes culminate in a personal growth plan.

Developing multicultural competence is challenging, time intensive, and requires commitment. Even though the process can be assigned to students as a course requirement, it is at heart a voluntary process. Teachers can enter and exit the process at will. Some teachers will choose not to

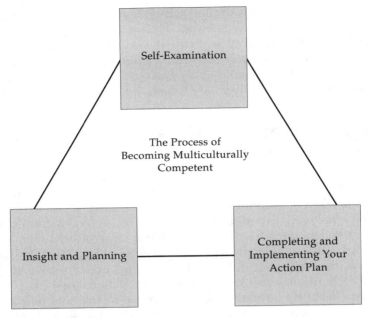

Figure 12.1
Developing Multicultural Competence

sincerely engage the process. They may, for example, find it difficult to see the importance of self-understanding and multicultural competence when they are immersed in competency-based, standards-oriented programs. However, even though everyone may not fully engage the process, it can serve as a foundation for future work.

The next three sections of this chapter are written directly to teachers and form a template for teachers to use to assess themselves, organize their activities, and plan the steps that they will need to take to increase their multicultural competence. Teachers are encouraged to insert themselves into the description below and visualize themselves as being in the process of becoming multiculturally literate.

Phase I. Self-Examination

Examining who you are and how you came to be the person you are today is a difficult task. It requires that you take a critical look at your ability to function as a cross-cultural teacher by asking hard questions and engaging in an honest search for answers. You will need to examine your personal background as well as your skills and knowledge of multicultural education.

Identify three colleagues you would like to work with as you engage this process. When you move to Phase II, you will need to get together with your colleagues and discuss your answers to the questions. Next, go to Table 12.1 and answer the questions. Record your answers in a notebook. As you answer the questions in Table 12.1, you may encounter concepts, theories, and scholars that are unfamiliar to you. Simply indicate that in your notebook. After you've answered the questions in Table 12.1, you will have a good sense of what you know as well as the gaps in your knowledge and skills. This part of the process can be daunting. You may be disappointed in your level of knowledge. However, it is important to remember that this is the first, not the last step in the process.

Phase II. Insight and Planning

When you enter this phase you should have completed all the questions in Table 12.1 and recorded your answers in your notebook. As a result of answering the questions, you should have an initial understanding of the skills, attitudes, and behaviors you need to work on. Contact the members of your group and arrange a time and place to meet and discuss the information in your notebook. When you meet, begin by sharing your responses to question 1. Allow each person in the group to respond to each question before moving to the next question. Compare and contrast your responses. Continue in that manner until you've discussed all the questions. Working together as a team, try to identify at least one resource that you will be able to turn to for additional information on each of the questions in Table 12.1. You will use that information in Phase III. It may take two to three sessions for you to discuss all the questions and identify resources.

Next, to get a broader view of your multicultural skills and knowledge, talk to students, parents, and colleagues at your school and let them know you are building your multicultural competency. Get their sense of how you are functioning with respect to diversity and find out if they have questions or concerns that you could help them with in your role as a cross-cultural teacher. Let them know that you will be gathering information and would be happy to share it with them. Record the information you gather in your notebook. This process will give you a better idea of how you can serve your school as well as some ideas on local resources and support. It will also let the school community know that you are concerned and available for help on diversity issues.

Review the information you gathered from your school community with your team of colleagues. After getting your team members' input, review all the information you've gathered: information from your school community as well as your answers to the questions in Table 12.1 and your list of resources. State in your own words what you believe you should know and be able to do to be an effective cross-cultural teacher in your school. Write your description in your notebook. This is your personal definition of cross-cultural teaching.

Make a list of all the things you can begin doing immediately to improve your ability to function as a cross-cultural teacher. For example,

Table 12.1
Assessing Your Multicultural Competences

The questions below are not intended to represent an exhaustive overview of multicultural knowledge. They can, however, serve as a departure point for thinking about your self awareness, knowledge and skills. Use these questions to generate new questions and new areas to explore.

1. **Self Awareness**
   a. Indicate the race, gender and social class of:
      - Most of your neighbors
      - Your doctor
      - Your dentist
      - The last five people who visited your home
      - Your best friend
      - Most of the people at the last social event you attended

      What insights can you draw about diversity in your life from your answers? Why do you think your profile has turned out as it did? What other questions would you add?
   b. Describe the first time you realized that there are many different races in the U.S.
   c. What did you learn about race, class, and gender in school?
   d. What did you learn about race, class, and gender from your parents and in your community when you were growing up?
   e. Over the years, what have you done to increase your multicultural awareness?
   f. Have you ever been a victim of discrimination? Describe the incidents.
   g. How would you describe your contact with and attitude and behaviors toward members of different ethnic, racial, gender, and social class groups?

2. **Knowledge**
   a. Language
      What languages and dialects are spoken by students in your school?
      What languages do you speak?
      In what ways can language empower as well as oppress individuals?
   b. Define and give examples of the concepts listed below. (This is not an exhaustive list).

• afrocentricity	• internment
• assimilation	• power
• colonialism	• prejudice
• discrimination	• racial conflict and riots
• ethnic self-help organizations	• racism
• ethnic group	• revolution
• exploration	• sexism
• immigration	• social class

   c. Discuss the work of the following theorists (this is not an exhaustive list).

• Gordon Allport	• Carl Grant
• James A. Banks	• Jacqueline Irvine
• Elizabeth Cohen	• Gloria Ladson-Billings
• Carlos E. Cortés	• Sonia Nieto
• Linda Darling-Hammond	• Valerie Ooka Pang
• Lisa Delpit	• Christine E. Sleeter
• Geneva Gay	• Janet Ward Schofield
• Carol Gilligan	• Robert E. Slavin

d. Can you discuss the histories and cultural characteristics of the following groups? Identify and discuss several key historical events and cultural characteristics for each of the groups. Discuss intragroup differences within each of the groups.
- African Americans—Identify the new immigrant groups from Africa
- Asian Americans—Identify the major groups in the U.S.
- European Americans—Identify several of the major groups in the U.S.
- Hispanics—Identify the major groups in the U.S.
- Native Americans—Identify several tribes

e. Structural Issues
Examine each item below and discuss how social class and gender equity may affect them.
- tracking
- assessment
- staffing
- school cimate

3. Skills
a. Construct an evaluation form and use it to evaluate the multicultural characteristics of the textbooks and trade books used in your clasroom.
b. Design a multicultural lesson that demonstrates how you could infuse multicultural content into the curriculum.
c. Design a lesson using cooperative learning.
d. Describe ways in which parents from diverse cultural backgrounds can be involved in schools.
e. Do the attitudes and behaviors of parents, students, teachers, or administrators have any implications for cross-cultural teaching?

4. Summary
a. Where are your informational gaps?
b. What would you like to know about ethnicity, race, gender, and social class in the United States?
c. Review some of your recent teaching experiences. How do you feel about the level of communication, empathy, and genuineness you were able to establish with your students from different racial and ethnic groups? Do you feel comfortable with your level of cross-cultural competence?

---

you might include such items as refusing to make assumptions about a student's background or ability based on the student's race or ethnic group. Next, list all the other goals you plan to work on along with the resources you will use to attain them. This list could include purchasing and reading books or taking courses or workshops on topics related to race, class, or gender at a local college or university. Rank your goals, placing those needing the least amount of work at the top of your list and those requiring the most work at the bottom. This is the first draft of your action plan.

Phase III. Completing and Implementing Your Action Plan

When you enter Phase III, you should be aware of what you need to do and how to do it. You will begin implementing your plan in this phase of the process. Changing behavior is not an easy task. Old behaviors are resistant to change because they are familiar and we are skilled in executing them. New behaviors are risky and unknown. It is reasonable to feel uncomfortable or afraid when trying new behaviors.

Begin the implementation process by carefully and thoughtfully reviewing the goals you identified in your notebook. On the outside of the notebook, write your definition of cross-cultural teaching. Use a separate page in your notebook for each of your goals. List your goal and state how you plan to achieve it. Start with your easiest goal on page one and work your way up to your most difficult goal. Each day do at least one thing to move you closer to achieving your goal. Record your activity in the notebook. Also note your reflections and insights on your actions and how they've affected your knowledge, attitudes, and effectiveness. Also note changes that friends, colleagues, and students mention they see in you and your work. After your program is underway, you may find that you need to reconceptualize, expand, or adjust parts of it.

Discuss what you are doing with colleagues who are interested in cross-cultural teaching. Some of your colleagues might like to participate in a similar program, and you may be able to start a group that can support its members as they engage the process of becoming cross-cultural teachers. You can also use this program when working with your students.

Cross-Cultural Teaching: A Process

Cross-cultural teachers are involved in a process of self-examination, education, and practice. They are attempting to increase their knowledge and to improve their ability to work more effectively with individuals from diverse ethnic and racial groups. They are aware of the impact of their behavior on their students and of their own issues in dealing with race and ethnicity. Their attempt to confront those issues helps them empathize and work more effectively with students who are confronting similar issues.

Cross-cultural teachers recognize the vast diversity of experiences, cultural forms, goals, perspectives, and realities that exist among and within U.S. ethnic groups. They feel comfortable with themselves and with individuals from diverse racial and ethnic groups. They are involved in a process that requires them to experience other cultures and to be open to those experiences. These attitudes and experiences equip them to be more effective teachers. By moving outside their own cultures, effective cross-cultural teachers are able to experience other cultures and learn how to function effectively in diverse cultural settings. Consequently, they are able to better understand their own culture and themselves. Becoming an effective cross-cultural teacher is an ongoing process, not a state of being. The ability to function cross-culturally and bring multicultural knowledge, skills, and perspectives to your classroom is personally and professionally enriching.

References

Allport, G. (1954). *The nature of prejudice*. Reading, MA: Addison-Wesley.

Baldwin, J. (1985). *The price of the ticket: Collected nonfiction 1948–1985*. New York: St. Martin's.

Banks, C. A. M., and Banks, J. A. (1989). Teaching for multicultural literacy. *Louisiana Social Studies Journal, 16*, 5–9.

Carnes, J. (Ed.). (1999). *Responding to hate at school*. Montgomery, AL: Teaching Tolerance.

Delpit, L. (1995). *Other people's children: Cultural conflict in the classroom*. New York: New Press.

Erickson, F. (2000). Culture in society and in educational practices. In J. A. Banks and C. A. M. Banks (Eds.), *Multicultural education: Issues and prospectives* (pp. 32–60). New York: John Wiley and Sons.

Jary, D., and Jary, J. (1991). *The HarperCollins dictionary of sociology*. New York: HarperCollins.

Pollard, K. M., and O'Hare, W. P. (1999). America's racial and ethnic minorities. *Population Bulletin, 54*(3), 3–13.

Stephan, W. (1999). *Reducing prejudice and stereotypes in schools*. New York: Teachers College Press.

U.S. Bureau of the Census. (1998). *Statistical abstract of the United States*. Washington, DC: U.S. Government Printing Office.

Vogt, W. P. (1997). *Tolerance and education: Learning to live with diversity and difference*. Thousand Oaks, CA: Sage.

chapter 13

The Role of the School in Deterring Prejudice

Ilene Allgood

Prejudice is pervasive and persistent. It exists in most people and it thrives in most institutions. Schools devoid of prejudice are rare yet attainable, and I would argue that only in prejudice-free environments can *all* students reach their maximum potential academically and socially. Unless schools address teachers' and students' biased attitudes, the learning process will suffer. School can be the place where prejudice is exacerbated or extinguished. Vigilance in deterring prejudice through the educational process is imperative because history has clearly shown us that silence and complacency allow the poison of prejudice to proliferate.

What Is Prejudice?

For the purposes of this chapter, prejudice is defined as an *attitude* one forms about others without first considering facts, history, or alternative perspectives prior to forming that attitude. In this manner, any judgments about or behaviors toward the object of the prejudice are based on preliminary, partial, or incorrect information: prejudgment. Without accurate information, we are left with half-truths, myths, or stereotypes on which to base our actions toward others. Prejudices can be embraced, denied, acted on, invisible to others, or even hidden from oneself. Since prejudices are attitudes, they can be private or made public. This choice depends on the *degree of acceptability* or conformity of a particular attitude in one's social structures (i.e., family, community, and society). Prejudices may be overt and intense, or dormant. Prejudices are simple, cognitively unsophisticated beliefs about our own group, other groups, or belief systems. They are what we think and how we feel and are the basis of how we act toward others. Prejudice is also systemic (i.e., pervasive within institutions) to the extent that schools still practice cultural imperialism and ethnic separatism (Banks 1994). All prejudices are insidious.

Where Do Prejudices Come From?

Several theories seek to explain why prejudices form and how they are perpetuated. Some are psychological, focused on the individual personality; others are sociological, focused on systematic explanations (Pate 1995). The research on prejudice indicates that searching for its causes is a first step in recognizing ways to eliminate it.

Prejudice has both psychological and sociological roots. One school of thought contends that prejudice is psychologically conditioned, largely predetermined by the human psyche (Adorno et al. 1982; Allport 1982; Barron 1953; Foley 1976; Plant, Telford, and Thomas 1965; Schaller, Boyd, and Yohannes 1995; Smithers and Lobley 1978). However, psychological remedies to address prejudice fail without consideration of the environmental or social factors that feed it. As a practical matter, prejudice cannot be easily modified on an individual level, nor are there any quick fixes to solve this complicated problem. The research on prejudice that explains it in social terms (as a result of cognitive conditioning) is more useful to the practitioner. (A fuller discussion of the causes of prejudice may be obtained from the research of Allport 1982; Rokeach 1960, 1973; Simpson and Yinger 1985; Stephan 1999; and Triandis 1971.) However, most researchers agree that prejudices are acquired through what we learn and what we are taught. This is why prejudice is stubbornly persistent.

The Relationship of Prejudice and Dogmatism

Another way to look at prejudice is as a cognitive entity—a way of thinking about others. Essentially, prejudice is an uncritical, nonreflective way of thinking, since it is the rendering of adverse judgments without critical examination.

Dogmatism may be looked at as an unsophisticated thought-processing aspect of prejudice. Dogmatism is defined as an inflexible, uncritical way of thinking (Rokeach 1960, 1972). It is a condition of closed-mindedness. Four decades of research studies have verified this strong correlation between prejudice and dogmatism (Adorno et al. 1982; Cotton 1993; Ehrlich 1978; Loria 1981; Martin and Morris 1982; Paul 1993; Richards and Gamache 1979; Rokeach 1960, 1972). High levels of dogmatic thinking are likely to indicate high levels of prejudice.

In the absence of critical analysis, a person can believe any assumptions. Uninformed assumptions made about groups of people and the individuals within the groups are called stereotypes. When a person rejects others based on these faulty assumptions, this rejection creates social schisms that are based on prejudice. But prejudice is complicated, and dogmatism is not the sole cause of prejudice. Rather, dogmatism can be a precursor of and provide impetus for prejudice (Adorno et al. 1982; Ehrlich 1978; Loria 1981; Richards and Gamache 1979; Rokeach 1960). When dogmatic thinking is prevalent in schools, this creates fertile ground on which prejudice may grow.

Academic and Cognitive Ramifications of Prejudice in Schools

Prejudice is difficult to quantify because of its various manifestations. Nevertheless, schools can measure the problems left in the wake of prejudice by examining lower academic achievement levels among disenfranchised minority students (Banks and Banks 1995; Bennett 1995; Diaz 1992; Palmer and Kalin 1991; Partenio 1985). Not only does prejudice obstruct the educational opportunities of students, but it also stifles their cognitive growth and impedes learning. Rokeach (1960) discovered that rigid thinkers performed significantly more poorly in analytical thinking than did nonrigid thinkers. Numerous other researchers have pointed out that dogmatism, the antithesis of cognitive flexibility, is the main barrier students face in acquiring transformative knowledge (Banks and Banks 1997; Dillon 1986; Kennedy 1991; Meyers 1986; Nichols and Stults 1985; Paul 1987, 1993; Symons et al. 1989). Moreover, there is evidence that dogmatism also has a negative effect on students' achievement levels in college (Martin, Grah, and Harris 1986). Conversely, a five-year longitudinal study disclosed that cognitive flexibility is directly related to greater college academic success (Goldman and Flake 1996).

Prejudice in teachers prevents transformative knowledge from being transmitted through the curriculum. Transformative knowledge is often transmitted when issues, concepts, and ideas are examined from various perspectives. Reevaluating existing knowledge paradigms is a common result of acquiring transformative knowledge.

Ramifications of Prejudice on Self-Esteem and Learning

Various complex dimensions of prejudice make it pernicious to its recipients. Prejudices may lead to unjustified actions directed toward others who are perceived as *different from* or *outside* the mainstream. Prejudices held by teachers will directly impact the academic achievement of their students. Prejudice may be transmitted to students in indirect ways.

For example, studies have demonstrated that when rigid attitudes are held about minority students' intellectual abilities, student performance will move in the direction of the teacher expectations, fostering a self-fulfilling prophecy (Cotton 1990; Eden 1992; Jones 1977). When teacher assertions are based on stereotypes of a group to which the student belongs, these faulty beliefs will ostracize students and directly impede their success in the classroom (Banks 1994, 1995; Bennett 1995; Goodlad 1984; Palmer and Kalin 1985; Partenio 1985; Rivilin and Fraser 1995; Sleeter 1985; Spencer, Carter and Steele 1993; Steele and Aronson 1995). Vital to this discussion is the fact that schools and teachers clearly affect, even control to some extent, the thinking patterns, attitudes, and behaviors of students in ways that can lead to a reduction in prejudging while improving their academic and social skills (Aviram 1987; Brophy 1983; Cooper and Tom 1984).

Ramifications of Prejudice on Students' Social Development

Not only does prejudice influence students' academic development adversely, but it hinders their social development as well. Studies have focused on this relationship between prejudiced thinking and students' attitudes toward their peers. For example, researchers found a significant difference between open-minded and closed-minded students in terms of the social distance (segregation) they maintained from others whom they perceived as outsiders. (Plant, Telford, and Thomas 1965). There is a tendency for rigid-thinkers to be more restrictive in their social interactions with those who differ from them culturally. (Rokeach 1960; Rosenfeld and Nauman 1969).

It appears that prejudiced people hold more negative attitudes toward others, and are also more likely to reject those who do not agree with their own perspectives of the dominant cultural norms (Ehrlich 1978). With U.S. schools becoming increasingly diverse along cultural, ethnic, and socioeconomic lines, some scholars argue that when prejudice prevails in school systems, students who differ from the majority culture of the school system are the ones most likely to be rejected or marginalized.

Prejudice and School Climate

School climates may be tolerant or intolerant of prejudice. If schools tolerate prejudice, there is an aspect of prejudice that makes it deleterious for everyone in the school setting: its preponderance to escalate. Left unchecked, prejudice tends to lead to active bigotry and hatred. This escalating nature of hatred can display itself in discrimination or acts of violence. When bigotry and hate rhetoric are expressed and given tacit approval on school campuses, alienation or violence may erupt (ADL 1997).

Discrimination

Discrimination is behavioral and involves action. Discrimination stemming from prejudice is a social problem and implies more than a benign making of distinctions. Racial discrimination involves behavior that is based on judgments devoid of critical consideration but is based on race (Flexner and Hauck 1987). Dr. Martin Luther King Jr., a champion in the battle against hatred and prejudice, made the following observation: "Morality cannot be legislated, but behavior can be regulated. Judicial decrees may not change the heart, but they can restrain the heartless" (1963).

Prejudice and the Potential for Violence

Prejudice and bigotry are attitudes. When these attitudes are expressed, they constitute hate speech, which may lead to violent action. We have seen evidence of this phenomenon throughout history. People have been persuaded to act on behalf of causes rooted in prejudice or extreme hatred. Sometimes marginalized youth gravitate to gangs or extremist groups that will accept them. Sometimes people act for unjustified and even immoral reasons.

Stanley Milgrim's classic study sheds light on the complexity of the relationship among people's personalities, attitudes, and behaviors. In this experiment, a person's proclivity to inflict physical pain on another human being, just because he was told to do so, is alarming (Milgrim 1974). This experiment speaks to the ease with which people will take action, even behave inhumanely, because of the power of another person's attitude or words.

The Internet provides educators and students with opportunities and challenges. The opportunities are widely known, but the threats to humanity are often covert. Hatred in the 21st century is high tech. Hundreds of hate mongers poison the web with virulent racism, anti-Semitism, homophobia, and anti-government rhetoric. For example, a high school student who is searching the Internet for information on the Holocaust may inadvertently enter a Holocaust denial site, which is dedicated to promoting that the Holocaust never happened. Other extremists target youth with their own brand of bigotry. Hate mongering in cyberspace ought to be regulated by responsible adults. The Anti-Defamation League has developed a computer software program called HateFilter® that can be used by parents to educate and protect children from hate on the Internet. ADL HateFilter® blocks access to hate-oriented sites and directs users to information provided by the League about the blocked sites.

The Pyramid of Hate

Consider Figure 13.1, the Pyramid of Hate (Anti-Defamation League 1998). This model describes various levels and intensities of prejudice that occur in societies, from the most minimal to the most extreme forms. Institutions vary regarding the level of prejudice they may harbor. Likewise, individuals within those institutions vary in terms of the levels of prejudice they may possess.

The base of the pyramid reflects the most subtle manifestations of prejudice, acts that are demonstrated indirectly. Even at this level, prejudice is not benign. Stereotyping occurs at this level. To stereotype is to broadly generalize about an entire group of people without regard to individual differences. Stereotypes are oversimplified assumptions. They are forerunners of prejudice that, when learned and culturally transmitted, frequently become dogmatically held ideas. Stereotypes link social groups to a constellation of faulty information. Examples of stereotyping in schools would be teachers who assume that all Asian students are good in math, or all African American students are lazy. Moreover, people often avoid information that is contrary to their stereotypical images of others. To further compound this problem, a bias in memory leads people to recall members of minority groups in negative terms more frequently than in positive ones (Hamilton and Rose 1980; Rothbart, Evans, and Fulero 1979).

Stereotypes persist because, as a categorizing technique, they serve a function—they justify and simplify the social world (Stephan 1999). Stereotyping is a process that is activated automatically (Dovidio, Evans, and Tyler 1986; Fazio 1997). Activation occurs on both the affective and cognitive levels. Unless there is a direct challenge to a stereotype, it will persist. In order for negative stereotypes to be modified, sufficient cognitive resources must be presented in a nonthreatening, noncompetitive atmosphere. It is far more difficult to weaken stereotypes than to strengthen them.

Though "acts of bias" might seem harmless, people who engage in these activities, (e.g., spreading rumors or telling ethnic jokes) generally don't consider the individual dimensions of the target group nor the effects these acts have on the individuals who identify with this group. Subtle acts of bias provide a foundation on which more intense forms of

PYRAMID OF HATE

ACTS
OF
EXTREME
VIOLENCE
Genocide
Murder   Terrorism
Rape   Lynching
Arson   Bombing

ACTS OF VIOLENCE
Hate Crime
Assault and Battery   Dehumanization
Desecration   Vandalism   Threats
Riots   Terrorism

ACTS OF DISCRIMINATION
Harassment   Employment discrimination
Housing discrimination   Educational discrimination
Social exclusion

ACTS OF PREJUDICE AND BIGOTRY
Scapegoating   Slurs/Name calling
Ridicule   Social avoidance   Spreading Rumors
Stereotyping (actions)

ACTS OF SUBTLE OR INDIRECT BIAS
Discussing feelings with like-minded others
Accepting negative information/screening out positive
Stereotyping   Jokes   Rumors

Acts of violence may be directed at individuals, institutions or entire communities. Community violence has a direct impact on individuals and violence directed at individuals also affects the community.

Figure 13.1
The Pyramid of Hate

Acts of violence may be directed at individuals, institutions, or entire communities. Community violence has a direct impact on individuals, and violence directed at individuals also affects the community. (© 1999 Anti-Defamation League)

prejudice may be built. To varying degrees, this type of prejudice may be "politically" acceptable within institutions. Nevertheless subtle acts of bias provide a comfort zone for prejudice. If school personnel are apathetic to these displays of prejudice, more intense hate is likely to emerge.

Overt forms of prejudice and bigotry include scapegoating. This is the deliberate action of blaming individuals or groups for things they did not do. Scapegoating promotes verbal aggression such as racial or ethnic epithets and physical or social avoidance. Scapegoating often springs from stereotypes because, when stereotypes are activated, people tend to pay more attention to what they expect rather than what is. In other words, information they receive is distorted by what they expect. For example, in a study conducted with White college students (Duncan 1976), a videotape of a Black person shoving a White person was interpreted as violence by 75% of the students. However, a videotape of a White person shoving a Black person was interpreted as violence by only 17% of the respondents. Moreover, when faced with the fact that African Americans score lower than Whites on national standardized achievement tests, many people inaccurately attribute this to a lack of intelligence on the part of African Americans. This conclusion scapegoats the victim and ignores critical situational factors (cultural bias) in the tests or inequitable educational opportunities.

Examples of Hate-Related Violence

As the Pyramid of Hate indicates, prejudice can easily elevate to a higher level of discrimination that manifests itself in harassment. Hatred, when not deterred, will often become more extreme and even explode into violence under certain circumstances. At the end of the 20th century, there have been several indications of prejudice elevating to violence around the United States.

In Jasper, Texas, James Byrd Jr., an African American, was chained to a pickup truck and dragged to his death by White supremacists. Across the South, Black churches were targeted and burned to the ground. A young man, Matthew Sheppard, was brutally beaten, tied to a barbed-wire fence, and left to die in the frigid temperatures of Laramie, Wyoming, because he was homosexual. At Columbine High School in Colorado, two teenage boys clad in black trenchcoats celebrated Hitler's birthday by massacring their peers and teachers, leaving 13 dead. Then, youth violence exploded again on a high school campus in Georgia, leaving four people wounded in its wake. During the Independence Day weekend of 1999, a man with affiliations to an organized hate group that promotes anti-Semitism and racism went on a shooting spree through Illinois and Indiana, targeting Jews, Blacks, and Asians, which ended with two dead and nine wounded. During that same summer, a gay couple was murdered, arsonists torched three Synagogues in Sacramento, California, and a gunman shot and killed his family, nine other people, and himself in Atlanta, Georgia. Also, another gunman with ties to an organized hate group took aim at preschool children and employees at a Jewish Community Center in Los Angeles, California, because he allegedly wanted "to give America a wake-up call to kill Jews." This is a chilling list of violent hate crimes that closed the 20th century. But the 20th century also saw the pinnacle of hatred (see the Pyramid of Hate) with the Holocaust, Armenian, Chinese, and other genocides.

What researchers have learned is that silence is not neutral—prejudice must be combated because it will not dissipate by itself. Prejudice has not been adequately addressed in the institutions or schools of U.S. society. However, a body of research in this area seeks to help educators who struggle with these issues.

Research on Prejudice Reduction

The school offers numerous ways to prevent or reduce the negative effects of prejudice even though children often enter school with preconceived attitudes about others. Once teachers acknowledge that prejudice is a problem that stems from faulty knowledge about those who are different, certain interventions can deter prejudice.

Multicultural education stresses that there are differences among people and groups. This is essential to a schoolwide plan of eliminating prejudice (Allgood 1998; Banks 1994, 1995; Briscoe 1991; Gay 1992, 1988; Grottkau and Nickolai-Mays 1989; Grossman 1991; Klugman and Greenberg 1991; Johnson and Johnson 1978; King 1983; Larke 1990a, 1990b; Lassiter 1984; Rogers, Miller, and Hennigan 1981; Pate 1992; Payne 1984; Pine and Hilliard 1990).

An effective way to accomplish the goal of reducing prejudice and dogmatism is through implementing sound multicultural and anti-bias programs, praxis, and curricula (Allgood 1998; Byrnes 1988; Cotton 1993; Howe 1992; Gay 1992; Pedersen 1994; Walsh 1988). Moreover, there is a need for teacher training in multicultural education that fosters critical thinking and dogmatism reduction in students and builds tolerance for diversity (Allgood 1998; Burstein 1989; Campbell and Farrell 1985; Foster 1989). There has been much discussion on the nature and content of these kinds of programs, but the literature indicates multicultural and anti-bias educational programs can have mitigating effects on some aspects of prejudice, such as dogmatic thinking. This is especially true when sound theories from pedagogy and andragogy are applied (Banks and Banks 1997; Cotton 1993; Derman-Sparks 1997; Gollnick and Chinn 1998; Knox, Lindsay, and Kolb 1993; Nissani 1989; Pang 1995; Parkay 1983; Simonton 1983; Sleeter and Grant 1987).

Equitable education requires that teachers relate to diverse students in unbiased ways. There is a clear correlation among variables such as prejudice, social distance, academic achievement, and dogmatism. Therefore, because dogmatism in education has negative implications for students, it is important to reduce dogmatism when it exists in pre-service and in-service educators.

A number of approaches are effective in reducing closed-minded attitudes. For example, the terminology one uses has a direct effect on the amount of prejudice amplification or remission that occurs. For example, referring to the traits of a group of people as "stingy," "pushy," or "cunning" will obviously have a deleterious impact. Describing another group as "philanthropic," "assertive," or "smart" will have a positive impact. Likewise, referring to a student as having "limited English proficiency" is vastly different than referring to him or her as "potentially English proficient." Behaviors, as well as traits, may be labeled positively or negatively. For example, a Haitian student who diverts his or her eyes from the teacher may be labeled as "disinterested" or "guilty." However, this behavior is more accurately a sign of "respect" and "deference" in Haitian culture. With increased semantic education (as with increased cognitive awareness), there is significant prejudice reduction, which has been measured on social distance scales (Black 1971).

A counter-stereotype approach, in which ethnic minority persons are presented in atypical roles, is also effective in diminishing prejudice (Freedman, Gotti, and Holtz 1983). Additionally, it was found that cultural immersion approaches alter attitudes (Ijaz 1981). This can be understood in the classic Native American adage of "walking in another person's moccasins" in order to fully appreciate the other person's viewpoint. Furthermore, approaches using values clarification improved racial attitudes and the social acceptability of diverse students (Lassiter 1984). Students exposed to more democratic or shared coping approaches, such as cooperative learning, show more positive racial and ethnic attitudes (Slavin 1979, 1990). Moreover, multicultural and cooperative approaches, such as heterogeneous teaming, appear to have long-range positive effects (Bennett 1979; Baker 1977; Banks 1994; Rogers, Miller, and Hennigan 1981; Sanders and Weisman 1990; Slavin and Oickle 1981; Sleeter and Grant 1987; Walberg and Genova 1983). When the approach is "team competitive," then winning must occur to diminish prejudice (Pate 1995).

A preponderance of the literature indicates that classrooms where multicultural practices and learning style theories are applied tend to be more effective in reducing rigid thinking and prejudice and stimulating cross-cultural communication (Briscoe 1991; Gay 1988; Grottkau and Nickolai-Mays 1989; Grossman 1991; Klugman and Greenberg 1991; Johnson and Johnson 1978; King 1983; Larke 1990a, 1990b; Pate 1992; Payne 1984; Pine and Hilliard 1990; Taylor 1987; Trachtenberg 1990).

The Cognitive Realm: Critical Thinking

A component of learning that is especially effective in reducing prejudice is "critical thinking." Critical (or reflective) thinking is examining an issue from multiple perspectives, reflecting on the issue, and then drawing conclusions based on this broad analysis of the issue. Thinking critically is the antithesis of dogmatic thinking (Byrnes 1988; Dillon 1986; Kennedy 1991;

Meyers 1986; Nichols and Stults 1985; Paul 1987, 1993; Symons et al. 1989; Walsh 1988). The ability to think critically correlates with reduced prejudice, especially in social interactions (Allport 1982). Critical reasoning also builds empathy among students (Gabelko 1988; Gallo 1989).

Dogmatism is an uncritical, rigid way of thinking that correlates strongly with prejudice. Cognitive qualities affect social attitudes. For example, cognitively sophisticated people are less prone to exhibit prejudice than those who are not (Davis and Fine 1975). Other findings from research indicate that persons who are high in ethnic prejudice or authoritarianism are comparatively more rigid in their problem-solving behavior, more concrete in their thinking, more narrow in their grasp of subject matter, and tend more toward premature closure in their perceptual processes than their less-prejudiced counterparts (Barron 1953; Becker 1954). Additionally, persons who hold more prejudice show a greater tendency to be intolerant of ambiguity and have more faulty memory patterns.

The cognitive propensity to over-generalize has been correlated with deficient critical thinking and is prevalent among highly prejudiced people (Pate 1995). Very prejudiced people are more dogmatic and tend to think in absolute terms. In contrast, cognitively sophisticated persons exhibit advanced critical thinking ability, have advanced retention skills, and also display less faulty generalizing practices. Therefore, these persons are less likely to engage in any form of stereotyping.

A body of research demonstrates that dogmatic attitudes and prejudices are extremely resistant to change from classroom intervention or anti-bias training (Washington 1981). Some maintain that the "prejudice habit" has an automatic, controlled, and even a rebounding effect if attempts are made to tamper with it (Cole 1997; Devine 1989; Dovidio 1993; Fazio 1997; Macrae et al. 1994).

Intervention efforts to diminish prejudicial thinking are effective when the cognitive and affective domains are both addressed (Butler 1982; Cove, and Love 1996; Wurzel 1980) and learning is expedited or restrained by emotion (Goleman 1995). Moreover, in one study at the college level, teaching in the affective domain was deemed more effective than other modes of instruction (Gee 1991).

A strategic prejudice-reduction framework, which addresses multicultural content in the cognitive, reflective, emotive and active domains, will reduce prejudicial thinking in students (Allgood 1998). Intervention efforts to diminish prejudice are more effective when, in addition to addressing affective domains, students engage in critical analysis of multicultural issues and carry out social action projects. (See Figure 13.2.)

Cognitive processing is self-regulating and includes a self-centering mechanism that strongly influences thought, affect, and action (Bandura 1991). Lower self-esteem correlates with higher prejudice levels. Attitude change involves a process of self-discovery. Methods such as anti-bias and

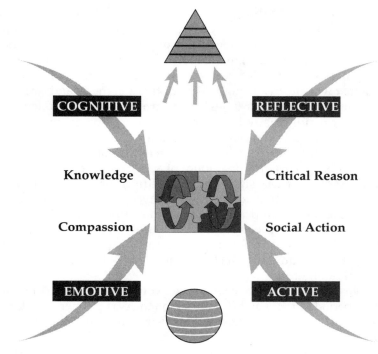

Figure 13.2
Prejudice Reduction Framework

sensitivity training, which promote ethnic self-worth, embrace cultural diversity, and open lines of communication, are one means of reducing prejudice (Byrnes 1988; Garcia, Powell, and Sanchez 1990; Foster 1989; Hart and Lumsden 1989; Mabbutt 1991; Pate 1988; Peck, Donaldson, and Pezzoli 1990; Rubin 1967).

Social conditions influence thinking by impacting personal belief systems and attitudes. Studies on group dynamics looked at the influences that groups have on their members. One study found that people tend to change their beliefs and attitudes in order to be consistent with the prevailing attitudes of the groups they join. In other words, "they tend to go along with the crowd" (Foley 1976). Another problem is a tendency for participants to provide politically correct responses or exhibit socially acceptable behaviors in some venues. When people from cultural minority groups are perceived as individuals, less stereotyping occurs (Katz 1973). Personal identification with people from marginalized (out) groups was found to reduce dogmatism and prejudice (Weiner and Wright 1973).

Research suggests that those Americans most likely to be anti-Semitic or racially prejudiced tend to be older and less educated than the general public. There is a higher degree of prejudiced thinking in the 50 and over age category (35%) than among respondents ages 30–49 (23%). However, persons in the 30 or under category had levels of prejudiced thinking that were nearly as high (31%) as those in the 50 and over group (Anti-Defamation League 1992). This is alarming, since it challenges the notion that prejudice is reduced in each successive generation. This study also revealed that other factors often believed to be linked with anti-Semitism and racism (such as income level, political ideology, religious affiliation, geography, or amount of actual contact with non-whites or Jews) appear to be less significant than education. Among the demographic factors, education (specifically the type that promotes reflective inquiry) is the most significant predictor of having less prejudiced attitudes. In other words, prejudice is more closely linked to a lack of educational attainment than with any other major demographic category. Schooling that reinforces reflective thinking can be significant in the diminution of bigotry.

Cognitive and attitudinal change takes considerable time. Any change requires a period of internal restructuring on the part of a person (Stotland, Katz, and Patchen 1972). The less ego-defensive a person is, the more likely there will be an attitude adjustment. The reverse is also true.

Changes in attitude do not necessarily change behavior or carry over into other situations (Miracle 1981). Behavioral change must be independently verified.

The Affective Realm: Psychological and Social Theories

Gordon Allport developed the Social Contact Theory of prejudice almost a half century ago, which has been the basis for much of the research that has followed (Allport 1982). He theorized that prejudicial characteristics, such as dogmatism, were woven into the fabric of personality. Many other early theories included the argument that the propensity toward prejudice stems from personality (Simpson and Yinger 1985; Adorno et al. 1982; Triandis 1971) or is attributed to a "natural" predisposition of humans to be wary of "outsiders" (Fishbein 1996). This fear of "foreign" things or people (without prior critical analysis) is termed xenophobia. Other authorities argue that prejudice is learned and taught (Anti-Defamation League 1998). Some see the problem as emanating from social frustration or rejection. This in turn leads to aggression that culminates in prejudicial or dogmatic-type thinking (Gaertner and Dovidio 1977).

The Active Realm: Service Learning

Another approach in education that is effective in reducing prejudice is service learning. Research on service learning in education shows that it has positive effects on reducing prejudicial tendencies, since it prepares youth for civic leadership (Boyte 1991; Calabrese and Schumer 1986; Conrad and Hedin 1991; Luchs 1981; MacNicol 1993; Newmann and Rutter 1983; Rolzinski 1990; Seigel and Rockwood 1993). For example, students serving food at soup kitchens as part of a project on world hunger learn about poverty; students helping to build homes for the needy through Habitat for Humanity gain self-esteem through their volunteerism and an appreciation for the plight of the less fortunate.

Courts are ordering "social remediation" by having convicted racists, for example, take part in organizations that advocate support for victims of violence and hatred. A couple of convicted neo-Nazis whose sentences included visits to Holocaust museums and conversations with Holocaust survivors have expressed a change of heart on issues that caused them to violate hate crime laws.

Teaching Strategies

Teaching methods can create classroom climates where students have opportunities to socialize and collaborate with each other. Such classrooms will reduce social distance and improve attitudes among diverse people if certain conditions are met (Allport 1982). Teachers must create opportunities for students to cooperate with each other while maintaining a climate of equity. This involves creating positive social norms, communicating clear objectives, reducing competitive anxiety, and maintaining high expectations for all students (Allport 1982; Selltiz and Cook 1963). This theory of prejudice reduction continues to be the most influential force in enhancing cross-cultural relationships among diverse students.

Increasing students' critical thinking skills is essential to prejudice reduction because critical inquiry is the antithesis of prejudiced thinking (Allgood 1998; Walsh 1988). Methods and lessons that stimulate high-level thought and encourage students to question or examine their own thinking are crucial. Students need to be taught to engage in thinking that is not "absolute" and exercise higher levels of thinking such as synthesizing, comparing, and distinguishing before reaching conclusions.

Research indicates that direct, sermonizing approaches to teaching tolerance are not as effective as other methods that incorporate more active student participation (Dent 1976). Methods such as service learning, case studies, or anthropological approaches (where prejudice is studied from the "outsider's" perspective) are far more effective (Pate 1992).

Classroom and Teaching Practices: Techniques, Content, and Materials

Cooperative learning has been shown to be an effective means for breaking down misconceptions that feed dogmatic thinking (Conrad 1988; Davis 1985; King 1983; Parrenas and Parrenas 1990; Sharan and Sharan 1992). Cooperative learning approaches include activities that use teaming such as Jigsaws and Cultural Quilts (Anti-Defamation League 1998). Dramatization, simulation, or role-playing activities have been shown to be effective (Gimmestad and DeChiara 1982; Byrnes and Kiger 1990). These activities are especially effective if they involve the affective and the "active" domains (participation). This principle was confirmed in studies measuring attitude changes toward persons with disabiliies. (Jones et al. 1981; Horne 1987). Furthermore, while a class discussion format had some effect on the interracial behaviors of White students, this technique did not necessarily affect their attitudes (Slavin 1979). Case-study techniques, designed to heighten an individual's insight into the psychodynamics of prejudice, were found to be effective in modifying attitudes in professional development programs (Merseth 1994). This approach is effective because cases stimulate analytical thinking and personal reflection (Klienfeld 1992; Richert 1991).

Television and movies are powerful educational resources. One study indicated that audio-visual materials (particularly television or films) had relatively long-lasting effects in improving negative attitudes toward ethnic minority individuals, the disabled, and in improving gender relations (Pate 1995). Also, using specific anti-bias material is effective in reducing prejudice (Seiter 1988; Hayes 1969). But materials alone are insufficient as a means of changing attitudes (Lessing and Clark 1976).

Culturally heterogeneous teams of presenters are more effective than homogeneous teams in promoting themes of tolerance. Furthermore, when facilitators model positive attitudes, they are more apt to generate prejudice reduction in participants (Kraus 1972). Another finding, which aggregates content with action, was that among teachers who developed and implemented their own bias-reduction materials, the development of these materials led to a decline in the prejudice level among teacher-developers (Moore 1977).

Schoolwide Considerations

Specific school policies and practices that reduce prejudice are rendered ineffective unless school leaders model respectful attitudes and behaviors toward diverse people and belief systems (Pate 1992). This includes attitudes toward differences in cultural and religious norms, ethnicity, language, physical ability, clothing, lifestyle, and age. Moreover, schools are most effective in reducing prejudice when teachers exhibit attitudes of zero tolerance toward prejudice, hatred, and discriminating practices. By actively combating prejudice when it emerges in their classrooms or in peer group interactions, teachers can significantly impact a positive school climate. School policies should also reflect intolerance for bigotry and discrimination.

The anti-bias mission of the school should encompass the totality of the institution and should be democratic, operative, dynamic, and equitable. Also, it must be pursued fairly. Schools need to be vigilant and promote diversity in areas such as school governance, policies, staffing, resources, curriculum, and assessments. For example, tracking practices that tend to feed prejudice by segregating and labeling students should be discouraged (Slavin 1989). Curricular decisions and testing practices should be scrutinized for cultural inequities. In staff development, teachers should be encouraged to teach in accordance with learning style research so that diverse students have multiple opportunities to absorb curricular content.

For institutions, as for individuals, the first step in eliminating subtle forms of prejudice is having the awareness that it exists. Schools that evaluate their own practices and climates are being proactive in thwarting prejudice.

Effective school practices reduce intolerance in an institution (Kyle 1985; Slavin 1979). These practices include: teaching methods to improve race relations, principals and teachers who behave equitably toward all students, institutional support for integration, expanding social interactions, zero tolerance levels for prejudice in any form, and a willingness on the part of the school staff to explore in-service opportunities of prejudice reduction (Stover 1990).

The Imperative to Create Prejudice-Free School and Classroom Climates

Why should the school have any role in preventing prejudice? After all, one could argue that as a free nation, aren't citizens guaranteed the right to free thought, even if that thought is biased? It would follow from this argument that the nation's schools, already saddled with massive curricular requirements, should not be further burdened with an imperative to deter or even reduce prejudice.

When prejudice goes from a thought to an action, it becomes discrimination. At this point, discrimination violates laws protecting the rights of individuals against unfair treatment on the basis of ethnicity, race, religion, gender, or age. Therefore, schools have a professional and ethical responsibility to help mold unbiased citizens, because this will ultimately reduce the strife caused by discrimination. At the beginning of the 21st century, most schools in the United States had not taken up the challenge of reducing prejudice in American society.

Conclusion

Prejudice exists in most people and societal institutions because it serves a function. It is a means for simplifying complexity and for categorizing people. Nevertheless, it is harmful. Since the nature of prejudice is to grow exponentially if left alone, ignoring prejudice in schools is tantamount to promoting it. Prejudice at any level must be combated.

Prejudices result in unfair assessments and judgments about others because they are based on dogmatically rigid, narrow thinking. Since dogmatism portends prejudice, researchers point out that counteracting dogmatic thinking with reflective analysis will lower the tendency for people to develop prejudice. Prejudice is learned, and since the purpose of schools is to advance learning, school becomes the most significant institution and education the most significant process for deterring it. Educators need to recognize and fully understand the nature of prejudice in order to eliminate it.

Caveat

Schools are paradoxical institutions because they are a means to alleviate the problems caused by prejudice but may also be instruments of its perpetuation. It requires nothing short of a total school commitment to eliminate prejudice from the school enviornemnt.

References

Adorno, T., Frenkel-Brunswik, E., Levinson, D., and Sanford, R. (1982). The authoritarian personality. New York: W. W. Norton.

Allgood, I. (1998). The development, implementation, and evaluation of a strategic prejudice reduction framework and its effect on dogmatism levels of college students. Doctoral Dissertation, Florida Atlantic University.

Allport, G. (1982). The nature of prejudice. Reading, MA: Addison Wesley.

Anti-Defamation League (1992). *Highlights from an Anti-Defamation League survey on anti-Semitism and prejudice in America*. New York: Anti-Defamation League of B'nai B'rith.

Anti-Defamation League. (1997). Schooled in Hate: Anti-Semitism on Campus. New York: ADL.

Anti-Defamation League. (1998). A World of Difference® Institute Training Manual, 8, 20. New York: ADL.

Aviram, O. (1987). The impact of school as a social system on the formation of student intergroup attitudes and behavior. *Journal of Educational Equity and Leadership, 7*(2), 92–108.

Baker, G. (1977). Multicultural education: Two preserve training approaches. *Journal of Teacher Education, 28*(3), 29–33.

Bandura, A. (1991, Dec.). Social cognitive theory of self-regulation. *Organizational behavior and human decision processes, 50*, 248.

Banks, J. A. (1994). *Multiethnic education: Theory and practice*. Boston: Allyn and Bacon.

Banks, J. A. (1995). Multicultural education and the modification of students' racial attitudes. In W. D. Hawley and A. W. Jackson, A.W. (Eds.), *Toward a common destiny: Improving race and ethnic relations in America* (p. 642). San Francisco, CA: Jossey-Bass.

Banks, J. A. and Banks, C. A. (Eds.). (1995). Handbook of research on multicultural education. New York: Macmillan.

Banks, J. A., and Banks, C. A. (1997). *Multicultural education: Issues and perspectives.* Needham Heights, MA: Allyn and Bacon.

Barron, F. (1953). Complexity-simplicity as a personality dimension. *Journal of Abnormal Psychology, 48,* 163–172.

Becker, W. C. (1954). Perceptual rigidity as measured by antiseikonic lenses. *Journal of Abnormal Psychology, 49,* 419–422.

Bennett, C. (1979). The preparation of pre-service secondary social studies teachers in multiethnic education. *The High School Journal, 62*(5), 232–237.

Bennett, C. (1995). Research on racial issues in American higher education. In J. A. Banks and C. A. Banks (Eds.), *Handbook of research on multicultural education.* (pp.663–681). New York: Macmillan.

Black, J. A. (1971). The effects of instruction in general semantics on ethnic prejudices as expressed in measurements of social distance. Unpublished doctoral dissertation, New York University.

Boyte, H. C. (1991, June). Community service and civic education. *Phi Delta Kappan, 71*(10), 765–767

Briscoe, D. B. (1991). Designing for diversity in school success: Capitalizing on culture. *Preventing School Failure, 36*(1), 3–18.

Brophy, J. (1983) Research on the self-fulfilling prophecy and teacher expectations. *Journal of Educational Psychology, 75,* 631–661.

Burstein, N. D. (1989). Preparing teachers to work with culturally diverse students: A teacher education model. *Journal of Teacher Education, 40*(5), 9–16.

Butler, D. (1982). *The reduction of racial prejudice through the use of vicarious experience.* Unpublished doctoral dissertation, University of Michigan, Ann Arbor.

Byrnes, D. A. (1988). Children and prejudice. *Social Education, 52*(4), 267–271.

Byrnes, D. A., and Kiger, G. (1990). The effects of a prejudice-reduction simulation on attitude change. *Journal of Applied Social Psychology, 20*(4), 341–356.

Calabrese, R. L., and Schumer, H. (1986). The effects of service activities on adolescent alienation. *Adolescence, 21,* 675–687.

Campbell, R. L., and Farrell, R. V. (1985). The identification of competencies for multicultural teacher education. *Negro Educational Review, 36*(3/4), 137–144.

Cole, J. (1997). *Beyond prejudice.* Ellensburg, WA: Growing Images.

Conrad, B. D. (1988). Cooperative learning and prejudice reduction. *Social Education, 52*(4) 283–286.

Conrad, D., and Hedin, D. (1991, June). School-based community service: What we know from research and theory. *Phi Delta Kappan, 72*(10), 743–749.

Cooper, H. M., and Tom, D. Y. H. (1984). Teacher expectation research: A review with implications for classroom instruction. *Elementary School Journal, 85,* 77–89.

Cotton, K. (1990). *Expectations and student outcomes* (Northwest Regional Educational Laboratory Monograph No. 7). Portland, OR: Northwest Regional Educational Laboratory.

Cotton, K. (1993, Nov.). Fostering intercultural harmony in schools: Research findings. *School Improvement Research Series (topical synthesis #7).* Portland, OR: Northwest Regional Education Laboratory and the Office of Educational Research, U.S. Department of Education.

Cove, P. G., and Love, A. G. (1996). *Enhancing student learning: Intellectual, social, and emotional integration.* (ERIC Document. [Online], Available: ED400741).

Davis, B. R. (1985). Effects of cooperative learning on race/human relations: Study of a district program. *Spectrum, 3*(1), 37–43.

Davis, E. E., and Fine, M. (1975). The effects of the findings of the U.S. National Advisory Commission on civil disorder: An experimental study of attitude change. *Human Relations, 28*(3), 209–228.

Dent, P. L. (1976). Curriculum as a prejudice reduction technique. *California Journal of Educational Research, 7*(1), 84–92.

Derman-Sparks, L. (1997). *Teaching/learning anti-racism.* New York: Teachers College Press.

Devine, P. G. (1989). Stereotypes and prejudice: Their automatic and controlled components. *Journal of Personality and Social Psychology, 56*(1), 5–18.

Diaz, C. F. (Ed.). (1992). *Multicultural education for the 21st century.* Washington DC: National Education Association.

Dillon, R. F. (1986). Issues in cognitive psychology and instruction. In R. F. Dillon and R. J. Sternberg (Eds.), *Cognition and instruction* (pp. 1–12), Orlando, FL: Academic Press.

Dovidio, J. (1993, April). The subtlety of racism. *Training and Development,* 51–57.

Dovidio, J. F., Evans, N., and Tyler, R. B. (1986). Racial stereotypes: The contents and their cognitive representation. *Journal of Experimental Social Psychology, 22,* 22–37.

Duncan, B. (1976). Differential social perceptions and attribution of intergroup violence: Testing the lower limits of stereotyping blacks. *Journal of Personality and Social Psychology, 34,* 590–598.

Eden, D. (1992). Leadership and expectations: Pygmalion effects and other self fulfilling prophecies on organizations. *Leadership Quarterly, 3*(4), 271–305.

Ehrlich, H. J. (1978). Dogmatism. In H. London and J. E. Exner Jr. (Eds.), *Dimensions of Personality.* New York: John Wiley and Sons.

Fazio, R. H. (1997). Categorization by race: The impact of automatic and controlled components of racial prejudice. *Journal of Experimental Social Psychology, 33,* 451–470.

Fishbein, H. D. (1996). *Peer prejudice and discrimination.* Boulder, CO: Westview Press.

Flexner, S. B., and Hauck, L. C. (1987). *The Random House dictionary of the English language* (2nd ed.). New York: Random House.

Foley, L. (1976). Personality and situational influences on changes in prejudice. *Journal of Personality and Social Psychology, 34*(5), 846–856.

Foster, L. A. (1989). Breaking down racial isolation. *Educational Leadership, 47*(2) 76–77.

Freedman, P., Gotti, M., and Holtz, G. (1983). A comparison of the effectiveness of two approaches to the reduction of stereotypical thinking. *Contemporary Education, 54*(2), 134–138.

Gabelko, N. H. (1988). Prejudice reduction in secondary schools. *Social Education, 52*(4), 276–279.

Gaertner, S. L., and Dovidio, J. F. (1977). The subtlety of white racism, arousal, and helping behavior. *Journal of Personality and Social Psychology, 35,* 691–707.

Gallo, E. (1989). Educating for empathy, reason, and imagination. *Journal of Creative Behavior, 23*(2), 98–115.

Garcia, J., Powell, R., and Sanchez, T. (1990, April). Multicultural textbooks: How to use them more effectively in the classroom. Paper presented at the annual meeting of the American Educational Research Association, Boston, MA. ED320 262.

Gay, G. (1988). Designing relevant curricula for diverse learners. *Education and Urban Society, 20*(4), 327–340.

Gay, G. (1992). Effective teaching practices for multicultural classrooms. In C. F. Diaz (Ed.), *Multicultural education for the 21st century.* (pp. 38–56). Washington D.C.: National Education Association.

Gee, J. B. (1991). New perspectives in teaching in the affective domain. (ERIC Document. [Online], Available: ED341659.)

Gimmestad, B. J., and DeChiara, E. (1982). Dramatic plays: A vehicle for prejudice reduction. *Journal of Educational Research, 76*(1), 45–49.

Goldman, B. A., and Flake, W. L. (1996). Is flexibility related to college achievement?: A five-year study. *Psychological Reports, 78,* 337–338.

Goleman, D. (1995). *Emotional intelligences.* New York: Bantam Books.

Gollnick, D. M., and Chinn, P. C. (1998). *Multicultural education in a pluralistic society.* New York: Macmillan.

Goodlad, J. I. (1984). *A place called school.* New York: McGraw-Hill.

Grossman, H. (1991). Multicultural classroom management. *Contemporary Education, 62*(3), 161–166.

Grottkau, B. J., and Nickolai-Mays, S. (1989). An empirical analysis of a multicultural education paradigm for preservice teachers. *Educational Research Quarterly, 13*(4), 27–33.

Hamilton, D. L. and Rose, T. (1980). Illusory correlation and the maintenance of stereotype beliefs. *Journal of Personality and Social Psychology, 39,* 832–845.

Hart, T. E., and Lumsden, L. (1989, May). Confronting racism in the schools. *OSSC Bulletin, 32*(9).

Hayes, M. (1969). An investigation of the impact of reading on attitudes of racial prejudice. (ERIC Document, Available: ED123319.)

Horne, M. D. (1987). Modifying peer attitudes toward the handicapped: Procedures and research issues. In H. E. Yuker (Ed.), *Attitudes toward persons with disabilities.* New York: Springer.

Howe, K. R. (1992). Liberal democracy, equal educational opportunity, and the challenge of multiculturalism. *American Educational Research Journal, 29*(3), 455–470.

Ijaz, M. A. (1981). Study of ethnic attitude of elementary school children toward Blacks and East Indians. (ERIC Document, Available: ED204448.)

Johnson, D. W., and Johnson, R. T. (1978). The effects of cooperative and individualized instruction on student attitudes and achievement. *Journal of Social Psychology, 104,* 207–216.

Jones, R. A. (1977). *Self-fulfilling prophecies.* Hillsdale, NJ: Lawrence Erlbaum.

Jones, T. W., Sowell, V. M., Jones, J. K., and Butler, L. G. (1981). Changing children's perceptions of handicapped people. *Exceptional Children, 47*(5), 365–368.

Katz, P. (1973). Stimulus pre-differentiation and modification of children's racial attitudes. *Child Development, 44*(2), 232–237

Kennedy, M. (1991, May). Policy issues in teaching education. *Phi Delta Kappan,* 661–666.

King, E. W. (1983). Promising practices in teaching ethnically diverse children. *Momentum, 14*(1), 38–40.

King, M. L., Jr. (1963) Strength to Love. New York: Harper Row.

Klienfeld, J. (1992). Learning to think like a teacher: The study of cases. In J. H. Shulman (Ed.), *Case methods in teacher education* (pp. 33–49). New York: Teacher College Press.

Klugman, J., and Greenberg, B. (1991). Program helps identify, resolve problems in multicultural high schools. *NASSP Bulletin,* 96–102.

Knox, W. E., Lindsay, P., and Kolb, M. N. (1993). *Does college make a difference?* Westport: Greenwood Press.

Kraus, S. (1972). Modifying prejudice: Attitude change as a function of race of the communicator. In Brown (Ed.), *Prejudice in children* (pp. 183–195). Springfield, MA: Charles C. Thomas.

Kyle, R. A. (1985). Reaching for excellence: An effective school sourcebook. In J. Lynch (Ed.), *Prejudice reduction and the schools.* New York: Nichols.

Larke, P. J. (1990a). Cultural diversity awareness inventory: Assessing the sensitivity of preservice teachers. *Action in Teacher Education, 12*(3), 23–30.

Larke, P. J. (1990b). The minority mentorship project: Changing attitudes of preservice teachers for diverse classrooms. *Action in Teacher Education, 12*(3), 5–11.

Lassiter, W. (1984). The impact of selected value clarification teaching strategies on attitudes toward ethnically diverse groups. Unpublished doctoral dissertation, Northern Arizona University.

Lessing, E. E., and Clarke, C. C. (1976). An attempt to reduce ethnic prejudice and assess its correlates. *Educational Research Quarterly, 1*(2).

Loria, B. R. (1981). Measuring the effectiveness of race relations seminars within the army medical department. Unpublished doctoral dissertation, Rutgers University.

Luchs, K. (1981). Selected changes in urban high school students after participation in community-based learning and service activities. Unpublished doctoral dissertation, University of Maryland.

Mabbutt, R. (1991). *Prejudice Reduction, What Works?* Reducing bias: Research notes on racism in America. Boise, ID: Idaho Human Rights Commission.

MacNicol, R. (1993, Sept.). Service learning: A challenge to do the right thing. *Equity and Excellence in Education, 26,* 9–11.

Macrae, C., et al. (1994). Out of mind but back in sight: Stereotypes on the rebound. *Journal of Personality and Social Psychology, 67*(5), 808–817.

Martin, J. D., Grah, C. R., and Harris, J. W. (1986). Closed-mindedness: Effect on achievement. *Psychological Reports, 59,* 611–614.

Martin, J. D., and Morris, D. A. (1982). Relationship of the scores on the Tolerance Scale of Jackson Personality Inventory to those in Rokeach's Dogmatism Scale. *Education and Psychological Measurement, 42,* 377–381.

Merseth, K. K. (1994, Nov.). Cases, case methods, and the professional development of educators. (ERIC Document [Online], Available: ED401272.)

Meyers, C. (1986). *Teaching students to think critically.* San Francisco: Jossey-Bass.

Milgram, S. (1974). *Obedience to authority: An experimental view.* New York: Harper and Row.

Miracle, A. (1981). Factors affecting interracial cooperation. *Human Organization 40,* (2), 150–4.

Moore, L. (1977). Training of childcare providers to use nonsexist approach to child development. (ERIC Document [Online], Available: ED178730.)

Newmann, F., and Rutter, R. (1983). *The effects of high school community service programs on students' social development.* Madison: University of Wisconsin Center for Educational Research.

Nichols, D. P., and Stults, D. M. (1985, Aug.). Moral reasoning: Defining issues in open and closed belief systems. *Journal of Social Psychology, 125*(4), 535–536.

Nissani, M. (1989, Aug.). An experimental paradigm for the study of conceptual conservatism and change. *Psychological Reports, 65,* 19–24.

Palmer, D. L., and Kalin, R. (1985, Jan.). Dogmatic responses to belief dissimilarity in the 'bogus stranger' paradigm. *Journal of Personality and Social Psychology, 48,* 171–179.

Palmer, D. L., and Kalin, R. (1991, April). Predictive validity of the dogmatic rejection scale. *Personality and Social Psychology Bulletin, 17*(2), 212–218.

Pang, V. O. (1995). The power of culture. In C. A. Grant (Ed.), *Educating for diversity* (pp. 341–358). Needham Heights, MA: Allyn and Bacon.

Parkay, F. W. (1983, March). An experienced-based multicultural program for reducing dogmatism among counselor trainees. *Journal of College Student Personnel, 24,* 160–161.

Parrenas, F. Y., and Parrenas, C. S. (1990). Cooperative learning, multicultural functioning, and student achievement. San Bernardino School District. San Bernardino, CA. (ERIC Document, Available: ED337540.)

Partenio, I. (1985). The relationship of teacher ratings and IQ: A question of bias? *School Psychology Review, 14*(1), 79–83.

Pate, G. S. (1988). Research on reducing prejudice. *Social Education, 52*(4), 287–289.

Pate, G. S. (1992). Reducing prejudice in society: The role of schools. In C. F. Diaz (Ed.), *Multicultural education for the 21st century* (pp. 137–149). Washington DC: National Education Association.

Pate, G. S. (1995). *Prejudice reduction and the findings of research.* University of Arizona. (ERIC Document, Available: ED383803.)

Paul, R. W. (1987). Dialogical thinking: Critical thought essential to the acquisition of rational knowledge and passion. In J. Baron and R. Steinberg (Eds.), *Teaching thinking skills: Theory and practice.* W. H. Freeman.

Paul, R. W. (1993). Critical thinking: *What every person needs to survive in a rapidly changing world.* Santa Rosa, CA: Foundation for Critical Thinking.

Payne, C. (1984). Multicultural education and racism in American schools. *Theory into Practice, 23*(2), 124–131.

Peck, C. A., Donaldson, J., and Pezzoli, M. (1990). Some benefits nonhandicapped adolescents perceive for themselves from their social relationships with peers who have severe handicaps. *Journal of the Association for Persons with Severe Handicaps, 15*(4), 241–249.

Pedersen, P. B. (1994) Multicultural training in schools. In P. B. Pederson and J. C. Carey *Multicultural counseling in school.* (pp. 225–238). Boston: Allyn and Bacon.

Pine, G. J., and Hilliard, A. G. (1990). Rx for racism: Imperatives for American schools. *Phi Delta Kappan, 71*(8), 593–600.

Plant, W. T., Telford, C. W., and Thomas, J. A. (1965). Some personality differences between dogmatic and non-dogmatic groups. *Journal of Social Psychology, 67,* 67–75.

Richards, H., and Gamache, R. (1979). Belief polarity: A useful construct for studies of prejudice. *Educational and Psychological Measurement, 39*(4), 791–801.

Richert, A. E. (1991). Using teacher cases for reflection and enhanced understanding. In A. Lieberman and L. Miller (Eds.), *Staff development for education in the '90s* (pp. 113–132). New York: Teachers College Press.

Rivlin, H. N., and Fraser, D. M. (1995). Ethnic labeling and mislabeling. In C. A. Grant (Ed.), *Educating for diversity* (pp. 371–379). Needham Heights: Allyn and Bacon.

Rogers, M., Miller, N., and Hennigan, K. (1981). Cooperative games as an intervention to promote cross-racial acceptance. *American Educational Research Journal, 1* (4), 513–516.

Rokeach, M. (1960). The open and closed mind. New York: Basic Books.

Rokeach, M. (1972). Beliefs, attitudes, and values. San Francisco: Jossey-Bass.

Rokeach, M. (1973). *The nature of human values.* New York: Free Press.

Rolzinski, C. A. (1990). *The adventure of adolescence: Middle school students and community service.* Washington, DC: Youth Service America.

Rosenfeld, H. M., and Nauman, D. (1969). Effects of dogmatism on the development of informal relationships among women. *Journal of Personality, 37,* 497–511.

Rothbart, M., Evans, M., and Fulero, S. (1979). Recall of confirming events: Memory processes and the maintenance of social stereotypes. *Journal of Experimental Social Psychology, 15,* 343–355.

Rubin, I. (1967). Increased self-acceptance: A means of reducing prejudice. *Journal of Personality and Social Psychology, 5,* 233–238.

Sanders, J. A., and Wiseman, R. L. (1990). The effects of verbal and nonverbal teacher immediacy on perceived cognitive, affective, and behavioral learning in the multicultural classroom. *Communication Education, 39*(4), 341–353.

Schaller, M., Boyd, C., and Yohannes, J. (1995, Mar.). The prejudiced personality revisited: Personal need for structure and formation of erroneous group stereotypes. *Journal of Personality and Social Psychology, 68*(3), 544–555.

Seigel, S., and Rockwood, V. (1993, September). Democratic education, student empowerment, and community service: Theory and practice. *Equity and Excellence in Education, 26,* 65–70.

Seiter, D. M. (1988). Reducing prejudice in the classroom. *Social Education, 52*(4), 302–303.

Selltiz, C., and Cook, S. W. (1963). The effects of personal contact on intergroup relations. *Theory into Practice, 2*(3), 158–165.

Sharan, Y., and Sharan, S. (1992). *Expanding cooperative learning through group investigation.* New York: Teachers College Press.

Simonton, D. K. (1983). Formal education, eminence and dogmatism: The curvilinear relationship. *Journal of Creative Behavior, 17*(3), 149–162.

Simpson, G. E., and Yinger J. M. (1985). Racial and cultural minorities: An analysis of prejudice and discrimination (5th ed.). New York: Plenum.

Slavin, R. E. (1979). Effects of biracial learning teams on cross-racial friendships. *Journal of Educational Psychology, 71,* 381–387.

Slavin, R. E. (1989). Cooperative learning and student achievement. In R. E. Slavin (Ed.), *School and classroom organization.* Hillsdale, NJ: Lawrence Erlbaum.

Slavin, R. E. (1990). Research on cooperative learning: Consensus and controversy. *Educational Leadership, 47*(4), 52–54.

Slavin, R. E., and Oickle, E. (1981). Effects of cooperative learning teams on student achievement and race relations: Treatment by race interactions. *Sociology of Education, 54,* (3), 174–180.

Sleeter, C. E. (1985). A need for research on preservice teacher education for mainstreaming and multicultural education. *Journal of Educational Equity and Leadership, 5*(3) 205–215.

Sleeter, C. E., and Grant, C. A. (1987). An analysis of multicultural education in the United States. *Harvard Educational Review, 57*(4), 421–444.

Smithers, A. B., and Lobley, D. M. (1978). Dogmatism, social attitudes, and personality. *British Journal of Social and Clinical Psychology, 17,* 135–142.

Spencer, S., Carter, K., and Steele, C. (1993, Aug.). Increasing African Americans' academic performance by reducing vulnerability to stereotypic evaluation. Paper presented at the 101st meeting of the American Psychological Association, Toronto, Ontario.

Steele, C. M., and Aronson, J. (1995). Stereotype threat and intellectual test performance of African-Americans. *Journal of Personality and Social Psychology, 69,* 797–811.

Stephan, W. G. (1999). Reducing prejudice and stereotyping in schools. New York: Teachers College, Columbia University

Stotland, E., Katz, D. and Patchen, M. (1972). The reduction of prejudice through the arousal of self-insight. In Brigham and Weissbach (Eds.), *Racial Attitudes in America.* New York: Harper.

Stover, D. (1990). The new racism. *American School Board Journal, 177, 6,* 14–18.

Symons, S., Snyder, B. L., Cariglia-Bull, T., and Pressley, M., (1989). Why be optimistic about cognitive strategy instruction? In C. B. McCormick, G. E. Miller, and M. Pressley (Eds.), *Cognitive strategy research.* New York: Springer-Verlag.

Taylor, O. L. (1987). *Cross-cultural communication: An essential element of effective education.* Washington: Mid-Atlantic Equity Center of the American University.

Trachtenberg, S. J. (1990, April). Multiculturalism can be taught only by multicultural people. *Phi Delta Kappan, 71*(8), 610–611.

Triandis, H. C. (1971). *Attitude and attitude change.* New York: John Wiley and Sons.

Walberg, H. J., and Genova, W. J. (1983). School practices and climates that promote integration. *Contemporary Educational Psychology, 8*(1), 87–100.

Walsh, D. (1988). Critical thinking to reduce prejudice. *Social Education, 52*(4), 280–282.

Washington, V. (1981). Impact of anti-racism/multicultural education training on elementary teachers' attitudes and classroom behavior. *Elementary School Journal, 81*(3), 186–192.

Weiner, M. J., and Wright, F. (1973). Effects of undergoing arbitrary discrimination upon subsequent attitudes toward a minority group. *Journal of Applied Social Psychology, 3*(1), 94–102.

Wurzel, S. T. (1980). The reduction of prejudice and stereotyping: A treatment to improve. Unpublished doctoral dissertation, Boston University.

chapter **14**

Educating for Human Rights

A Curricular Blueprint

Ricardo L. García

Education for human rights teaches universal ethics about human dignity. It teaches students to respect the rights of individuals so they can better practice their own rights—the first steps toward moral competence and social responsibility. The ethics of human rights attempt to transcend the values and norms of all societies and cultures. Their intent is to allow people to practice their own cultures without violating the rights of others with whom they may or may not share cultures.

You could say the ethics of human rights are ideal constructs of justice. They are ethics that define the parameters necessary for all people to experience dignity throughout their lives. The human-rights approach is based on a philosophy of human interdependence, or on the idea that the fates of all humans are linked. Much like the line of John Donne's poem, "No man is an island, entire to itself," the human-rights approach operates on the belief that all humans are members of one community—the human community—their individual fates are inextricably linked to the fates of others.

The Universal Declaration of Human Rights issued in 1948 by the General Assembly of the United Nations included this statement about human rights:

> Recognition of the inherent dignity and of the equal and inalienable rights of all members of the human family is the foundation of freedom, justice, and peace in the world.

208

This declaration boldly asserted the faith that peace was possible if all people would commit themselves to human rights, if all humans regardless of their affiliation with groups—gender, ethnic group, nation, race, religion, and social class—commit themselves to the belief that individuals are entitled to a dignified life.

The Universal Declaration of Human Rights was issued as nations were moving from a world at war to a world at peace. The hope was that humanity had learned war has no winners. All are losers, and among them, the noncombatants and the innocent often suffer the most. The ethical imperative of the postwar era was "we had better learn to live together in peace or we shall destroy each other in war." Now, at the dawn of the 21st century, this imperative still holds true. The traditional enemies of people—ignorance, poverty, hunger, violence, disease—like the Four Horsemen of the Apocalypse, still run rampant across the land.

We have become better at fighting some of these enemies. During the past five decades, we have become more effective at waging war. We have even developed weapons that will kill people in their homes without damaging their houses. Without the inconvenience of rebuilding structures, conquerors can move into the undamaged houses of the vanquished. Yet even barring the windows will not protect these "victors" from the nuclear rain and winds another aggressor can use to annihilate the plants and animals that serve as food for all the combatants.

We are better at waging war against disease. We have developed "wonder" drugs, vaccines, and preventative medicines that ameliorate suffering and pain, thereby extending the quality and quantity of life. Is it progress, then, to claim that we have achieved parity at both saving and killing life? Absolutely not! I would argue we are better at killing than at saving life, although we have attained high levels of technical competence in both areas.

How do we make use of our high level of technical competence? We have centuries of experience with teaching people to save and to kill life. We have less experience with teaching that helps people understand how to use knowledge in a socially responsible manner, especially in an interdependent, pluralistic world. We need to rise to a new plateau of competence, to a level of moral proficiency where we use our newfound knowledge to improve the conditions of life and learn to live together in peace. World peace, like charity, should begin at home. If we cannot learn how to get along with our neighbors and other people within our communities and nations, we can hardly hope to learn how to get along with people who live in other continents.

Educators should begin building a world for peace within their own local schools and communities. Educators and schools cannot achieve this ideal alone. What they can do is seek to improve the relationships within their own classrooms by fostering the belief we are all interdependent members of the human community who should treat each other with respect. In the words of the first President of Mexico, Benito Juarez,

"Respeto de los derechos de tu vecinos es el salvación de todos." That is, respect for the rights of your neighbors is everyone's salvation.

Schooling as a Community Affair

Throughout the United States, as in most nations, schools are embedded in communities. In a larger sense, they are embedded in a variety of communities and are affected by what happens within their respective states, the country as a whole, and of course, the world. What these variegated communities have in common are people—human beings who collectively form a human community.

The human community consists of billions of people who speak different languages and practice different cultures. While vast differences in ideologies, religions, and values attest to the human community's plurality, all the people share an interdependence of fates. We all live on the same planet, breathe the same air, and drink the same water. The storage of toxic wastes in the desert of New Mexico, the destruction of the rain forests of Brazil, and the precipitation of acid rain in highly industrialized regions of Europe all affect the air we breathe and the water we drink, regardless of where we live.

Schools and educators play a role in shaping the human community. Schools and their teachers are legally mandated to teach the values, knowledge, and skills necessary to enable students to think and act for themselves within a democratic society. Furthermore, schools are morally challenged to prepare their students to live within the broader human community as socially responsible citizens (i.e., they also teach morality). While schools will reflect the prevailing values and cultures of their local communities, and while transmission of the basic skills and knowledge of academic disciplines may prepare students to live within their respective communities, the schools and their teachers are challenged to prepare students to live in a pluralistic, globally interdependent human community. Schools should not only be mirrors that reflect the values and beliefs of their local communities; they should also be windows to the world that exists beyond their own communities.

The global challenge places schools and teachers in the position of responding to political, economic, religious, and social forces existing outside the school's neighborhood while concurrently responding to the values and aspirations of the people within the local community. Teachers can work toward the goal of creating socially responsible humans by construing the classroom as a social contract entered into by students and teachers in which human rights play a central role in the day-to-day classroom routine.

Rights as Fundamental Principles

Rights are not merely high-sounding ideals. Rights are fundamental principles we can use to guide relationships with other people. They are social in character and exist within a socially interactive context. Rights are given to each of us by the people in the communities in which we live. Rights function within the context of a group or community and prescribe the behavioral parameters allowed individuals within it.

Rights define the kind and degree of freedom individuals are allowed within their communities. Too much or too little freedom would be destructive to a human group. Too much freedom would create social chaos and disorder; too little freedom would smother individual creativity and stymie communal development by imposing stifling conformity. Within any group or community, there exists a need to balance the rights (freedoms) of the individual with the rights of all the people in the group. As such, rights are correlative: for the rights given to the individual within a community, there exists a concurrent responsibility to respect the rights of others.

There are important differences between the kinds of rights that people enjoy. *Civil rights* are granted to individuals by their governments and are supposed to protect individuals from the arbitrary behavior of the state's leaders. The 12th-century charter of Henry I and the 13th-century charter of John (the *Magna Carta*) were agreements between British kings and their barons. The charters stated the rights of the king and the barons, which served to limit the power of the king. The principle that laws should limit the power of governments and protect the individual from the arbitrary behavior of government officials emerged from these charters. In the late 18th century, the Bill of Rights was added to the United States Constitution to specify the rights vested in citizens, protecting them from the arbitrary behavior of those in power. However, for more than a century, the Bill of Rights limited only the powers of the national government, not those of state or local governments.

The potency of civil rights lies within the power of the laws behind them. However, civil rights are only as good as the people who enforce them. For example, even though the Thirteenth Amendment of the U.S. Constitution freed all African American slaves in 1865, thereby granting them civil rights, Jim Crow laws were enacted soon after that effectively blocked African Americans from practicing their civil rights. How did this happen? It happened because officials failed to enforce the civil rights granted to African Americans by the Thirteenth, Fourteenth, and Fifteenth Amendments to the Constitution. The civil rights of African Americans were sacrificed in order for Rutherford B. Hayes to assume the office of president. This 'compromise of 1876' held nothing of value for African Americans.

Cultural rights refer to the prerogatives of group membership. For example, as a member of a certain cultural group, individuals are entitled to a sense of community and historical connectedness. In other words, individuals within the group are linked by common traditions, customs, and symbols that provide them with a feeling of belonging to a group, which in turn forges a self-identity for the individuals. Further, the individuals are entitled to the knowledge they are linked to a long history of events and people, thereby preventing social alienation.

To maintain the group's prerogatives, its members conceive certain behaviors as appropriate or inappropriate for the security or perpetuation of the group. Cultural rights are focused on the group's need to maintain conformity and order within it. Cultural rights protect the group from the arbitrary behavior of individual members. Cultural rights have the power of customs and traditions to enforce them. Minimal deviations from the group's norms are accepted; extreme deviations are punished through banishment or ostracism. If individuals wish to remain within the group and receive its protection and security, then they must conform to the group's norms.

Civil and cultural rights are limited in their scope. They exist within the context of a given province, such as a nation or an ethnic group. Protection of civil rights varies over time and with different groups. Cultural rights are limited to members of a particular group, thereby depriving nonmembers of rights gained by group membership or conformity to its norms.

Human rights, on the other hand, are universal in scope. They apply to all humans in all parts of the world. They transcend the provinciality of civil and cultural rights, but they do not exist in legally formulated constitutions or governments, nor do they necessarily exist within historically established ethnic or cultural groups. Consequently, human rights do not have the legal power of civil rights or the emotional power of cultural rights. Human rights exist as constructs of perfect justice, emphasizing what people hold in common in a globally interdependent community. Allegiance to human rights is voluntary.

The Roots of Human Rights

Human rights are based on a philosophy of human dignity and consist of a cluster of ethics regarding individuals and their relationship with others. They operate on the faith that human relationships can be governed by ethics that transcend all cultural differences.

Ancient Greek philosophers believed that the world was organized in a balanced, harmonious order. As a part of the natural order of things, humans were ultimately controlled by laws held by their respective group, nation, or tribe. The greatest virtue was to know the laws and live in conformity with them, i.e., the greatest virtue was to live in harmony with humans in a group. The Ancient Greeks perceived individuals as "corporate persons" whose duty was to join a group (ethnic group, religion, nation, tribe) and then pursue its interests. In short, people existed for groups. During the latter parts of the European Middle Ages, scholars shifted the focus from people as corporate persons to people as individuals. As individuals, people were free to join groups. Scholars such as John Locke, Jean-Jacques Rousseau, and Adam Smith stressed the individual nature of social interaction. Smith, for example, argued that if individuals were allowed to pursue their own self-interests without mercantile interference, then both the individual and the nation could prosper. This was the basic thesis of Smith's classic text *The Wealth of Nations*. The English philosopher John Locke is credited for formulating the philosophy of political individualism and freedom. "The state of nature has a law to govern it," he postulated in *On Civil Government*, published in 1689. Locke wrote that "reason teaches all mankind ... being all equal and independent, no one ought to harm another in his life, health, liberty, or possessions." Thomas Jefferson placed Locke's notion of individual rights and moral equality in the Declaration of Independence.

Human rights germinated as a consequence of the union between the Ancient Greek notion of group conformity and the European worldview of people as individuals entitled to freedom of action. Human rights are based on the following *a priori* assumptions:

- *All humans are members of one race, the human race.* Humans may differ culturally, intellectually, and physically, but these differences are subordinate to the fundamental humanity shared by all people. In other words, being human takes precedence over any differences.

- *Humans exist as ends in themselves.* Individuals are not born to serve masters, although they are free to submit their fates to a master, such as a government, a teacher, or a God.

- *Humans are ethically equal.* The belief in human rights acknowledges the existence of cultural, intellectual, economic, political, and physical inequalities. Yet the existence of these inequalities does not justify unethical treatment of humans.

- *Humans live in communities.* All people live within a civil society and a human society. The civil society consists of the individual's state, province, or nation in which citizenship is held. The human society is the totality of all humanity. There are no national boundaries to the human society. Rather, the society is governed by those rights that dignify individual humans—we are all global citizens.

- *Within the human society, for every right there exists a concurrent responsibility.* If all humans are to have rights, all must respect the rights of others. Mutual respect of rights is the axle that keeps the wheel of human rights moving.

These assumptions—all people are members of the human race and are ends in themselves, entitled to equal treatment, with the duty of showing respect for the rights of others—are succinctly summarized in the preamble of the Declaration of Independence:

> We hold these truths to be self-evident, that all men are created equal, that they are endowed by their Creator with certain unalienable rights, that among these are Life, Liberty, and the pursuit of Happiness.

Life, liberty, and the pursuit of happiness are fundamental human rights. How can they be taught in the classroom?

Human Rights in the Classroom

Human rights really cannot be taught didactically; students are more apt to practice the ethics they experience rather than the ethics they are told to embrace. In other words, human rights should be *caught* rather than *taught.*

Of course, human rights in action are hardly possible without education, or freedom from ignorance. Schools and teachers have the responsibility of educating all of their students so they may exercise their human rights. But teachers should work toward the goal of creating socially responsible students who are able to live in a pluralistic and globally interdependent human community by treating the classroom experience as a social contract entered into by students and teachers alike. Social responsibility can be caught by the students, rather than taught, in the daily interplay of the classroom as a social contract.

A social contract is an agreement among humans made to protect the rights of individuals so they may pursue their better interests. In pursuits of interests, individuals can benefit the community and themselves. Students in a classroom—operating on a social contract—enter into an agreement with their teachers and the other students to respect the rights of others while pursuing their own interests.

In the classroom, pursuit of interests means learning. The classroom is a community of scholars engaged in learning. They hold in common the overall goal of learning whatever the teacher has to offer. While students may differ in terms of class, ethnicity, gender, language, race, religion, and physical or intellectual capabilities, they are nonetheless a community sharing an interdependence of fates. As a community, they stand or fall, depending on the quality and quantity of learning that occurs within their classroom. Individual students have a responsibility to the community to initiate activities that allow all of them to learn. They are all duty-bound to take learning into their own hands.

While pursuing learning, students should respect the rights of other students to learn. Students should be encouraged to pursue learning competitively and cooperatively so long as individual students are responsible for their own learning. There is no pedagogical justification for making all learning activities competitive. Often, students can help each other learn. Excessive use of competitive modes lends itself to "win at any cost" learning strategies in which there are only a few winners and many losers. The approach, used excessively in the United States and in other nations, is inimical for learning social responsibility. The same is true with the excessive use of a cooperative approach that might cause learning to drop to a very low common denominator if students do not feel individual responsibility for the group's accomplishments.

What follows is a human-rights blueprint that incorporates the rights of life, liberty, and the pursuit of happiness into a classroom context. The blueprint can be used as a guide for operating a classroom as a social contract intended to foster learning of academic subjects as well as social responsibility.

Preamble

The classroom operates as a community of scholars who are engaged in learning. The individual's right to learn is protected and respected by all scholars. Scholars should initiate learning, teachers should initiate instruction, balancing the rights of individuals with the rights of other individuals in the community.

A. The Right to Exist, or Safe Occupancy of Space

The classroom is a physically safe learning environment.

- Classroom fixtures and furnishings are in good repair and otherwise nonhazardous.
- The classroom is well ventilated and well lighted, and the temperature is comfortable.
- The teacher does not allow students to physically harm each other.
- The teacher does not allow throwing of objects or other risky behavior that endangers students.

B. The Right to Liberty or Freedom of Conscience and Expression

The teacher:

- Allows students to assert their opinions.
- Fosters respectful student dissension as a means for rational understanding of issues and divergent opinions.
- Enforces dress and hairstyle codes that allow for individual differences.
- Fosters examination of each student's ethnic or cultural heritage. Teachers should help students become "ethnically literate" about their own individual cultural backgrounds as well as the backgrounds of others.

C. The Right to Happiness or Self-Esteem

The classroom is a safe, emotional learning environment that fosters self-esteem. The teacher:

- Fosters respect for self and others.

- Fosters linguistic and cultural respect by using linguistically and culturally relevant curriculum materials telling the students their language and culture are welcome in the classroom community.
- Fosters respect for cognitive and learning diversity by reasonably accommodating differing cognitive and learning style preferences.
- Disciplines students fairly, insuring some students are not punished more severely than other students for the same infractions.
- Does not foster name-calling, elitist, racist, or sexist slurs, or stereo-typical expressions in the classroom.
- Does not reveal confidential documents, term papers, or notes to the whole class without the permission of the author.
- Does not reveal grades or remarks on class projects or term papers to the whole class without permission of the student.

Conclusion

Human-rights instruction for the 21st century requires teachers to prepare students to act as socially responsible individuals within a pluralistic, globally interdependent human community. Socially responsible individuals require more than technical competence; they require the ability to function with diverse peoples, cultures, and languages. They need to be morally competent individuals who are able to transcend cultural differences without denigrating the differences of others.

The human-rights approach evolved as a means by which students can be taught fundamental ethical principles to govern all of their human relationships. The approach requires schools and teachers to conduct their classrooms as a community of scholars in pursuit of learning. Students take responsibility for their own learning; teachers, as leaders of the classroom community, help students enter a social contract in which everyone has rights and concurrent responsibilities to respect the rights of others to learn.

As disputes and differences of opinion emerge, the teacher guides students through negotiations to help them develop skills in conflict resolution without recourse to violence. The ultimate hope is that if students can learn to resolve differences peacefully in their classrooms, they will have the moral competence to resolve differences peacefully within the broader human community.

References

Juarez, B. Quotation cited by my father, Manuel A. García, from the oral tradition.
Locke, J. *On Civil Government. The second treatise.* Chicago: Great Books Press, 1947.
Universal Declaration of Human Rights. New York: United Nations, 1948.

chapter **15**

Responding to the Critics of Multicultural Education

What All Educators Should Know

Carlos F. Diaz

$\mathbf{A}$s anyone who has ever tried to change curriculum knows, schools are inherently conservative institutions. The previous chapters have persuasively suggested that traditional school practices have not served many of our students well, and absent significant change, gaps in educational achievement among students of different cultural backgrounds can be expected to remain wide or even to increase in the future.

Educators who support a multicultural curriculum and school environment must understand that their efforts will not always meet with unqualified support. There will be instances when students, parents, administrators, or teachers will react to these changes with trepidation, fear, or outright opposition. Multicultural curricular reform can generate controversy in some educational settings. This potential for controversy should not be discussed tangentially, but must be fully understood by all educators. The topics that follow are issues that represent potential obstacles to multicultural curricular change.

Opposition to multicultural education has one positive dimension; it means that multicultural education is being taken seriously by its critics. When this field was in its infancy, critics were relatively few and many of those may have assumed that, like other passing trends in education, this effort to reform the school and curriculum would simply go away.

However, the scholarship that undergirds multicultural education has increased significantly and remains a viable force in education.

The topics that follow are issues that represent potential obstacles to multicultural curricular change.

Temporary Curricular Notion

Recently, one of my students remarked after class, "Everything you are teaching me makes sense to me, but how do I know it is not a fad?" One logical barrier to implementing multicultural education is that teachers will invest time and energy learning the multicultural dimensions of their subjects, and then emphasis in this area simply disappears. Historically, the mainstream or macrocultural perspective has dominated the curriculum of American public schools. While this curricular caricature of American society has been in place for generations, the reality of American life has always been multicultural in nature.

No one can predict the cycles of future emphasis in curriculum, but teachers who develop multicultural literacy and incorporate these perspectives into their teaching can be certain that their teaching practices will be congruent with the heterogeneity present in this nation as well as in the world.

Is It Social Reconstructionism?

In the 1930s, the progressive movement in American education faced a major cleavage. Works like *Dare We Build a New Social Order?* by George Counts challenged progressive educators to inculcate a particular set of values and conclusions in students. Mainstream progressive education should give students a wide range of information and the ability to ask probing questions, and the conclusions should be left to students themselves.

A multicultural curriculum, appropriately conceived and presented, does not attempt to force any conclusions on students. However, educators and pupils must be prepared for possible shifts in outlooks as each of them is exposed to a much broader range of information and perspectives. For instance, how might student or public opinion be affected on the issue of public-school integration if all parties had a full understanding of the case law, timetables, and enforcement practices that occurred from 1954 to the present? Most Americans have opinions, and often strong ones, on the need and mechanisms for integrating public education. Few, however, can articulate a historical perspective on this issue and base their judgment mainly on life experience. A multicultural curriculum would provide all students with a wide range of information and the analytical tools to apply that knowledge to issues like school integration and many other topics that receive cursory attention in the curriculum.

Critics of multicultural education such as Webster (1997) question its commitment to a more equitable society. He states, "Should multicultural-ism not be divested of a concern with issues of racial oppression and racial justice? After all, such a concern does essentialize racial differences" (p. 73).

It is certainly possible (some would argue desirable) that, if the school curriculum presents issues that involve historical inequities, some stu-dents may look at contemporary society to see if these inequities persist. Webster questions whether "motivating students to act on patterns of dis-empowerment, discrimination and deprivation" is an appropriate role for education. The only way for schools to totally avoid having students examine the equity dimensions of societal norms and practices is not to teach about issues that have equity implications. This would be an unreal-istic and artificial restriction on the curriculum.

In attempting to infuse multicultural perspectives, educators should present unifying themes in society as well as circumstances that may be less flattering to our national image. The curriculum should not take the posi-tion that events be presented from the perspectives of "victims and victim-izers." Likewise, topics should not be glossed over or omitted because they illustrate unequal power relationships or do not contribute to a unified notion of American society. Societal unity, in this or any other society, can-not rest on a manufactured consensus or a selective presentation of facts.

Does Multiculturalism Politicize the Curriculum?

A number of authors have written about potentially dangerous elements in multicultural education. Chester Finn (1990) distinguishes between con-structive and destructive multicultural education. In the latter category, he includes curricula that are, "designed to tell a particular group about them-selves, their ancestors, their unique qualities, how superior they are, and how oppressed they have been. In contrast, constructive multiculturalism "draws on the ideas, customs and historical contributions from all our var-iegated groups into a unified curriculum that everyone studies" (p. A40).

A potential danger in this artificial dichotomy is that topics that are legitimate, but may not particularly contribute to the unifying theme, are dismissed as destructive multicultural education. Issues such as institu-tional racism and linguistic or gender discrimination are the types of top-ics that are legitimate areas of study, but prime candidates for dismissal as destructive multiculturalism.

Diane Ravitch (1990) distinguishes between the cultural-pluralist and the particularistic approach to multicultural education. The former "accepts diversity as fact, and the latter seeks to attach students to their ancestral homelands as a source of personal identify and authentic "cul-ture" (p. A44). It is certainly possible for students to become so engrossed in their ancestral culture that they develop ethnocentrism. However, it is equally possible for students to take identification with a narrow definition of nationalism to similar extremes. The development of a positive identification with an ancestral culture does not constitute a negative consequence of a multicultural curriculum. James Banks (1988) suggests that individuals must develop positive ethnic identifications before they can develop a clarified national identification.

Others critics of multicultural education like Spaeth (1997) argue that "The emphasis on group identity, on comfortable environments for minority students, and on total school transformation points to a divisive movement, concerned not so much about what students should be learning as about how they learn and how they feel about themselves" (p. 3). There is nothing inherently contradictory about being concerned that students feel comfortable in the classroom and having significant academic expectations. Also, the charge that studying any subject from multicultural perspectives cements group identities (and by implication politicizes students) is a hollow one.

A monocultural or multicultural curriculum may be presented in a highly politicized manner. However, teaching multiculturally does not, by definition, cement ethnic identities and preclude a positive national identity. Few, if any, of the critics of multicultural education question whether the traditional (and largely monocultural) curriculum promoted an artificial national identity by excluding copious amounts of information about ethnic/cultural groups found in the United States. These critics also fail to address the issue of whether the traditional curriculum was itself "politicized" by including so little information about the nation's ethnic minority groups.

The curriculum should present the essential elements of the American Creed (dignity, individual freedom, equality of opportunity) as well as instances when society has veered from those lofty values. Efforts at defining appropriate multicultural content only as topics that contribute to a unifying theme are inherently suspect. They are attempts to filter multicultural content through a neoconservative prism and, in effect, define those ethnic perspectives deemed legitimate. This insistence on a unifying theme, where it may or may not be present, adds an artificial criterion in teaching that is likely to interfere with critical thinking and analysis. The goal of education should be to expose students to a wide range of information and allow them to draw their own conclusions. Attempts to limit the perspectives students learn, however well intended, will detract from this goal.

Another caveat about the potential politicizing tendencies of multicultural education is the possibility that some educators will define multicultural perspectives as "special interests." These educators generally view themselves as defenders of traditional and wholesome tendencies in curriculum and attempt to diminish efforts toward multicultural curricular reform with the "special-interest" label. Meanwhile, these critics of multicultural education portray themselves as representing positive, unifying, and national interests.

Restructuring the Canon

Taking a new look at the canon of knowledge and how it is presented in our public schools is an area that is certain to generate some controversy. An appropriate multicultural curriculum goes far beyond sprinkling traditional subjects with selected heroes, heroines, and accomplishments of persons of color. A restructured canon of knowledge will sometimes challenge the imagined worlds that many students inhabit.

Many traditional concepts taught in American schools will have to be reexamined or qualified. When we teach that Christopher Columbus discovered America, we need to qualify that the term "discovery" applies to making the existence of the Americas public to Europeans. Otherwise, teachers risk leaving the impression that places don't exist until Europeans see them.

The qualification or redefinition of a number of traditional concepts is likely to spawn some opposition from fellow educators who often contend that this task is too complex. Another contention is that revising the curriculum to reflect multicultural themes and perspectives is a laudable goal but cannot be undertaken because there isn't enough time to teach current content. This view assumes that all current material enjoys priority status and multicultural perspectives represent curricular frills. An appropriate question to those who contend this is: "Does the existing curriculum give an appropriate representation of the diversity found in American society?" If not, it is an appropriate task for teachers and administrators to reexamine the status quo.

Many teachers will feel highly constrained by the existing curricular guidelines in their subjects. These guidelines may be viewed as limiting what could or should be taught in a subject, rather than as a minimum standard for course content. Curriculum guidelines must be viewed as malleable. Teachers have always interpreted the emphasis given to various topics and the manner in which curricular guidelines are met. Also, educators should be willing to serve on groups that periodically revise guidelines to insure they are reflective of nonsexist and multicultural perspectives.

Greeman and Kimmel (1995) caution that "resistance to diversity is embedded in institutional structures" (p. 360). They also note that parochialism among teacher candidates, teachers, professors of education, communities, and school districts perpetuate the status quo.

Parks (1999) cites a Ford Foundation study of college students in Florida. This study reported that 58% of students believed that diversity education created division and conflict. Clearly, findings such as these indicate that multicultural topics do not yet enjoy the same academic legitimacy as the more traditional, monocultural curriculum. Parks (1999) also cited that 40% of university students described diversity education as nothing more than "political correctness." More African American and Hispanic students than White students expressed this view. This suggests that some students of color view changes in the curricular canon skeptically and representing obligation more than sincerity.

To the extent that the curricular canon has changed to reflect multicultural perspectives, support has been greater for changes at the periphery (elective courses) than at the core (required courses). The latter carry the highest academic value, reach the greatest number of students, and are most resistant to alteration.

Multicultural Education Represents an Academic Quota System

Some resistance will emanate from those who claim multicultural education seeks to elevate to curricular status the perspectives of women, ethnic minority groups, and persons of color that could not have passed traditional and rigorous standards for curricular inclusion. In effect, these critics argue that multicultural curricular reform represents an attempt to force diverse perspectives in areas of instruction where they are not really warranted (Krauthammer 1990).

Topics such as the writing of the United States Constitution must reflect that this document was written by a White, elite, male segment of the American population at that time. However, it is entirely appropriate to raise questions in teaching this subject, such as "Why were there founding fathers and no founding mothers?" "How were the interests of people not present during the writing of the Constitution treated by the document?" It is important to discuss these issues, or we risk leaving the impression that the only types of people at the time capable of constructing such a document were those who received an invitation to the Philadelphia convention. To raise these questions is not being unduly divisive but encouraging a full exploration of how the Constitution framed the United States government and the legal positions of people living at that time.

Moore (1996) reminds us that, "What is taught, who teaches it and what is considered important reflect the values of those who select the curricula, mandate teaching methodologies and design the textbooks. The conflict, therefore, is about resources, needs and values" (p. 23).

Harris and colleagues (1997, p. 15) point out the following characteristics of the mainstream curriculum.

1. Little or no representation of other ethnic or cultural groups.
2. Language, terms, and concepts used only by the majority race.

3. Representation of ethnic groups only in relation to various holidays.

4. Stereotyped or distorted portrayals of ethnic groups.

Suggestions that the only way to remedy the above-mentioned problems is to infuse trivia about ethnic groups are wrong, if not downright offensive. Clearly, infusion of content into the curriculum should meet commonsense standards of significance, but educators do not have to bend these standards in order to make the curriculum much more pluralistic.

Potential for Community Resistance

There are two, often diametrically opposed, views of the role of public schools. One suggests that the experiences students have in school should be a direct reflection of that community's views and values. The other view holds that schools should provide students with a "window to the world" and teach information and perspectives that may not be widely discussed in the community. Depending on the nature of the community, these two views are not necessarily conflicting.

The goal of reflecting diversity in the curriculum can meet community or parental resistance. This is particularly true if it results in students learning material that was not part of their parents' academic experience. In one south Florida school district, plans were implemented to fully integrate African American content throughout the American history curriculum. In most settings, the plan went well, but resistance was particularly strong in high schools with the highest median income. Well-educated parents lodged complaints such as: "Why does my son/daughter need to learn this information when I don't know this and I am a successful person?" Another objection was: "How is this material going to relate to higher SAT scores or help students find better jobs?" It is regrettable when segments of the public and policy makers define a good education strictly as having good verbal and quantitative skills measured by standardized tests. A broad liberal education comprises a pluralistic knowledge base that goes far beyond good skills.

This example helps illustrate that resistance can emanate from any point along the income or education continuum. Educators must communicate to their constituents that multicultural perspectives provide more varied and accurate conceptions of an academic discipline. These perspectives are valuable for all students but are particularly needed by students living in small, homogeneous communities.

In any community, multicultural education can face resistance merely because students are being taught material their parents don't recognize or understand. This problem has occurred in other areas (new mathematics), and efforts to evolve the curriculum will always meet with some opposition from those who expect total congruence between what was taught to parents and what is taught to their children.

Educators must not be dissuaded from multicultural curricular reform by the possibility of resistance. However, there are some points to keep in mind in this effort:

- Know your community and try to forecast and address possible objections in advance.
- Ensure that new information or perspectives being incorporated fit well within the academic discipline.
- When adding new course information that is not treated in the textbook, document it well.
- Enlist in advance the support of departmental colleagues, school administration, and district curriculum specialists to the highest degree possible.
- Correlate new information to the maturational level of students.
- Inform students/parents in advance when new material will be taught.
- Encourage parents to review new material and discuss it with you.

Potential for Resistance From Colleagues

Many colleagues view curriculum as a dynamic entity in the educational process and will be eager to present their disciplines from multicultural perspectives. Others, however, may see a multicultural focus in the curriculum as an added burden to be shouldered. Lack of familiarity with new content and cultural perspectives can promote feelings of obsolescence.

If multicultural curricular review is teacher initiated, care must be taken to share new materials and expertise with colleagues who don't have that familiarity. When school districts initiate curricular review, it should be followed by workshops, courses, or other opportunities for faculty to become conversant with new materials and issues. Resistance to new approaches often melts when educators are comfortable with new academic content.

Colleagues may also be reluctant to become involved in multicultural curricular review if they think that this activity may label them as reformers. Teachers' behavior is molded, to a degree, by the school and district administration in which they work. Not all teachers regard curricular reform with the same zeal, but there are always less prominent roles that these colleagues may feel comfortable taking.

Some teachers may question the effectiveness of multicultural education in teacher preparation, the impact of a multicultural curriculum, or the need for culturally sensitive pedagogy. Additionally, differences of opinion may arise between teachers who have taken courses in multicultural education and those who have not. Ironically, school administrators who typically have more average years of experience than the faculty they supervise, are less likely to have a clear grasp of research in multicultural education.

Webb-Johnson and colleagues (1998) note a continued need to research the effectiveness of multicultural education. They also cite Gay's observation that there is still a considerable gap between multicultural education theory and practice (p.8). Continued research in multicultural education may stem concerns from colleagues who are skeptical about its effectiveness, but it is likely to have little or no effect on the objections of educators who are philosophically opposed to multicultural education.

Another caveat regarding resistance from colleagues is that multicultural education goes beyond curricular review. It gives legitimacy to considering students' cultures and life experiences in the educational process. A few educators take the position that they teach "subjects" and not "students." They contend that academic content doesn't change depending on the background of the class. These educators are confusing product with process.

Multicultural education does not advocate changing exit criteria or competencies based on the cultural composition of the class. It does suggest, however, that teachers should be familiar with the research on the relationship of gender and cultural background to the learning process and adapt their teaching strategies where necessary (Cazden and Mehan 1989). The affective filter through which students learn is of major importance, and research on the significance of classroom atmosphere needs to be part of every teacher's preparation.

Finally, research on classroom interaction between teachers and students strongly suggests that female students and students of color do not receive proportional attention from their teachers (AAUW, NEA 1992). These practices are often unintentional. However, all students need to be treated with similar dignity and attention, in practice as well as in theory.

Conclusion

For multicultural education to move beyond its current stage in American education, it is imperative that its advocates understand the strength it brings to the curriculum as well as the pitfalls to its implementation. Critics of multicultural education have argued that open and legitimate discussion of cultural differences in schools will promote ethnic balkanization. Supporters of multicultural education have generally felt that the failure to recognize the pluralistic nature of this nation and world in the curriculum has contributed little to building a national consensus (Viadero 1990). It also has not added to students' abilities in critical thinking.

With regard to multicultural perspectives, too many of our students inhabit "imagined worlds." These imagined worlds are composed of people largely like themselves and are places where knowledge of other cultural traditions is limited and diversity is seen with skepticism. Worldviews are rooted almost exclusively in their national identity as Americans.

Too many of our students do not understand that the information they possess may be incomplete or that it doesn't allow them to think critically. These short-comings are not confined to any particular region of the nation or to the public sector of education. The relative dearth of knowledge about the non-European roots of American society can be found in students of differing ability and achievement levels who study in public and private schools.

Significant knowledge about the role of women and racial and ethnic minority groups remains largely the province of academic specialists. Shifting information about these groups from the periphery to the core of the curriculum is among the goals of multicultural education.

Currently, multicultural education is seen by some as an effort primarily benefiting students of color. It must be seen as an attempt to broaden the perspectives of all students, particularly those who are members of the majority group. This latter conception, although more difficult to implement, has a much broader intellectual base.

For multicultural education to succeed in the 21st century, it must have significant support among White educators: after all, these educators make up the great majority of this nation's teachers. Sleeter (1999) notes that unless White educators learn about multicultural education though scholarship and dialog with a diverse cross-section of their peers, many will agree with the conservative critics of multicultural education. She also suggests that all educators familiarize themselves with professional literature written by scholars of color as a way of understanding and addressing diverse perspectives in their classes (pp. 275–76).

All educators also need to reflect on the notion that there are attitudinal derivatives of knowledge, or lack of knowledge. Students rightfully posit their trust in schools to distill a highly complex body of knowledge and to teach them a representative sample of the whole. If there are entire areas, traditions, or groups absent from what schools choose to impart, it is not an illogical conclusion for students to think that there was not much substance in those areas. It follows that students' academic experiences can support misperceptions, or even prejudice, by default if not by design.

Understanding who opposes multicultural education and why they do so allows educators who support this endeavor to frame responses to these arguments appropriately and not to be caught by surprise. A very fundamental point supporting multicultural education is that very few topics are taught more accurately monoculturally than multiculturally. The leading scholars in multicultural curriculum theory neither assail nor diminish the importance of the Western tradition in the U.S. school curriculum. Rather, they advocate teaching that tradition along with other traditions that have historically been untaught or undertaught. If the critics are able to mischaracterize multicultural as anti-Western tradition, then it will surely fail. If the advocates of multicultural education can convince the American public that multicultural education represents a "Western cultural tradition plus" concept to enhancing the curriculum, then its prospects are bright.

Multicultural education seeks to reduce the gap between the academic distillation of the human experience portrayed in schools and the world students perceive. It redefines the notion of a "liberally educated person" to include individuals who are literate in the totality of the history and cultures that constitute the United States. In short, multicultural education is a curricular vehicle through which formerly inaudible voices can be heard.

References

American Association of University Women; National Education Association (NEA). (1992). *How schools shortchange women.* Washington, DC: NEA.

Banks, J. A. (1994). *Multiethnic education: Theory and practice* (3rd ed.). Boston: Allyn and Bacon.

Cazden, C. B.; Mehan, H. (1989). Principles from sociology and anthropology: Context, code, classroom, and culture. In M. Reynolds (Ed.), *Knowledge base for the beginning teacher* (pp. 47–57). New York: Pergamon Press and American Association of Colleges for Teacher Education.

Finn, C. E. (1990). Why can't colleges convey our diverse culture's unifying themes?" *Chronicle of Higher Education,* 13 June, A40.

Greenman, N., and Kimmel, E. (December 1995). "The road to multicultural education: Potholes of resistance." *Journal of Teacher Education, 46*(5), 360–368.

Harris, J., Stephens, J., Sandrige, R., and Donellan, R. (April 1997). From minority to majority: The students and faculty of tomorrow. *Journal of School business affairs, 63*(1), 13–18.

Krauthammer, C. (1990). Education: Doing bad and feeling good. *Time,* 5 February, 78.

Moore, P. (Spring 1996). Multicultural Education: Another Look. *Update on law related education.* Chicago: American Bar Association.

Parks, S. (April 1999). Reducing the effects of racism in the schools. *Educational leadership, 56*(7), 14–18.

Ravitch, D. (1990). Multiculturalism, yes; particularism, no. *Chronicle of Higher Education,* 24 October, A44.

Sleeter, C. (1999). Curriculum controversies in multicultural education. In M. Early and K. Rehage (Eds.), *Issues in curriculum: A selection of chapters from past NSSE yearbooks.* Chicago: University of Chicago Press.

Spaeth, C. (1997). *Multicultural education in Minnesota.* St. Paul: Minnesota Association of Scholars.

Viadero, D. (1990). Battle over multicultural education rises in intensity. *Education Week, 10*(13), 1.

Webb-Johnson, G., Artiles, A., Trent S., Jackson, C., and Velox, A. (January/February 1998). The status of research on multicultural education in teacher education and special education: Problems, pitfalls and promises. *Journal of Remedial and Special Education, 19*(1), pp. 7–15.

Webster, Y. (1997). *Against the multicultural agenda: A critical thinking alternative.* Westport, CN: Praeger.

LIST OF CONTRIBUTORS

Ilene Allgood

Ilene Allgood is the associate director of the Anti-Defamation League (ADL) in the Palm Beach region of Florida and is also an adjunct professor at Florida Atlantic University, specializing in multicultural education. Allgood received her doctorate in education from Florida Atlantic University and has a strong research interest in prejudice reduction and multicultural education. She has written and presented on a variety of topics pertaining to prejudice reduction, multiculturalism, equity in schools, critical vs. dogmatic thinking, English for speakers of other languages, anti-Semitism, the Holocaust, and First Amendment issues. She developed a curricular model for reducing prejudice in schools. This *Strategic Prejudice Reduction Framework (SPRF)* was found to be significantly effective in lowering dogmatism levels. As ADL regional director of education, Allgood is in charge of a broad range of educational programs. Among those is A WORLD OF DIFFERENCE® Institute, which offers comprehensive, proactive anti-bias and cultural awareness programs to schools, community organizations, law enforcement agencies, colleges, and workplaces. Allgood serves on numerous boards, committees, and coalitions whose mission is focused on halting prejudice and discrimination.

Cherry A. McGee Banks

Cherry A. McGee Banks is associate professor of education at the University of Washington-Bothell. She has contributed to such journals as *Phi Delta Kappan, Social Studies and the Young Learner, Educational Policy, Theory Into Practice,* and *Social Education.* She is associate editor of *The Handbook of Research on Multicultural Education,* and co-author of *Teaching Strategies for the Social Studies* (with James A. Banks). Banks is on the editorial boards of *Educational Foundations, Multicultural Perspectives,* and *American Educational Research Journal.* In 1997, she received the Distinguished Teaching Award from the University of Washington—Bothell.

James A. Banks

James A. Banks is professor and director of the Center for Multicultural Education at the University of Washington, Seattle. He has written or edited more than a dozen books in multicultural education and in social studies education. Banks is a past president of the National Council for the Social Studies (NCSS) and the American Educational Research Association (AERA). His books include *Teaching Strategies for Ethnic Studies; Educating Citizens in a Multicultural Society; Teaching Strategies for the Social Studies;* and *Cultural Diversity and Education: Foundations, Curriculums and Teaching.* He is the editor of *The Handbook of Research on Multicultural Education,* of the Multicultural Education Series of books published by Teachers College Press, Columbia University, and is a member of the Board on Children, Youth, and Families of the National Research Council of the National Academy of Sciences.

Jane Bernard-Powers

Jane Bernard-Powers is professor of elementary education and department chair at San Francisco State University. Her interest and work in gender has focused on gender in curriculum, teaching, and teacher preparation. Publications include *The Girl Question in Education.*

Andre J. Branch

Andre J. Branch is assistant professor of multicultural education in the School of Teacher Education at San Diego State University. His research projects include studies of teacher-facilitated ethnic identity development through curriculum, and pre-service teachers' conceptions of multicultural education. *Learning to Value Cultural Differences* and *Understanding Multicultural Education* are consulting workshops he provides for K—12 and college and university educators.

Patsy Ceros-Livingston

Patsy Ceros-Livingston is a professor of education in the College of Education at Florida Atlantic University. She is also a practicing psychologist in clinical, school, and forensic psychology. She has published in the areas of measurement and assessment of special populations and serves as an expert witness in various courts regarding measurement and assessment issues. She is a consultant to schools and businesses and serves on many professional and university committees with a focus on assessment issues.

Carlos F. Diaz

Carlos F. Diaz is professor of multicultural education at Florida Atlantic University. He is coauthor of *Global Perspectives for Educators* and contributing author to *Teaching Strategies for Ethnic Studies* and *Teaching in America.* Diaz has procured and directed grants providing 240 teachers with full scholarships to earn a master's degree with areas of specialization in multicultural education and ESOL. Diaz has received two Excellence in Undergraduate Teaching and two Teaching Incentive Program awards at Florida Atlantic University.

Ricardo L. García

Ricardo L. García is professor of education in Teachers College at the University of Nebraska—Lincoln. His research areas encompass bilingualism, second language acquisition and development, sociocultural factors in teaching and learning, and storytelling as an instructional tool for teaching culture. His current textbook, *Teaching for Diversity*, was published by Phi Delta Kappa International in 1998. Currently, he is seeking a publisher for two books of fiction, *On the Way to San Francisco Bay* and *Coal Camp Days in Chicorico*.

Geneva Gay

Geneva Gay is professor of education and associate of the Center for Multicultural Education at the University of Washington—Seattle. She is the recipient of the 1990 Distinguished Scholar Award, presented by the Committee on the Role and Status of Minorities in Educational Research and Development of the American Educational Research Association, and the 1994 Multicultural Educator Award, the first to be presented by the National Association of Multicultural Education. She is internationally known for her scholarship in multicultural education, particularly as it relates to curriculum design, staff development, classroom instruction, and culture and learning. Her writings include more than 110 articles and book chapters, *At the Essence of Learning: Multicultural Education* (Kappa Delta Pi, 1994), and co-editorship of *Expressively Black: The Cultural Basis of Ethnic Identity* (Praeger, 1987). Her professional service includes membership on several national editorial review and advisory boards, such as the *National Alliance of Black School Educators Journal, Educational Forum, Social Studies*, and the Advisory Council of the Black Family Studies Program at Philander Smith College in Little Rock, Arkansas.

Sonia Nieto

Sonia Nieto is professor of language, literacy, and culture in the School of Education, University of Massachusetts at Amherst. Her scholarly work focuses on multicultural education, the schooling of language minority and immigrant students, the education of Latinos in the United States, and Puerto Ricans in children's literature. She has written a number of books, including *Affirming Diversity; The Light in Their Eyes: Creating Multicultural Learning Communities;* and *Puerto Rican Students in U.S. Schools*. She has also written many book chapters and articles in such journals as *Harvard Educational Review, Theory Into Practice*, and *Educational Forum*. Nieto has worked extensively with teachers and schools and serves on several national boards and commissions that concentrate on educational equity and social justice. Her awards include the Human and Civil Rights Award from the Massachusetts Teachers Association in 1989, the Educator of the Year Award from NAME, the National Association for Multicultural Education, in 1997, and the New England Educator of the Year Award from Region One of NAME in 1998. She received an Annenberg Senior Fellowship for 1998–2000.

Valerie Ooka Pang

Valerie Ooka Pang, professor of teacher education at San Diego State University, earned a doctorate at the University of Washington in 1981. She was a Spencer Foundation postdoctoral fellow and studied achievement and test anxiety in Asian American students from 1987–1989. She is presently a senior fellow with the Annenberg Institute for School Reform, holding an academic appointment to Brown University. Pang received the 1997 Distinguished Scholar Award from the American Educational Research Association's Standing Committee on the Role and Status of Minorities in Education. Her articles have appeared in *The Handbook of Research on Multicultural Education, Harvard Educational Review, The Kappan, Theory and Research in Social Education, Multicultural Education, Educational Forum, Equity and Excellence,* and *Social Education.* Pang is a member of several professional committees and serves as a consultant to private and public institutions with interest in education.

Rodolfo Puente

Rodolfo Puente is a graduate student at California State University, Monterey Bay, where he recently completed his B.A. degree in liberal studies. He works for the office of Student Outreach and Recruitment, and aspires to completing a Ph.D. in the near future.

Angela Rhone

Angela Rhone was born in Jamaica, West Indies, where she received her primary and secondary education. She received her bachelor's and master's degrees in English education at Brooklyn College and New York University and her doctorate in curriculum and instruction at the University of North Carolina at Greensboro. She is an assistant professor at Florida Atlantic University and teaches the foundations, goals, and history of multicultural education to undergraduate and graduate students. Graduate classes include Race, Class, and Gender in Education as well as Teaching the African American Student. Her teaching has been recognized by a Teaching Incentive Program Award at Florida Atlantic University.

Dilys Schoorman

Dilys Schoorman is assistant professor of multicultural and global education at Florida Atlantic University. She received her doctoral degree in curriculum theory from Purdue University. Her research interests include the internationalization of higher education curricula, immigrant education, and strategies for increasing multicultural and global awareness among future teachers.

Christine E. Sleeter

Christine E. Sleeter is a professor in the Center for Collaborative Education and Professional Studies at California State University, Monterey Bay, where she coordinates the Master of Arts in Education program. She consults nationally in multicultural education and multicultural teacher education. Her awards include the National Association for Multicultural Education Research Award, the AERA Committee on the Role and Status of Minorities in Education Distinguished Scholar Award, and the University of Wisconsin—Parkside Research Award. She has published numerous books and articles in multicultural education; her most recent books include *Multicultural Education as Social Activism* (SUNY Press), *Developing Multicultural Teacher Education Curricula* with Joseph Larkin (SUNY Press), *Multicultural Education, Critical Pedagogy, and the Politics of Difference* with Peter McLaren (SUNY Press), and *Making Choices for Multicultural Education* with Carl A. Grant (John Wiley). In addition, she edits the book series *The Social Context of Education* for SUNY Press.

Karen Swisher

Karen Swisher received her Ed.D. in educational administration from the University of North Dakota. She is the interim president of Haskell Indian Nations University in Lawrence, Kansas. Prior to this interim appointment, Swisher served as vice president for academic affairs. She also served as chair of the Teacher Education Department and was instrumental in securing accreditation for the newly developed Elementary Teacher Education Program. Other university experience includes faculty positions at Arizona State University and the University of Utah. Swisher's teaching and research focus on the education of American Indians/Alaska Natives and multicultural education in general.

INDEX

Multicultural Education for the 21st Century

C A R L O S   F.   D I A Z

Sixteen prominent contributors examine the goals, challenges, and possibilities of multicultural education in today's classrooms. *Multicultural Education for the 21st Century* offers a wide range of perspectives that inspire critical reflection and lively debate. This collection shows teachers how to incorporate effective teaching practices into multicultural classrooms.

C O N T R I B U T O R S

Ilene Allgood	Geneva Gay
Cherry A. McGee Banks	Sonia Nieto
James A. Banks	Valerie Ooka Pang
Jane Bernard-Powers	Rodolfo Puente
Andre J. Branch	Angela Rhone
Patsy Ceros-Livingston	Dilys Schoorman
Carlos F. Diaz	Christine E. Sleeter
Ricardo L. Garcia	Karen Swisher

A B O U T   T H E   A U T H O R

Carlos F. Diaz is the co-author of *Global Perspectives for Educators* (1999) and is a contributor to *Teaching Strategies for Ethnic Studies* by James A. Banks and *Teaching in America* by George Morrison. He has also procured and directed grants that have provided 240 teachers with full scholarships to earn master's degrees with areas of specialization in multicultural education and ESOL.

Visit us on the Web at www.awl.com

Pearson Education

ISBN 0-321-05417-2

90000

9 780321 054173